CW01372094

INDIAN
MADE EASY

Anurag Aggarwal

SIMPLE, MODERN
RECIPES FOR EVERY DAY

cover illustration by Jordan Amy Lee
photography by Rita Platts

Quadrille

4	Foreword
6	Introduction
8	The Fundamentals of Indian Cooking
18	BREAKFAST
38	VEGETABLE CURRIES & LENTILS
62	MEAT-BASED DISHES
86	RICE DISHES & BREADS
108	SNACKS, SOUPS & SALADS
128	PUDDINGS
150	SPICE BLENDS, SAUCES & ACCOMPANIMENTS
170	MEAL COMBINATIONS
182	Index
188	Acknowledgements

FOREWORD

I was born and brought up in North India in a small town called Gurgaon. Being part of a traditional family, I was blessed to witness and experience the wide array of societal cultural themes and traditions. And food was the underlying thread which connected all the beads of these, from birth to death, religion, festivals, celebrations, charity, economy and lifestyle in general. Its influence almost becomes part of one's DNA and it's hard to differentiate whether we eat to live or live to eat!

Growing up in an average middle-class household, there was always an expectation to do well in life and to follow the tried and tested careers. In those days, there were three very popular paths to choose from: medicine, engineering and finance. Most of my immediate and extended family members were from a science or engineering background, but I decided to pick finance instead. To the outside world, I had done very well, but deep down I always knew that my heart lies in arts and creativity. My family, especially my dear, late mother, always encouraged my inclination towards arts and food.

My mother was the greatest influence on my love for cooking. She not only used to cook very delicious food, but it was a medium to express her unconditional love for the family – that was very touching. I used to cook along with her, and that was my training ground for understanding the flavours and fundamentals of Indian cuisine. It was all so normal for us, and I couldn't have imagined 30 years ago that one day I would be writing about it in my own cookbook, in this foreign country which I now call my home.

After moving to the UK in 2010, my professional path followed the field of finance, but my passion for cooking kept growing. Together with my wife, I used to watch many cookery programmes, and it was fascinating to learn about diverse cuisines. My cooking style was constantly evolving with the influence of different cultures and the availability of new ingredients. Missing India and its unique dishes, as well as a lack of access to Indian ingredients (online shopping for curry leaves was not very common a decade ago!) encouraged me to start looking at my home cuisine with a new perspective. Food is not all about recipes, dishes or ingredients to me. It is also very much about the nostalgia and stories it carries with it. So, I started exploring all the easily available ingredients and fresh produce in the local supermarkets and focused on how I could recreate my favourite Indian dishes without compromising on the flavours or the nostalgia.

While my Indian culinary skills were evolving, the conflict between my formal profession in finance and the voice of my foodie heart was growing louder. One thing led to another and I eventually gathered the courage to take the very first step towards pursuing cooking as my full-time profession. Being part of *MasterChef UK* 2023 and earning my place as one of three finalists has given me an acknowledgement and confidence to progress further on my culinary journey. I find food and cooking to be the best medium to express myself and to share the love and my stories with the whole world through my food. I sincerely hope that while reading this book, not only will you enjoy cooking and eating, but that you'll also be able to feel the nostalgia behind each recipe and share the story further.

Thank you for reading this book and becoming part of my story.

Anurag

@anuragfoodstory

FOREWORD

INTRODUCTION

I believe that food is a universal language. It has the unique strength to communicate beyond physical and political borders, cultures, race, religion and power. With the advances in globalization and technology, everything is within reach. As an Indian by birth, settled in the UK, I see no reason why I can't experience the same emotions that I enjoyed for 30 years before moving continents while relishing my country's amazing cuisine.

I appreciate the differences between cultures and cuisines, and I do understand that it can be very daunting at times to cook something from scratch, especially when it comes to Indian food, if you are not familiar with the dish. The long recipes, unique cooking techniques and tools, unusual ingredients and the language barrier can be overwhelming.

But as I mentioned in the foreword, food is not all about recipes, dishes or ingredients to me. It is also very much about the nostalgia and stories that come with the food. This book is my humble attempt to share the same nostalgia with you, using simple step-by-step recipes made with ingredients that are available in your local supermarkets, along with tips and tricks and clear explanations of specific cooking techniques.

Cooking should be fun, and you should be able to share it with your family and friends through the window of Indian cuisine. After learning the fundamentals here, you will soon master all the recipes and even be able to add your own spin. There is no right or wrong when it comes to food, it's all about what you enjoy cooking and eating.

I hope this book will serve as a foundation course in Indian cuisine for you. You will learn about the different spices and their flavour profiles and how they can work together. You will discover the staple Indian dishes and what non-Indian ingredients or fresh produce can be used seamlessly as replacements. You will also develop ideas and understanding about the Indian vegetarian dishes and uncover suggestions for pairing multiple dishes to make a complete meal.

THE FUNDAMENTALS OF INDIAN COOKING

Ingredients can be the same across many cuisines, and yet using specific quantities, techniques and tools for different recipes results in unique dishes and flavours. You can say that these are the key differences among dishes from different cultures.

In this section, I will share and explain a few fundamentals of Indian cuisine in terms of techniques, ingredients and tools. This is by no means an encyclopedia of Indian cookery, but it is a very good place to start as you to embark on this culinary journey. I have covered less common and sometimes regional ingredients, as most of the common spices – like ground coriander, turmeric or cumin – need no introduction.

INGREDIENTS

Ghee (clarified butter) vs oil
Made by clarifying butter, ghee has a very high smoking point. Therefore, it tastes very aromatic and nutty, and you need to use about two-thirds of the quantity compared to any other cooking oil. Using ghee instead of oil enhances the taste and texture of Indian curries and other dishes.

Personally, I prefer to cook with ghee. However, if the recipe calls for oil, I suggest any neutral cooking oil such as sunflower or vegetable oil.

Paneer (Indian cottage cheese)
This is fresh and unsalted Indian white cheese. Traditionally, it is made at home by curdling the milk and draining it through muslin cloth (cheesecloth), then pressing it under some weights. Nowadays it is easily available in stores. It has a firm texture and can be used raw in dishes for a soft and creamy feel, or it can be fried or griddled, if you want to add some texture to it.

Roti/chapati flour
Finely-milled wholemeal (wholewheat) flour is used to make rotis as it has a high fibre and protein content. It is very different to the plain (all-purpose) flour and wholemeal flour that we generally get in the supermarkets. It is commonly available in Indian stores, online or in large supermarkets. An easy replacement is half plain flour and half wholemeal flour.

Semolina (cream of wheat) or sooji
This pale yellow flour is processed from durum wheat and can be coarse, medium or fine. In batters and as part of doughs, it cooks up to a crispy texture. Generally, fine semolina is available in supermarkets and coarse/medium versions can be bought in Indian stores or online.

Besan or gram flour
Made from ground channa daal (split brown chickpeas), this is nutty in flavour and grainy in texture. It is versatile and can be used for batters, fritters and even for sweets. It is also gluten free and works very well to thicken sauces and marinades.

Poha
Flattened, beaten or pounded parboiled rice, used in snacks or breakfast dishes. It only needs soaking or frying. Buy this online or from Indian stores (it can't be made at home).

Curry leaves
Hailing from the southern region of India, curry leaves add a pungent aroma and a hint of sweetness to savoury dishes. Find them fresh or dried in Indian stores, large supermarkets or online.

Dhaniya (fresh coriander/cilantro)
Although fresh coriander doesn't need an introduction, I have mentioned it here because this is the king of herbs when it comes to Indian cuisine. Whenever you are in doubt about which herb to use to garnish, always go for fresh coriander.

Gud (jaggery)
Unrefined dehydrated cane sugar juice. This is almost fudge-like in texture and flavour, adding a caramelly sweetness to dishes. The closest replacement will be soft dark brown sugar. Jaggery is commonly available in Indian stores, large supermarkets or online.

Imli (tamarind)
Tamarind comes in two forms, either as pulp or as a pressed block with seeds and lots of fibre. The dominant flavour is sour, but it has some sweet notes as well. Tamarind is used extensively in south Indian dishes and dips. It is commonly available in Indian stores, online or in large supermarkets.

Ajwain (carom) seeds
This spice comes from the ajwain herb. It is bitter in taste and has a thyme-like aroma. Said to be medicinal, the seeds help reduce the 'heavy' feeling of certain foods, which is why we most often use them in curries, batters and fried snacks.

Eno
Effervescent fruit salts (Eno is a specific brand) are traditionally used to relieve indigestion, but make amazing instant raising agents. They are commonly available in Indian stores or online.

Kasoori methi (dried fenugreek leaves)
This is the dried form of the fresh green herb methi, or fenugreek, which is bitter in taste. When crushed within your palms and added to rich curries, these leaves add a subtle bitter note and provide an amazing balance for the dish. Commonly available in Indian stores or online.

Hing (asafoetida)
This fine yellow powdered resin has a pungent, sulphurous smell. That's why we use this in very small quantities, mainly for tempering or at the start of a curry base for a hint of umami. Commonly available in Indian stores, large supermarkets or online.

Black salt
This is mined from quarries rather than harvested from the sea. It is generally pink/greyish in colour and a bit less salty than sea salt. It is a must for the Indian street food/chaat recipes. It is commonly available in Indian stores, large supermarkets or online.

Amchoor (dried mango powder)
Amchoor is a powder made from ground dried unripe green mangoes, which is very sour and earthy. These mangoes are only available in specialty stores so it will be best to buy the powder ready-made. You can find it in Indian stores, online or in large supermarkets. It adds a sour element to dishes and as it is dry itself, it works best in the dry curries or fillings where we don't want to add any extra moisture from lime or lemon juice.

Anardana (dry pomegranate seed powder)
This is made from ground dried pomegranate seeds. It is very sour, sweet and a bit gritty. It is readily available in Indian stores, online or from large supermarkets. In addition to sourness, it provides a nice textural element. Depending on the dish, you can use it in coarse powder form or even as whole dried seeds.

Chillies
Heat has a special place in almost every Indian dish, especially curries, and this comes from chillies. There is a huge variety of fresh, dried and powdered chillies, all at different points on the Scoville scale. As a rule of thumb, I suggest buying a medium red chilli powder. Follow the recipe as given to determine how spicy you like it, then venture out into the world of chillies.

TECHNIQUES

Making a dough

The quality of your dough and the technique you use to make it are critical for getting the desired result for flatbreads and similar dishes. In the following chapters, I have used different kinds of doughs. However, this one is the basic technique. It can be customized if you want to introduce other elements like flavourings, fats or vegetables.

Dough-making is a mix of art and science, therefore there is no perfect recipe. Over time you will develop a feel for when it is right!

- In a large bowl, sift in 250g (9oz) plain (all-purpose) flour and make a little well in the middle.

- Measure out 125ml (4fl oz) water. Add half to the well then, using your fingers, start mixing the dry flour towards the centre to incorporate. After 1–2 minutes, you will get a very dry and crumbly dough.

- Now using your whole palms, start kneading the dough while adding the rest of the water, a little at a time. The dough will start coming together and you will have an even ball after 3–4 minutes.

- Dust some extra flour on a flat surface and start kneading the dough ball using both heels of your palms alternately.

- If the dough still feels a bit dry, add a splash more water, or if it is too wet, then dust with more flour. The proportion of the water in the dough will depend on the type/quality of the flour.

- In a few minutes, you will have a very smooth dough. Cover it with a damp dish towel and let it rest for 30 minutes, before using it to make any flatbreads, etc.

If you want to add other ingredients like flavourings, oil or vegetables, use the same techniques for the dough but you will find you may need more flour or water to get the same consistency.

THE FUNDAMENTALS OF INDIAN COOKING

TOOLS

Most of the tool/utensils mentioned below are not essential, but they are very helpful in recipes from my cuisine. They can all be bought very easily online or from large supermarkets.

Measurement reference

Every household has unique utensils and different-sized pots, pans or cups. I recommend getting a set of measuring spoons and a set of digital scales, if you can – they are inexpensive and make everything much easier to measure.

Non-stick pans with lids

These are essential to my style of cooking. A non-stick coating encourages one to use less oil in the cooking as the food won't get stuck to the base.

Having lids for your pots and pans is also very helpful as it conserves energy. Plus the dish cooks in its own juices rather than by added water (unless a recipe specifically calls for a certain quantity of water), giving it a richer taste and a better texture.

Be wary that whether you're using your pans on an electric, induction or gas hob (stove) can impact timings and, sometimes, taste. I don't suggest refitting your whole kitchen to use this book! But be mindful that if your heat source is electric or works on induction, you may need to adjust cooking times to get the textures you're looking for.

Tava (large, flat, open, non-stick pan)

A tava is essential for Indian cooking. We use it for making flatbreads, crêpes, toasties, and even sometimes to grill meat and veg. You can always use a large frying pan (skillet) as a replacement.

Pressure cooker

This is a wonderful cooking vessel (though is not essential for this book), especially as it can reduce the cooking time of many dishes by almost a third, while also achieving a very soft and almost melt-in-the-mouth texture for meat and pulse dishes cooked this way.

If you do want to use one I suggest buying a small, 3-litre (5¼-pint) pressure cooker. The internal steam helps to cook

THE FUNDAMENTALS OF INDIAN COOKING

the food at a very fast speed, so you can adapt many recipes where the method includes cooking a dish in a covered pan. Start by reducing the cooking time by one-third. It depends on the quantity and ingredients, but with some trial and error you should be able to get the timings right.

Idli mould
These are specific moulds used to steam idlis (see page 22). They can be bought online or from Indian stores. The closest replacement will be a multiple round egg poacher insert, if that fits in your steamer.

Steamer
Some dishes call for steaming. There are many options to go for, such as metal or bamboo steamers that can be used on the hob (stovetop), or even plastic, microwaveable steamers. Choose what will be most versatile in your kitchen, depending on your usage and kitchen appliances. Sometimes, an idli mould comes with its own steaming vessel.

Belan (rolling pin)
Indian rolling pins are a bit different to the traditional dowel (straight cylinder) type and are much closer to the French style with tapered ends. The narrow handles help you to apply the most pressure with the least amount of effort to make thin roti or other similar flatbreads.

Small powerful spice grinder and blender
Indian spice grinders and blenders are generally small with a very powerful motor. This results in finely ground powders, pastes and batters. For a replacement, appliances like a bullet blender work equally well for most dishes.

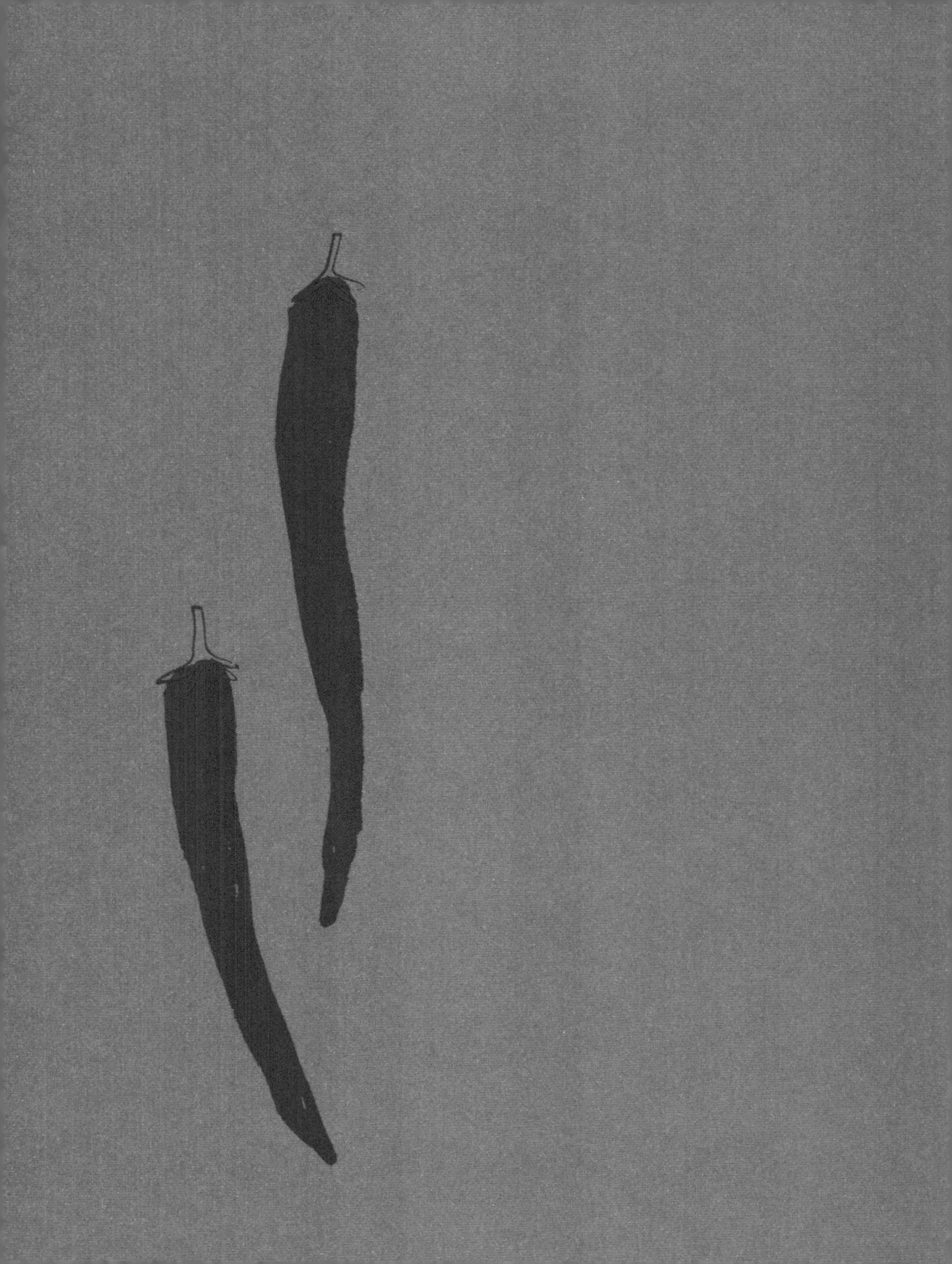

breakfast
NASHTA

Breakfast is the most important meal of the day. This is not just a cliché for me, but a reality. When I think about breakfast, I immediately get transported back to my childhood days. I can almost feel the same aroma and freshness of those lovely mornings when I was rushing to get ready for school and my mother was busy making a healthy and delicious breakfast. Weekend breakfasts used to be even more special and elaborate.

Steaming masala chai, the aroma of melting butter on stuffed flatbread, vibrant poha (flattened rice) dishes, ghee on toast or a masala omelette with loads of tomato ketchup on the side were not just breakfast items for me, but a precious part of my childhood which I will always cherish.

POTATO TOASTIES

(ALOO SANDWICH)

This is one of the easiest yet most delicious recipes I can recall from my childhood. I can still feel the crunch of a freshly-grilled aloo sandwich, made in a hand-held sandwich press over the open gas flame. The compressed golden edges oozing with a fluffy potato-ey centre is nothing short of a wonder. And when you take the first bite after dipping the sandwich in tomato ketchup and the Mint and Coriander Chutney, you will be transported to some other world!

Makes 4

400g (14oz) waxy potatoes, peeled, boiled and cooled

100g (3½oz) deseeded green (bell) pepper, finely diced

100g (3½oz) red onions, finely diced

2 tbsp chopped fresh coriander (cilantro)

½ tsp finely chopped green chilli

½ tsp grated fresh peeled ginger

1 tsp salt

1 tsp ground coriander

¼ tsp Garam Masala (see page 155)

¼ tsp red chilli powder

½ tsp anardana (pomegranate seed powder)

8 large slices of soft white bread (don't use a chewy bread like sourdough, or anything with a hard crust)

2 tbsp ghee or butter, softened

To serve
Tomato ketchup

Mint and Coriander Chutney (see page 162)

Masala Chai (optional; see page 34)

In a mixing bowl, use a fork to break the potatoes into a chunky mash. Then add the green pepper, red onion, fresh coriander, green chilli and ginger. Tip in the salt and all the spices and mix together, without making it too mushy.

Divide the mixture into four equal portions. Spread each portion evenly over a slice of bread, top with another slice and then, using your palm, press down gently, so that the mixture doesn't spill out.

Spread some ghee or butter on the outer sides of each sandwich.

Toast each sandwich in a non-stick frying pan (skillet) over a medium heat, using a flat spatula to gently press the sandwich down for extra crunch, until golden brown on both sides. Alternatively, if you have an electric sandwich grill, you can use this – but I feel that cooking these in a frying pan makes them taste even better.

Slice each sandwich in half diagonally. Serve with ketchup and Mint and Coriander Chutney, and a nice cup of Masala Chai, if you like.

Easy swap
Instead of green pepper, you can use any other vegetables like peas, spring onions (scallions), etc.

BREAKFAST

STEAMED SEMOLINA CAKES
(IDLI)

Idlis, famous in South India, are little fluffy pillows of semolina. On their own, they don't have any prominent flavours, but the mild tang of yoghurt combined with the savoury semolina makes them very comforting. Traditionally these are made with fermented rice and lentil batter. My take is much simpler, using semolina and an instant raising agent (Eno).

Makes 12–16

300g (10½oz) coarse semolina (cream of wheat)
200ml (7fl oz) natural (plain) yoghurt
3 tbsp oil
1 tbsp lime or lemon juice
2 tsp granulated sugar
½ tsp salt
2 tsp Eno
Oil, for brushing

To serve
Smoked paprika
Desiccated (dried shredded) coconut
Chopped fresh coriander (cilantro)
Your choice of chutneys and salsas (such as the Onion Tomato Chutney on page 163 and the Peanut and Chilli Salsa on page 169)

Add all the ingredients, except the Eno and oil, to a mixing bowl with 100ml (3½fl oz) of water. Mix well to a very thick batter. Rest for 10 minutes, then mix in 20–30ml (½–1fl oz) more water as the batter will have thickened further as the semolina absorbs the liquid.

Now add the Eno and mix well. The batter should almost double in size. Rest for 5 minutes and mix again to deflate the batter.

Get a steamer ready, brush some oil on an idli mould (see page 17) and then spoon enough batter into each cavity so that it fills up completely (do not overfill). Place the filled mould in the steamer, cover and steam over a medium heat for 12 minutes. Remove from the heat and leave covered for another 10 minutes. (Alternatively, if you don't have an idli mould, use an oiled 15–20cm (6–8in) round cake tin: fill it to 2cm (¾in) thickness with batter, then follow the steaming instructions above. Simply slice the steamed cake into shapes of your choice. Or use an egg poacher!)

Open the steamer carefully, take out the idli mould and leave to cool. Once cool, use a spoon to scoop out the cooked idlis.

Serve them hot, garnished with smoked paprika, desiccated coconut and coriander, with a little chutney or salsa for dipping.

Easy swaps
Swap the Eno for ½ tsp bicarbonate of soda (baking soda) and ½ tsp lime juice.

Feel free to add ground spices, such as turmeric and smoked paprika, and robust veg, like onion, grated carrots and chopped peppers to the batter.

PEA-STUFFED FLATBREAD
(MATAR PARATHA)

Parathas are almost synonymous with breakfast in many north Indian households. The story in my home was no different. On many occasions I awoke to the irresistible smell of these flatbreads. They can be made with so many delicious, seasonal fillings like onion, spinach, carrots, paneer or peas. The pea version is my favourite so I would like to share it with you lovely people. I can imagine the happiness on your face when you take a bite of your very first matar paratha! The recipe makes too much filling – save the leftover filling for later or use it to make a toastie (see page 20).

Makes 4

For the dough
125g (4½oz) plain (all-purpose) flour, plus extra for dusting
125g (4½oz) roti flour
¼ tsp salt
½ tsp ajwain (carom) or fennel seeds
1 tbsp ghee or oil

For the filling
1 tbsp ghee or oil
1 tsp cumin seeds
1 tsp ground coriander
½ tsp red chilli powder
½ tsp ground turmeric
½ tsp crushed fennel seeds
¼ tsp ground ginger
2 tsp salt
300g (10½oz) frozen peas
Ghee or oil, for frying

To serve
White Butter (see page 36)
Cranberry Relish (see page 167)

For the dough, combine the ingredients in a bowl with 150ml (5fl oz) of water and mix to make a dough (see page 14). Cover the bowl with a damp dish towel and leave to rest for 30 minutes at room temperature.

For the filling, heat the ghee in a small frying pan over a medium heat, then add the spices and salt. Once aromatic, add the frozen peas. Cook for a minute, then gently crush the peas using a potato masher. Continue to cook until the excess moisture has evaporated. Set aside to cool completely.

Once the dough has rested, knead it again for 1–2 minutes, then divide and shape it into 4 equal-sized balls. Take a ball and use both thumbs to make a deep cavity. Fill with 3–4 teaspoons of the cooled pea mixture – don't add too much or it will become difficult to roll out later – then reshape it into a ball, enclosing the filling. Lightly press it to make a small disc. Dust well with flour, then use a rolling pin to roll it into a wide circular shape. The sizes may differ, but they should be evenly thick, all around 5mm (¼in). Repeat with the remaining dough and filling.

Using a large, flat, non-stick pan or tava, cook the paratha, one at a time, over a medium heat for 2 minutes on each side. Reduce the heat to low, spread ⅓ teaspoon of ghee or oil on each side, then fry until golden and flaky, about 1–2 minutes per side. Remove from the pan and serve with the White Butter and Relish.

You can also freeze these for later use – just reheat in a hot pan from frozen, with a little oil, for around 2 minutes per side.

BREAKFAST

GRAM FLOUR PANCAKES
(BESAN CHILLA)

In comparison to many internationally famous sweet pancakes, Indians prefer savoury versions which are made from gram flour, rice, lentils or semolina as a breakfast item. They are such a good source of protein and provide an opportunity to incorporate many vegetables and spices as well. This gram flour version is very delicious, filling and a healthy way to break your fast!

Makes 6

250g (9oz) gram flour (besan)
100ml (3½fl oz) natural (plain) yoghurt
100g (3½oz) red onions, finely chopped
50g (1¾oz) spinach, finely shredded
½ tsp chopped green chilli
2 tbsp chopped fresh coriander (cilantro)
1 tsp ground coriander
¼ tsp red chilli powder
¼ tsp ground turmeric
½ tsp salt
¼ tsp freshly ground black pepper
Oil, for frying

To serve
Tomato ketchup
Mint and Coriander Chutney (see page 162)

Add all the ingredients except the oil to a mixing bowl, pour in 100ml (3½fl oz) of water and mix well to get a thick, pourable consistency which is spreadable. Rest the batter for 15 minutes and then add a little more water or gram flour to adjust the consistency, as required.

Heat a tava (see page 15) or large, flat, non-stick pan over a medium heat until hot, then spoon in around 100ml (3½fl oz) of the batter (about half a large ladleful). Using the same ladle or a serving spoon, and using a circular motion, gently spread out the batter to make a 15–18cm (6–7in) disc.

Drizzle 1 teaspoon of oil around the edges and on top of the pancake, then cook over a low-medium heat for 3–4 minutes until the underside is golden brown – you should be able to flip it using a flat spatula or palette knife. If you break the pancakes while flipping, don't worry, just pour a little batter into the cracks when cooking the other side.

Cook on the other side until it turns golden brown. Keep the heat at low-medium, otherwise it will burn on the outside and remain undercooked inside.

Transfer the pancake to a plate and keep warm, covered with tin foil, while you cook the rest in the same way.

Serve the pancakes warm with the ketchup and the Chutney.

Easy swap
You can replace the vegetables with any of your choice, making sure they are finely chopped and not very watery.

MASALA OMELETTE

Growing up in India, masala omelette was the only egg dish I was exposed to. I would never have known that an omelette has its origins in Persia and is a classic French dish. That's the thing about food – it's not about the technicalities behind it, it's all about your connection to it. For me, an omelette will always be this dish – a warming masala omelette with the freshness of coriander and the kick of green chillies.

Makes 1

2 large eggs
2 tbsp milk
4 tbsp chopped red onion
2 tbsp chopped tomato, deseeded
¼ tsp chopped green chilli, or to taste
1 tbsp chopped fresh coriander (cilantro)
¼ tsp salt
¼ tsp Garam Masala (see page 155)
1 tbsp butter

To serve
Ghee Toast (see page 36) or fresh bread
Tomato ketchup

Break the eggs into a small mixing bowl, add the milk and whisk together for a minute.

Add the red onion, tomato, green chilli and fresh coriander and mix well. Sprinkle in the salt and Garam Masala and mix again.

Melt the butter in a non-stick pan, then evenly pour the egg mixture into the pan.

Cook over a medium heat until nicely browned underneath, then gently flip the omelette over and cook the other side until browned all over. This Indian-style omelette needs to be cooked thoroughly to get some colour on both sides rather than a classic omelette where we look for a pale and soft finish.

Serve hot with Ghee Toast or fresh bread and a little ketchup.

Easy swap
Swap out the garam masala for freshly ground black pepper.

SAVOURY VEGETABLE FLATTENED RICE WITH PEANUTS

(POHA)

Sometimes for breakfast I want to eat something very nice and filling but not too heavy. This dish satisfies that craving perfectly. Fluffy parboiled rice with vibrant vegetables, crunchy peanuts and lots of fresh coriander makes for a hearty yet light dish for a great start to the day.

Serves 4

- 200g (7oz) dry poha (flattened rice)
- 2 tbsp oil
- 50g (1¾oz) whole raw peanuts (skin on)
- 1 tbsp black mustard seeds
- 1 tbsp curry leaves
- 1 tbsp grated fresh peeled ginger
- 2 green chillies, finely sliced
- 100g (3½oz) onions, chopped
- 100g (3½oz) small potatoes, peeled and diced
- 1½ tsp salt
- ½ tsp ground turmeric
- 3 tbsp lemon juice
- 100g (3½oz) frozen peas
- 100g (3½oz) tomatoes, chopped
- 2 tbsp chopped fresh coriander (cilantro), to garnish

To serve (optional)
Ghee Toast (see page 36)
Masala Chai (see page 34)

Rinse the dry poha in a sieve (strainer) under cold running water for 30 seconds, then leave to drain.

In a heavy-based, non-stick pan (with a lid), heat the oil over a medium heat, then lightly fry the peanuts for 2–3 minutes, or until golden and crispy. Set them aside on a plate for later.

Using the same oil and pan, fry the mustard seeds. Once they start sputtering, add the curry leaves, grated ginger and green chillies and cook over a medium heat for another minute. Now add the onion and potatoes, sauté for 2 minutes, then cover the pan and simmer for 5 minutes until the potatoes are fully cooked.

Stir in the salt, turmeric and lemon juice, then tip in the frozen peas and cook for another 2 minutes.

Fluff up the poha and add to the pan with the chopped tomatoes and half the peanuts. Mix well. Cover and simmer for 2 minutes.

Serve hot, with the remaining peanuts and the fresh coriander. For a more filling breakfast, enjoy with Ghee Toast and a cup of Masala Chai.

Easy swaps

You can use shop-bought, ready-roasted peanuts if you prefer. (Or, if you're allergic or just don't like them, simply leave them out.)

Replace the 200g (7oz) of dry poha with 250g (9oz) of cooked bulgur wheat or giant couscous.

Swap out the curry leaves for fresh or dried bay leaves.

Pictured overleaf.

SPICED EGG ROLLS

(EGG BHURJI PAV)

This dish reminds me of the busy streets of Mumbai. Many roadside carts sell this during the morning rush hour or even late at night. It can be a tasty and handy little breakfast or an evening snack to enjoy on the go. For the short while I lived in Mumbai, I was always amazed by those street vendors and their cooking skills in such a minimal set-up, working like nothing short of robots!

Makes 2

2 tbsp butter or oil

½ tsp chopped green chilli

50g (1¾oz) red onions, chopped

50g (1¾oz) tomatoes, chopped

¼ tsp salt

¼ tsp red chilli powder

¼ tsp Garam Masala (see page 155)

3 large eggs

1 tbsp chopped fresh coriander (cilantro)

1 tsp smoked paprika, plus extra for sprinkling

2 soft white bread rolls, cut in half

2 tbsp mayonnaise

2 tbsp tomato ketchup

Masala Chai (see page 34), to serve

In a frying pan (skillet), melt 1 tablespoon of the butter or oil over a medium-high heat, then add the green chilli and red onion. Sweat for a minute, then add the tomatoes.

Stir in the salt, chilli powder and Garam Masala, turn the heat up to high and cook for another minute.

Break the eggs into the pan and continue stirring over a high heat. It will take hardly any time before you get scrambled eggs. Do not let the eggs overcook or become dry. Stir in the fresh coriander. Transfer the scrambled egg mixture to a bowl and keep warm.

Without cleaning the pan, use it again to melt the remaining butter or oil over a medium-high heat and add the smoked paprika. As soon as it starts bubbling, place the halved bread rolls, cut-side down, into the pan.

Let the bread rolls absorb all the paprika butter and reduce the heat to low so that the rolls nicely crisp up. Now flip the rolls to fry the other side until crisp.

To assemble, take the bottom half of each roll, spread generously with the mayo, spoon in half of the egg bhurji, sprinkle some extra smoked paprika over the top and drizzle with the tomato ketchup. Cover with the top half of each roll and gently press it down. Enjoy hot with a nice cup of Masala Chai.

Easy swaps
Why not enjoy this with Roti (see page 88) or Paratha (see page 90) instead of the bread rolls?

You can add any vegetables which do not need to be cooked much, like (bell) peppers or peas.

BREAKFAST

MUST-HAVE SIDES

MASALA CHAI

Just like the blood in our body is the connecting medium for all our organs, nerves, muscles, etc, masala chai plays a similar role at breakfast time. It's not exactly a dish, but without it any other breakfast dish is incomplete. My mother always used to say that tea is like petrol for my body; I need it to keep going. Let's fuel your engines as well with this delightful hot drink!

Serves 1 (makes 250ml/9fl oz)

1 tsp black tea leaves (or 1 tea bag)
1 tsp granulated sugar
4 black peppercorns
2 cloves
2 green cardamom pods
Very small piece of cinnamon stick
1cm (½in) piece of fresh ginger, peeled
50ml (1¾fl oz) milk

Bring 200ml (7fl oz) of water to the boil in a small saucepan, then add the tea and sugar.

Lightly pound all the spices in a mortar and pestle, then add to the brewing tea and simmer for 2–3 minutes.

Now add the milk, and once it comes to the boil, simmer for another 5 minutes.

Strain the tea through a sieve (strainer) and enjoy the hot and warming cuppa!

Easy swaps
Swap the sugar for a sugar-free option or honey, or it can be skipped altogether.

Cow's milk can be replaced with a dairy-free/plant-based option of your choice.

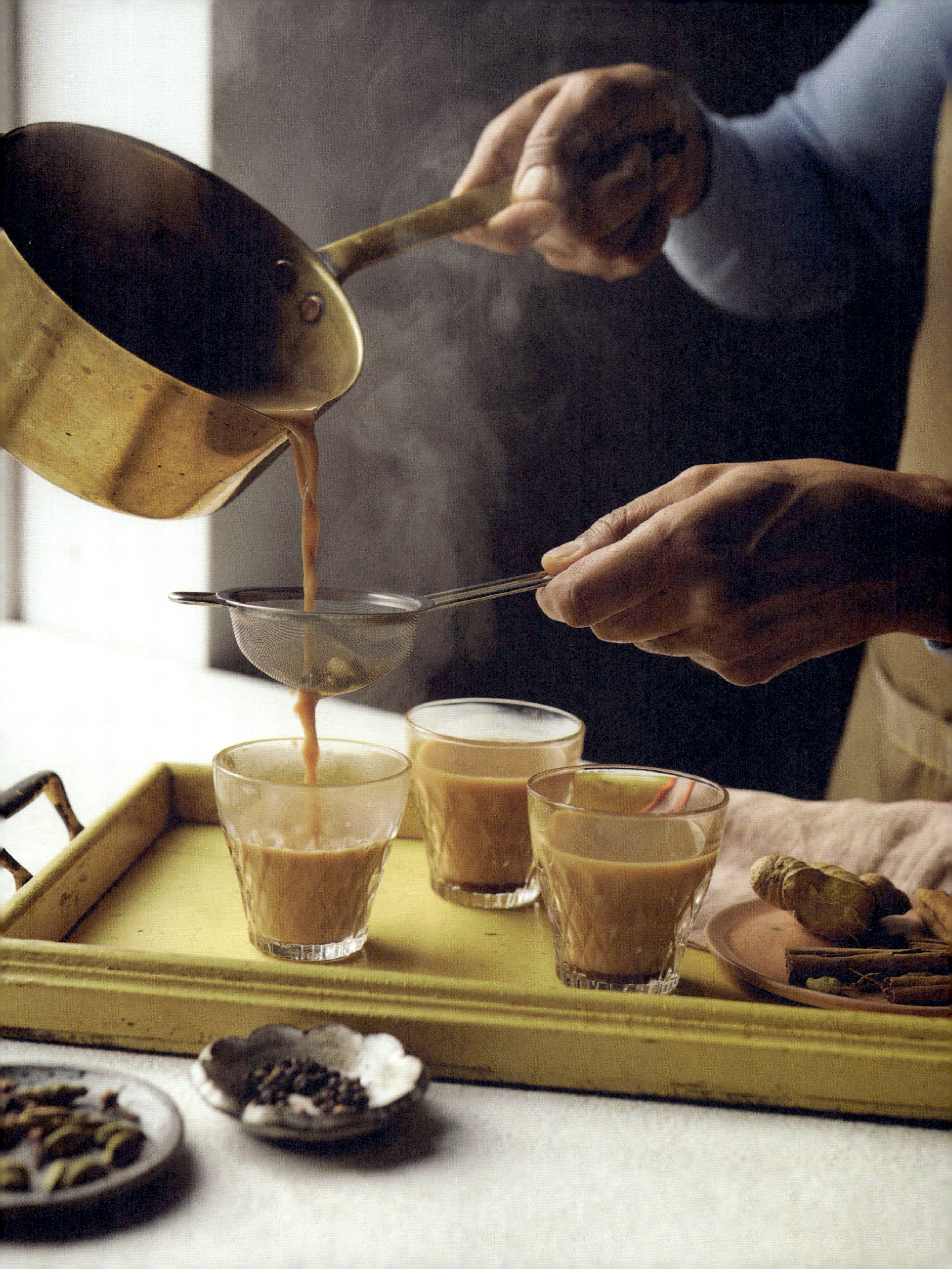

MUST-HAVE SIDES

GHEE TOAST

Think buttered toast, but very exclusive and classic. There is something special about this simple side – the deep earthy aroma of ghee, the salt sprinkles and the crispy dark golden edges of the toast. It's just mesmerizing. I am more than happy to have these with a cup of masala chai. Actually, calling it a side is not justified at all! Just be aware that after you taste ghee toast, you might make your toaster redundant!

Serves 2

2 tbsp ghee
4 thick slices of white bread
½ tsp salt, plus extra for serving

Spread the ghee on both sides of the bread slices and then sprinkle one side of each with the salt so that it gets stuck to the surface.

Take a non-stick frying pan (skillet) and place it over a low-medium heat.

Add one or two slices of bread (depending on the size of your pan) at a time into the pan.

Gently press down on the slice(s) using a flat spatula, on the edges only, and cook for 2 minutes on each side until golden brown.

Slice the toasted slices in half diagonally and sprinkle a little more salt over before serving while still hot.

WHITE BUTTER
(MAKKHAN)

Traditionally, ready-made yellow butter was not very common in India. Instead, people skimmed the cream from fresh whole milk and made butter by churning it, often in earthenware pots. There are many references to this butter in Lord Krishna's childhood stories as per Hindu culture. This butter is always white in colour. It's not oily, thanks to the water content, and is naturally sweet, with a slight tang. It's perfect with stuffed flatbread or for topping leafy curries. This is what's clarified to make ghee.

Makes 250g (9oz)

500ml (17fl oz) double (heavy) cream, chilled
200ml (7fl oz) ice-cold water
50ml (1¾fl oz) soured cream, chilled

Whisk the chilled double cream in a bowl using a hand-held electric whisk or a stand mixer until it splits. Keep whisking it and all the solids should come together.

Now add the ice-cold water and chilled soured cream and whisk again for 2–3 minutes, or until it looks curdled.

Strain it through a muslin cloth (cheesecloth) set over a bowl for 30 minutes at room temperature, then tie the cloth to squeeze out all of the water.

While it's still soft, use a small ice-cream scoop to scoop out small balls of the butter. This is best fresh, but the butter balls will keep in an airtight container in the fridge for 3–4 days.

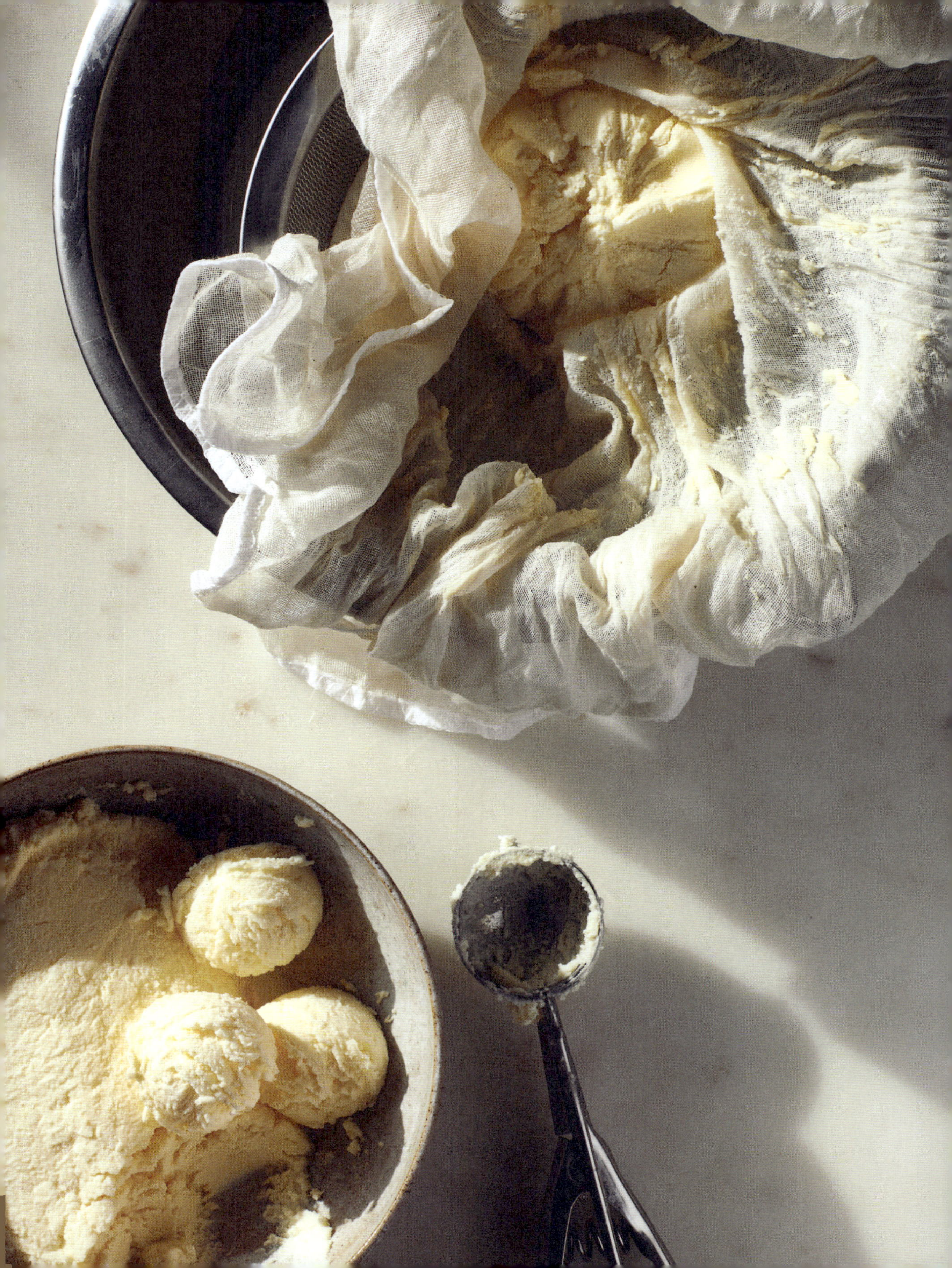

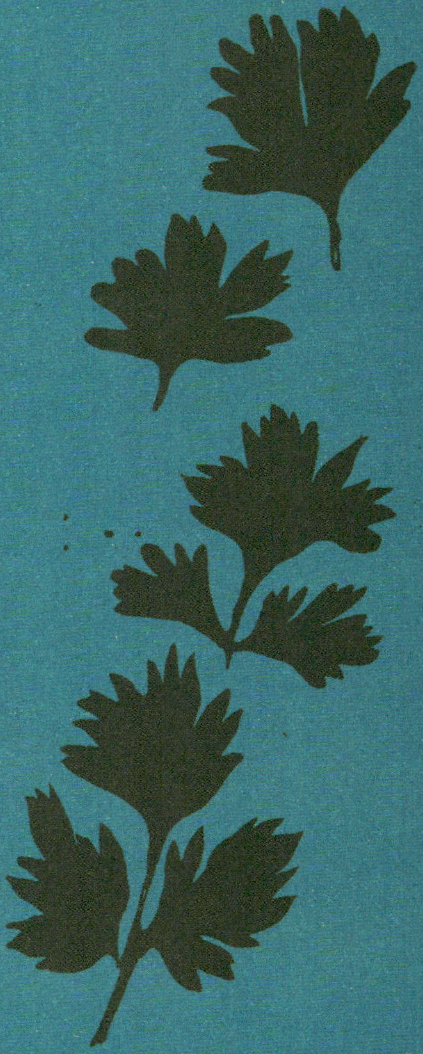

vegetable curries & LENTILS

What's for dinner? I am sure this is the most common question in all households when our tummies start making interesting sounds, signalling to please feed us something good. The urge for 'something good' can be annoying at times with our busy lifestyles!

This section will focus on some of the must-have veg curries and lentil dishes, which absolutely deserve to earn an Oscar for 'something good'. They are delicious, healthy and easy to make. They are also great options for batch cooking so that you can enjoy the same main dish with different side dishes, such as rice instead of chapati on a later day during the week. With my own very busy lifestyle and demanding young family, batch cooking and planning the meals for the whole week saves us lots of time without compromising on the taste and health aspects of our diet.

I was brought up in a vegetarian family and only started eating meat-based dishes in my late teens. As a result, the vegetarian options come very naturally to me when I think about meal planning. It's not at all a forced or conscious effort to eat something plant-based. Regional North Indian cuisine is inherently vegetarian, therefore it kills two birds with a single arrow – my cravings for traditional Indian dishes and meeting my five-a-day target.

POTATO AND PEA CURRY
(ALOO MATAR)

This wonderful curry reminds me of winters in India. With peas being ubiquitous during the colder months, my mother would make this curry so often that we siblings would complain and say, 'Oh, not again,' when it was served. Yet after such a love–hate relationship with this dish, its simplicity brings nostalgia and I want to share it with you out of love for my mother.

Serves 4

2 tbsp ghee or oil

½ tsp cumin seeds

1 green chilli, finely sliced, or to taste

1 tsp grated fresh peeled ginger

1 garlic clove, crushed

200g (7oz) red onions, chopped

200g (7oz) tomatoes, chopped

1 tbsp Curry Masala (see page 154)

1 tsp salt

200g (7oz) frozen peas

300g (10½oz) boiled peeled potatoes, cubed

A dash of double (heavy) cream, if you want to reduce the spice level (optional)

1 tbsp chopped fresh coriander (cilantro), to garnish

To serve
Paratha (see page 90), Roti (see page 88) or Jeera (Cumin) Rice (see page 105)

In a heavy-based pan (with a lid), heat the ghee or oil over a medium heat until hot, then add the cumin seeds. Once they start popping, immediately add the green chilli, ginger and garlic and cook over a medium heat for 1–2 minutes.

Now add the red onion and sweat for 5 minutes, then add the tomatoes and cook for another 2 minutes.

Tip in the curry masala and salt and keep cooking over a medium heat for 5 minutes, or until the oil separates.

Add the frozen peas and cubed potatoes and mix well. Pour in about 200ml (7fl oz) of water and bring to the boil. Cover the pan and simmer for another 5 minutes.

The curry should have a thick and wet consistency, so adjust the amount of water accordingly and adjust the spices to your taste. If it is too spicy, you could add a dash of cream.

Serve hot, garnished with the fresh coriander. This goes so well with Paratha, Roti or Jeera Rice.

Easy swaps
For a more special take on this, use roasted or fried potatoes.

Using the same curry base, you can cook any other vegetables or meat instead of the potatoes – just adjust the water level and cooking time as needed.

French (green) beans are a great substitute for the peas.

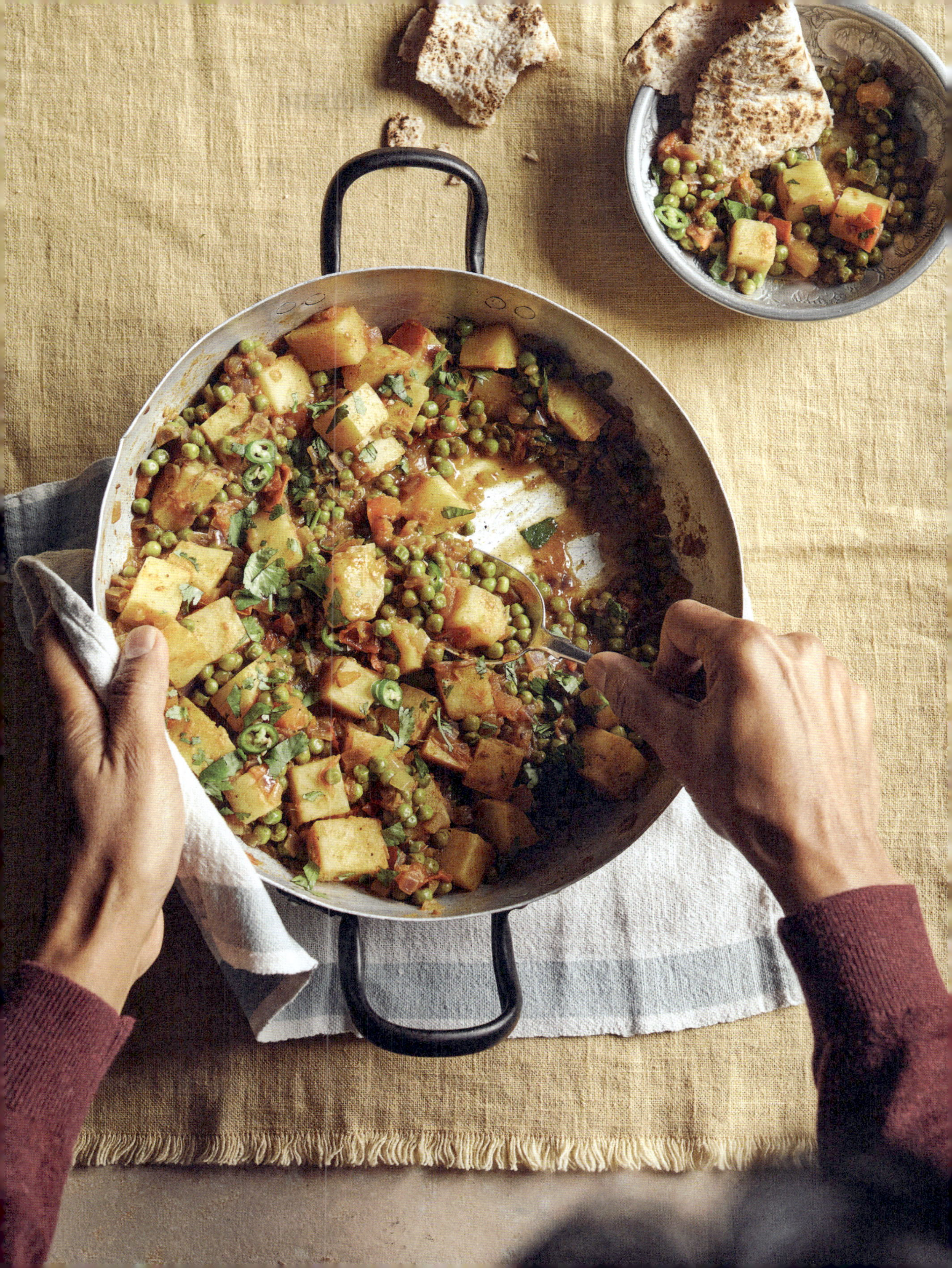

ROASTED CAULIFLOWER
(TANDOORI GOBHI)

A love of cauliflower runs in my family, and it is considered to be a very exclusive vegetable for use in dry curries for special occasions. When I moved to the UK, I struggled to produce the same flavour that I used to get in India. Then I realized that cauliflower grown outside of India has a very high water content, so when I cook it using the same old recipe, the outcome is not very appealing. That inspired me to create this recipe, whereby roasting this kind of cauliflower, rather than cooking it in a pan, produces a better dish!

Serves 6

200g (7oz) tomato passata (strained tomatoes)
1 tbsp Ginger Garlic Paste (see page 159)
1 tsp salt
1 tsp ground coriander
½ tsp red chilli powder
½ tsp ground turmeric
½ tsp Garam Masala (see page 155)
2 tbsp dried fenugreek leaves (kasoori methi)
4 tbsp oil
500g (1lb 2oz) cauliflower florets (see tip)

To garnish
Double (heavy) cream
Chopped fresh coriander (cilantro)

Preheat the oven to 200°C/180°C fan/400°F/Gas 6.

In a bowl, mix together all the ingredients, except the cauliflower, to make a marinade.

Coat the cauliflower florets thoroughly in the marinade and leave to marinate for 5 minutes.

Spread the cauliflower florets evenly over a baking sheet and roast in the oven for 30 minutes, or until cooked and slightly charred.

Serve hot, garnished with some cream and fresh coriander.

Tip
If time permits, remove the unprepped cauliflower from the fridge a day in advance and leave it at room temperature. This will help it to dry out, reducing the water content. Alternatively use a not-too-fresh cauliflower for a better texture.

Easy swap
Swap out the dried fenugreek leaves for 2 tsp dried curry or mint leaves.

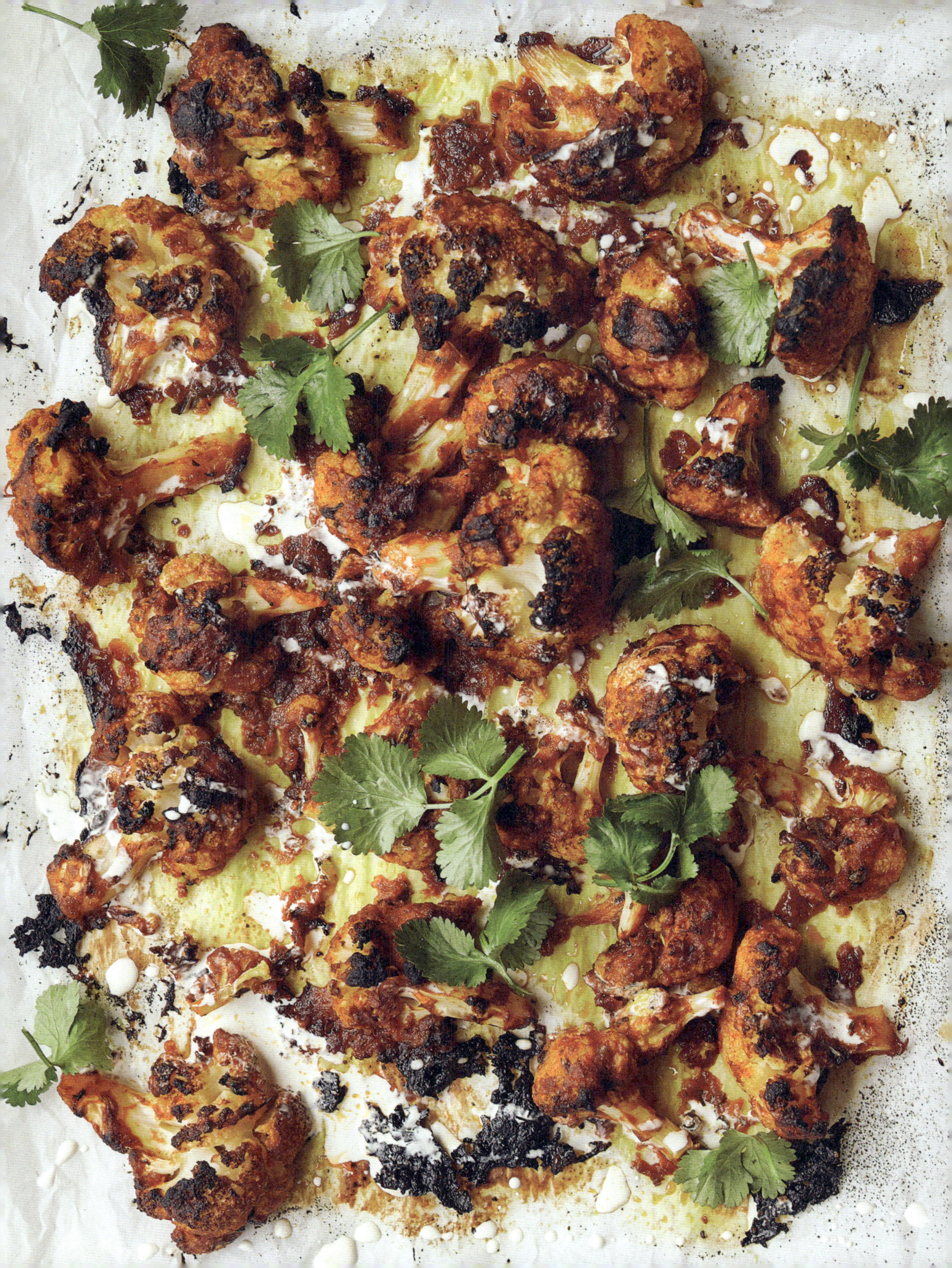

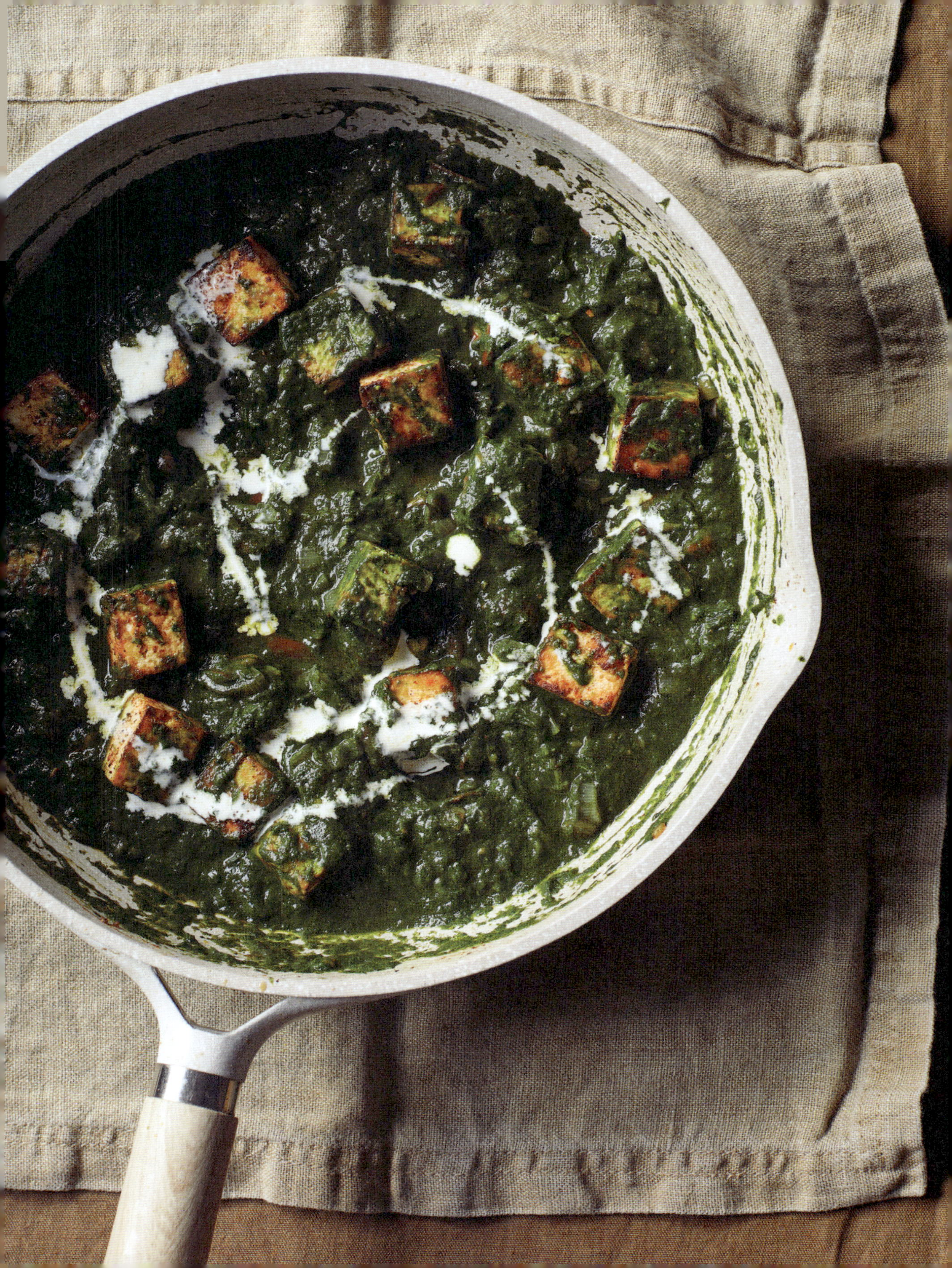

SPINACH AND INDIAN COTTAGE CHEESE CURRY

(PALAK PANEER)

Few dishes are special enough to grace the table only during celebrations. Palak paneer is one of them. For vegetarians, paneer provides a rich source of protein. On its own, it is very mild, but it's a great carrier for strong and earthy flavours like spinach. Being a celebratory dish, this recipe is surprisingly simple to make. I hope you will embrace the chance to taste the authentic Indian home-cooked version of the British Indian restaurant saag paneer for the first time!

Serves 4

250g (9oz) baby spinach, rinsed
240ml (8fl oz) boiling water
200g (7oz) paneer
1 tsp smoked paprika
2 tbsp ghee or oil
100g (3½oz) white onions, finely chopped
1 tsp chopped garlic
1 tbsp Curry Masala (see page 154)
100g (3½oz) tomatoes, chopped
¼ tsp Garam Masala (see page 155)
2 tbsp double (heavy) cream, to garnish

To serve (optional)
Paratha (see page 90) or Naan Bread (see page 98)
Mixed Salad (see page 59)

Vegan option
To make this vegan, swap the paneer for tofu, sweetcorn or mushrooms and pan-fry in the same way. Use plant-based cream, or skip it altogether.

Add the baby spinach and boiling water to a pan and cover with a lid. Cook over a high heat for 5 minutes. Drain the spinach through a sieve (strainer) and cool it under cold running water. Drain well. Now blend it into a smooth purée – you may need to add a splash of water, depending on your blender – and set aside to use later.

Cut the paneer into 16 small, equal cubes and coat in the paprika.

In a heavy-based pan, heat the ghee or oil. Fry the paneer cubes over a high heat, just enough to get some colour on all sides. It should not take more than 1–2 minutes. (Alternatively, skip this step to retain a soft texture.) Remove to a plate.

Using the same pan, tip in the onion and garlic and sweat over a medium heat for 5 minutes, then add the curry masala. Cook for another minute, then once it starts sticking to the pan, add the chopped tomatoes – they will deglaze the pan.

Add the spinach purée and mix well. Do not cook it for long or over a high heat – just enough to heat up the purée – or you will lose the vibrant colour of the spinach. The curry should be thick and wet; add a splash of water, if needed.

Add the pan-fried paneer to the pan, sprinkle over the Garam Masala and mix, then finally garnish with the cream and serve with Paratha or Naan bread, and lots of salad on the side.

VEGETABLE CURRIES & LENTILS

KIDNEY BEAN CURRY
(RAJMA)

Most Indians would never call this a rajma on its own: it is always referred to as 'rajma chawal', which is a combination of a kidney bean curry with rice. There's a bangers-and-mash kind of relationship between rajma and chawal (rice). I still haven't met an Indian who doesn't like rajma, and it's definitely a family favourite. Traditionally, it is cooked using dried kidney beans which are soaked overnight and then pressure cooked. My recipe is customized to get the same flavour in a very short time, without the need for a pressure cooker!

Serves 6

2 tbsp oil
½ tsp cumin seeds
4 cloves
2 dried bay leaves
2 garlic cloves, crushed
5cm (2in) piece of fresh ginger, peeled and cut into thin matchsticks/ julienne
200g (7oz) red onion paste (made by blending red onions with a splash of water)
1½ tsp salt
2 tsp Curry Masala (see page 154)
300g (10½oz) tomato passata (strained tomatoes)
2 x 400g (14oz) cans of red kidney beans, undrained
¼ tsp Garam Masala (see page 155)
2 tbsp chopped fresh coriander (cilantro), to garnish

To serve
Jeera (Cumin) Rice (see page 105)
Vegetables of your choice

In a deep pan, heat the oil over a medium heat and then add the cumin seeds, cloves and bay leaves. Once the whole spices start sputtering, add the garlic and ginger. Cook over a medium heat for a minute, then add the red onion paste and keep cooking until it gets some colour, around 5 minutes.

Now add the salt and Curry Masala and, once it starts sticking to the pan, tip in the tomato passata. Keep cooking over a medium-high heat until the oil separates. (This step is very important to achieve the deep flavour and correct texture.)

Tip in the red kidney beans together with their brine/liquid and mix well. Adjust the consistency by adding 200ml (7fl oz) of water and bring to the boil. It's important to add enough water here as the spices can be overpowering otherwise. Cover the pan and let it simmer for at least 15–20 minutes, until thick and soupy.

Adjust the spices to your taste and add a splash more water, if you like, then mix in the Garam Masala.

Garnish with the fresh coriander and serve hot with the Jeera Rice and vegetables.

Easy swaps
You can use chickpeas (garbanzo beans) or any other robust canned beans of your choice.

If you don't have a blender, just very finely chop the red onion.

VEGETABLE CURRIES & LENTILS

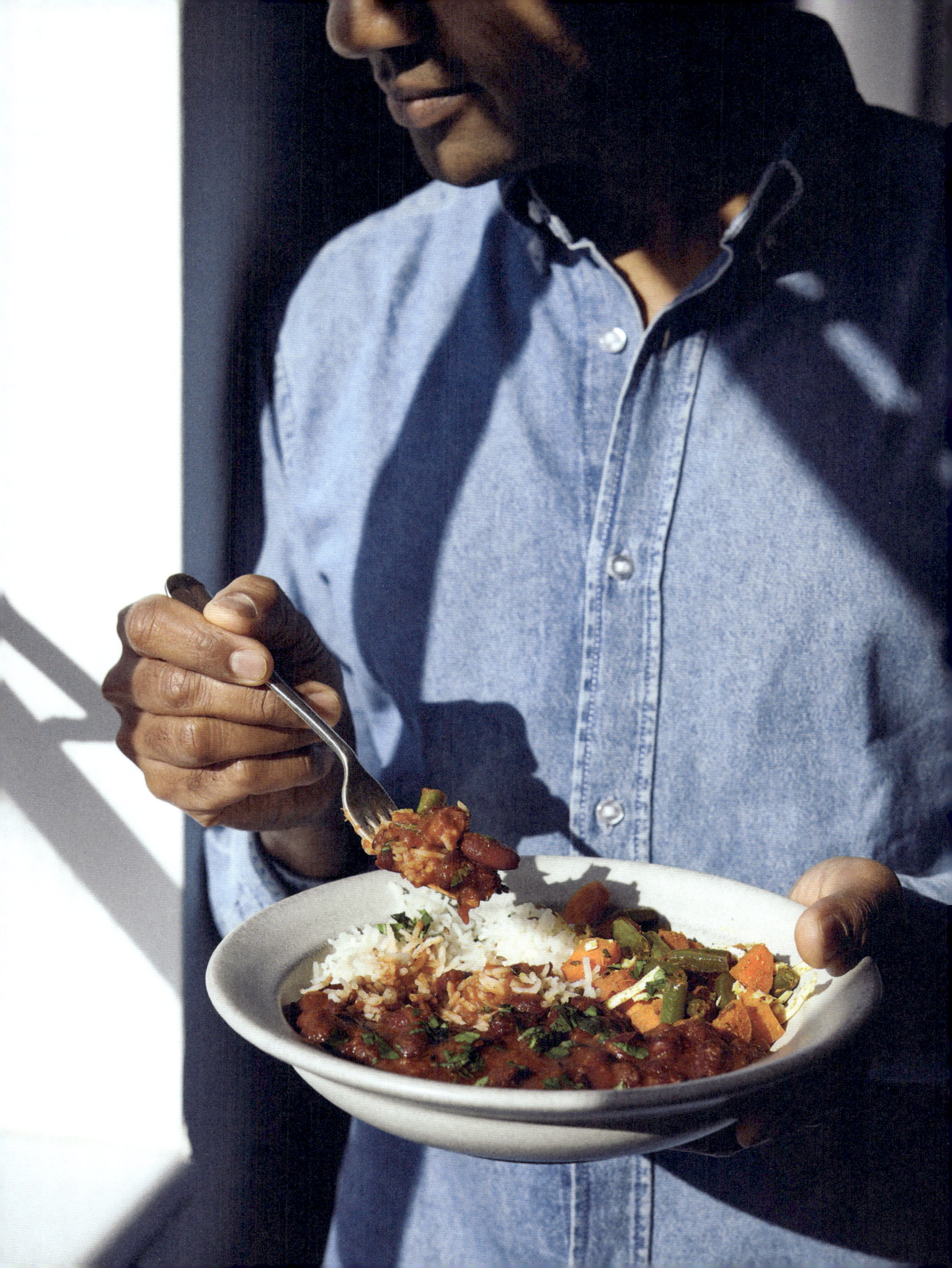

CARROTS AND BEANS
(GAJAR FALI)

Growing up back in India, eating seasonal vegetables was part of our lifestyle. Not only do they taste amazing, I feel that we should design our diets around the seasons and geography we live in. Bright and vibrant red carrots are synonymous with North Indian winters. This dry curry is a fantastic side to any lentil dish and rice or wheat-based meal. (See more meal combinations in chapter 7, starting on page 170). It's light in spices, to retain the natural sweetness of the carrots and the vibrancy of the beans. It's a clever way to incorporate healthy veg into your meal alongside your protein and carbs.

Serves 4

500g (1lb 2oz) carrots
200g (7oz) French (green) beans
2 tbsp oil
½ tsp cumin seeds
1 tsp salt
½ tsp ground turmeric
½ tsp Curry Masala (see page 154)
¼ tsp Garam Masala (see page 155)
2 tbsp grated paneer, to garnish
Handful of dried fenugreek leaves (kasoori methi), to garnish (optional)

Firstly, prepare the carrots and beans. Peel and trim the carrots, then slice in half lengthways and cut into 5-mm (¼-in) thick slices. Top and tail the beans and cut into 5mm (¼in) pieces. (If your vegetable pieces are bigger or smaller than this, you'll need to adjust the cooking time accordingly.)

In a heavy-based, non-stick pan (with a lid), heat the oil over a medium heat and add the cumin seeds. Once they start sputtering, tip in the carrots and beans. Add the salt and turmeric and mix well over a high heat, then reduce the heat, cover with the lid and simmer for 10 minutes.

Carefully open the lid and let the condensed steam fall back into the pan. Add the Curry Masala and Garam Masala, mix well and cook over a medium heat for another 5 minutes without the lid. At this stage, the carrots and beans should be fully cooked without being mushy or raw.

Serve hot, garnished with the grated paneer and, if you can, the dried fenugreek leaves – the bitterness will balance the sweetness of the carrots.

Easy swap
Try replacing the French beans with frozen garden peas, but add them towards the end of cooking when you add the Curry Masala, as they don't need long to cook.

BASHED AUBERGINE
(BAINGAN BHARTA)

In Indian cuisine, baingan (aubergine/eggplant) has a dual reputation of love and hate. The people who love it generally like to eat it in the form of this dish, which is smoky, earthy and comforting. Bharta is a Hindi term, which means to bash something to a pulp. If I have been barbecuing, I like to cook some aubergines over the residual heat ready for making this dish later – I just peel them and then freeze the cooled flesh and defrost before use.

Serves 4

600g (1lb 5oz) aubergines (eggplants)

2 tbsp oil

½ tsp cumin seeds

1 tsp finely chopped garlic

1 tbsp finely chopped fresh peeled ginger

1 green chilli, finely sliced

200g (7oz) red onions, finely chopped

1½ tsp salt

½ tsp ground turmeric

¼ tsp red chilli powder

1 tsp ground coriander

200g (7oz) tomatoes, sliced

1 tbsp lime juice

¼ tsp Garam Masala (see page 155)

2 tbsp chopped fresh coriander (cilantro), to garnish

To serve
Paratha (see page 90) or Roti (see page 88), if serving warm, or toasted bread or pitta if serving cold

Mixed Salad (see page 59)

Cucumber Raita (see page 59)

Preheat the oven to 240°C/220°C fan/475°F/Gas 9, or preheat a BBQ.

Pierce the aubergines with a sharp knife in a few places and cook in the oven for 20–25 minutes, or over a gas flame or BBQ, turning occasionally, until the skin is almost burnt/charred all over and the inside is fully cooked and soft. Remove from the heat and set aside to cool completely.

Once cool, carefully remove the burnt skin from the aubergines. You will be left with smoky, soft flesh. (Don't worry if it is a bit too burnt – you might just need to peel off a thicker layer of skin.) Place the flesh in a bowl and use a fork to gently break it down into a very chunky mash. Set aside.

In a deep, non-stick pan, heat the oil over a medium heat, then add the cumin seeds. Once they start sputtering, tip in the garlic, ginger and green chilli. Once they start taking on some colour, increase the heat to high and add the red onion.

After a minute or so, once the onion is translucent, add the salt, turmeric, red chilli powder and ground coriander and cook for another minute. Very soon the mixture will start sticking to the pan: immediately add the tomatoes and aubergine pulp. Increase the heat to high, stir continuously for 6–8 minutes, until most of the moisture has evaporated and the oil starts to separate.

Now add the lime juice and Garam Masala, mix well, then remove from the heat. Garnish with the fresh coriander and serve hot with flatbread, salad and raita, or cold, with toasted bread or pitta.

Pictured overleaf.

VEGETABLE CURRIES & LENTILS

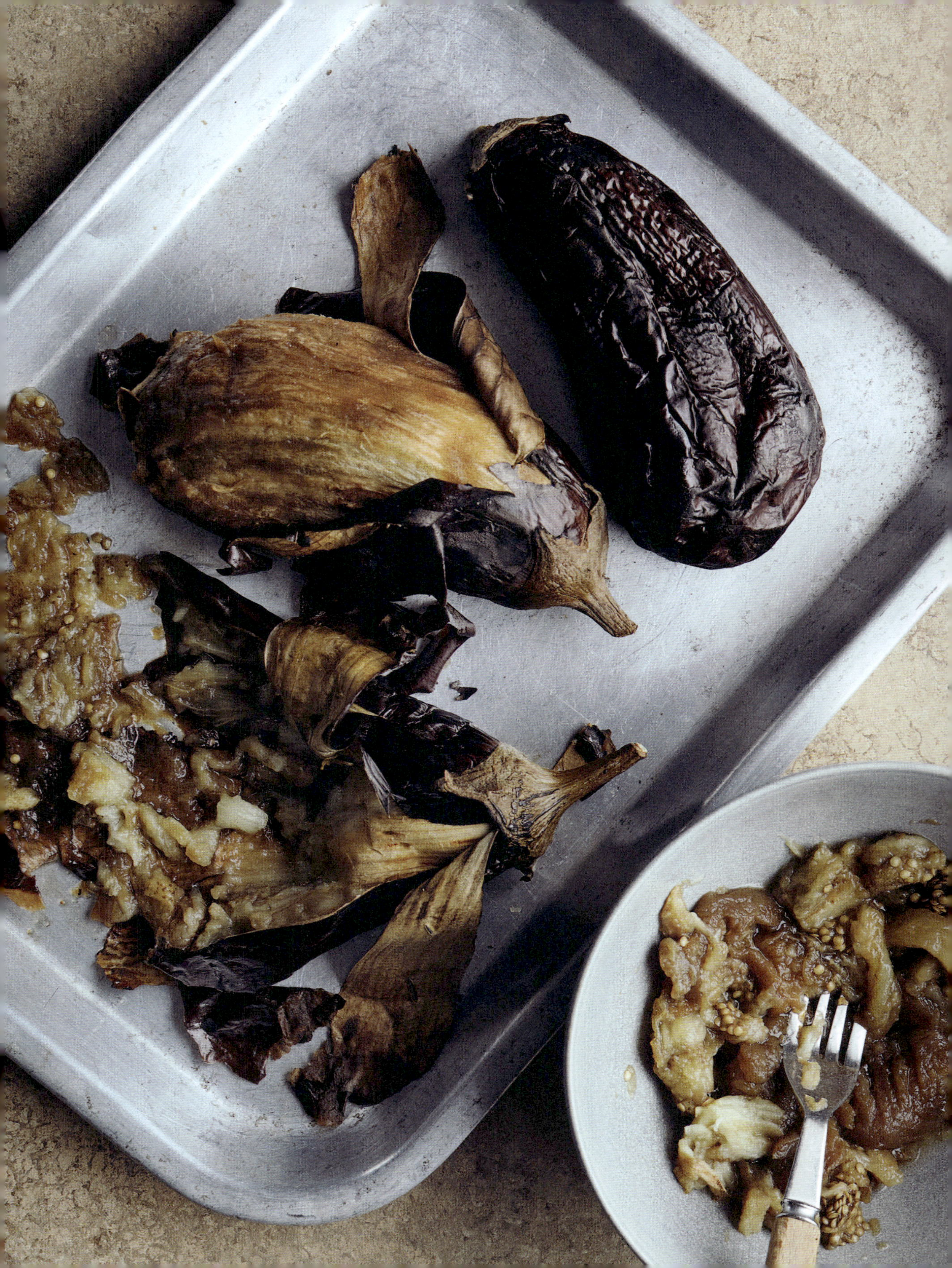

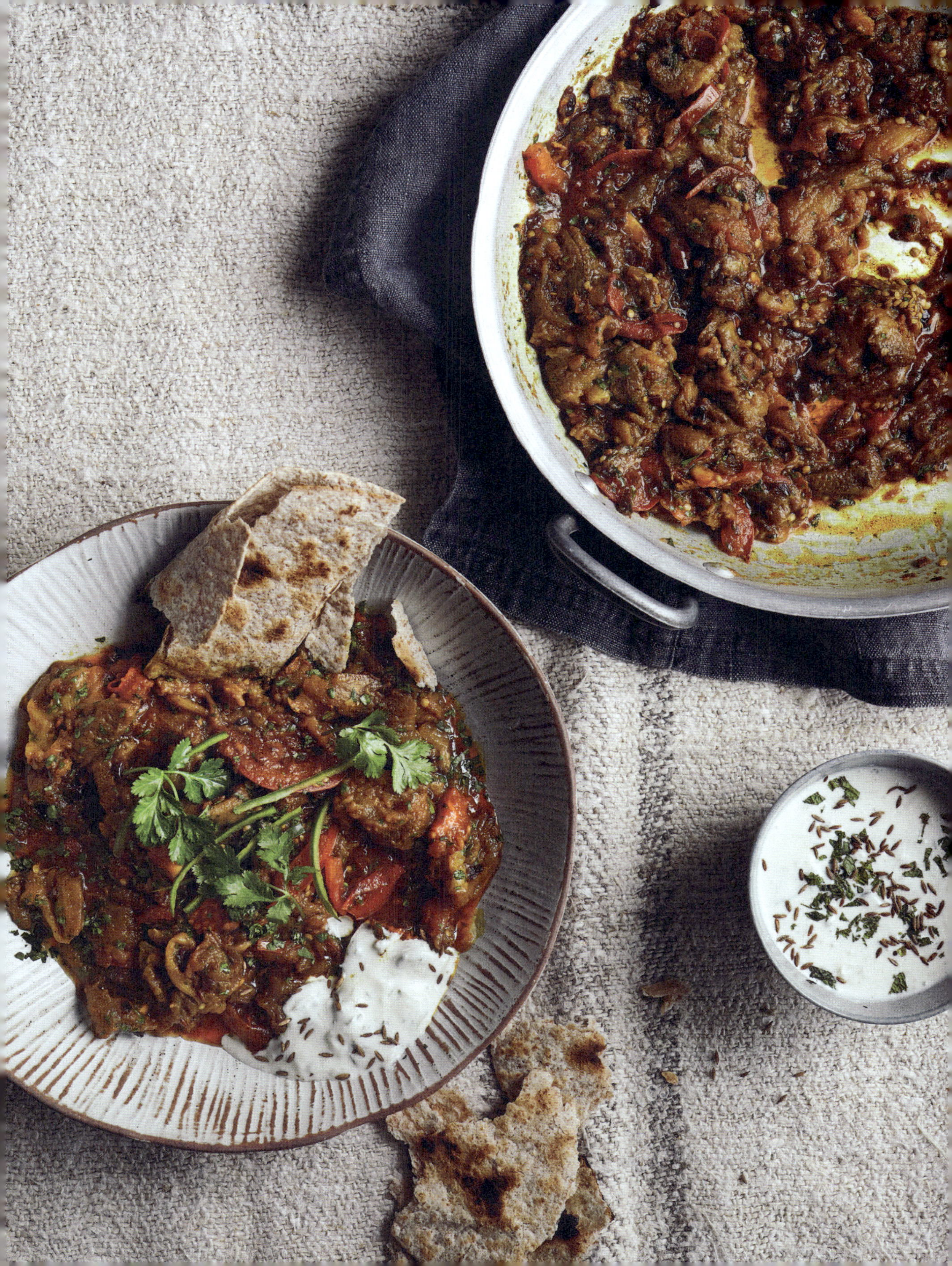

PANEER TIKKA

In any Indian restaurant, paneer tikka is one of the most famous dishes among vegetarians. Grilled (broiled) large paneer cubes with a charred spicy crust and a creamy centre, paired with vibrant peppers and red onion, then drizzled with mint yoghurt and finished with a squeeze of fresh lime and a generous sprinkle of chaat masala – what's not to love? This dish is very versatile and can be served as a side, starter or main (wrapped inside a flatbread, such as a paratha or naan).

Serves 4

- 500g (1lb 2oz) paneer, cut into 4cm (1½in) cubes
- 1 large red (bell) pepper, deseeded and cut into 4cm (1½in) chunks
- 1 large green (bell) pepper, deseeded and cut into 4cm (1½in) chunks
- 1 large red onion, cut into 4cm (1½in) chunks
- Oil, for brushing

For the marinade

- 2 tbsp oil
- 1 tbsp Greek-style yoghurt
- 1 tsp Ginger Garlic Paste (see page 159)
- 1 tsp cornflour (cornstarch)
- 1 tsp salt
- 1 tsp ground cumin
- 1 tsp ground turmeric
- ½ tsp red chilli powder, or to taste
- ¼ tsp Garam Masala (see page 155)
- 1 tbsp lime juice

For the garnish

- 2 tbsp Mint and Coriander Chutney (see page 162)
- 4 tbsp Greek-style yoghurt
- 1 tbsp Chaat Masala (see page 153)
- 2 tbsp lime juice
- 50g (1¾oz) red onion rings
- 2 tbsp chopped fresh coriander (cilantro)

4 x wooden skewers, soaked in water for at least 30 minutes before use

In a bowl, mix all the marinade ingredients together, then add the paneer cubes and toss to coat. Cover and leave to marinate for at least 1 hour at room temperature, or refrigerate overnight.

When you are ready to cook, preheat the grill (broiler) to high (or if using an oven grill, preheat the grill to 240°C/475°F/Gas 9). Bring the paneer cubes back to room temperature, if they have been chilled.

Thread the paneer cubes onto 4 wooden or metal skewers, alternating them with the pepper and red onion chunks.

Brush with some oil and cook under the hot grill (or in a large, non-stick frying pan/skillet over a medium heat) for about 7 minutes, then turn over and cook for a further 5 minutes, until the outside of the paneer is nicely charred and golden.

Meanwhile, in a small bowl, mix the chutney and yoghurt together to make a mint dip.

Sprinkle the Chaat Masala over the hot and sizzling paneer tikka, squeeze over the lime juice, drizzle over the mint dip and garnish with the red onion rings and fresh coriander, then serve.

Easy swap
Use firm tofu in place of the paneer, if you prefer.

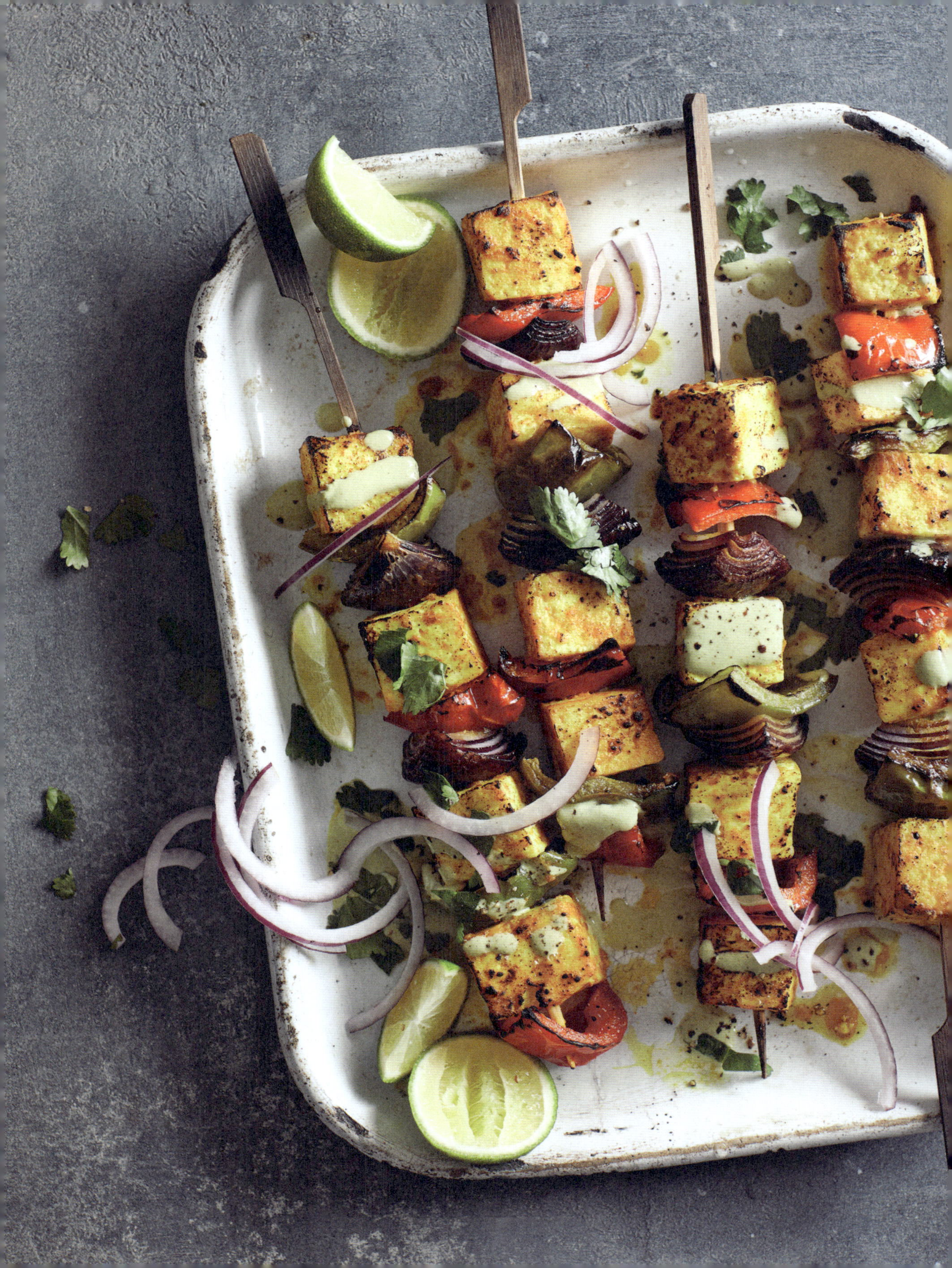

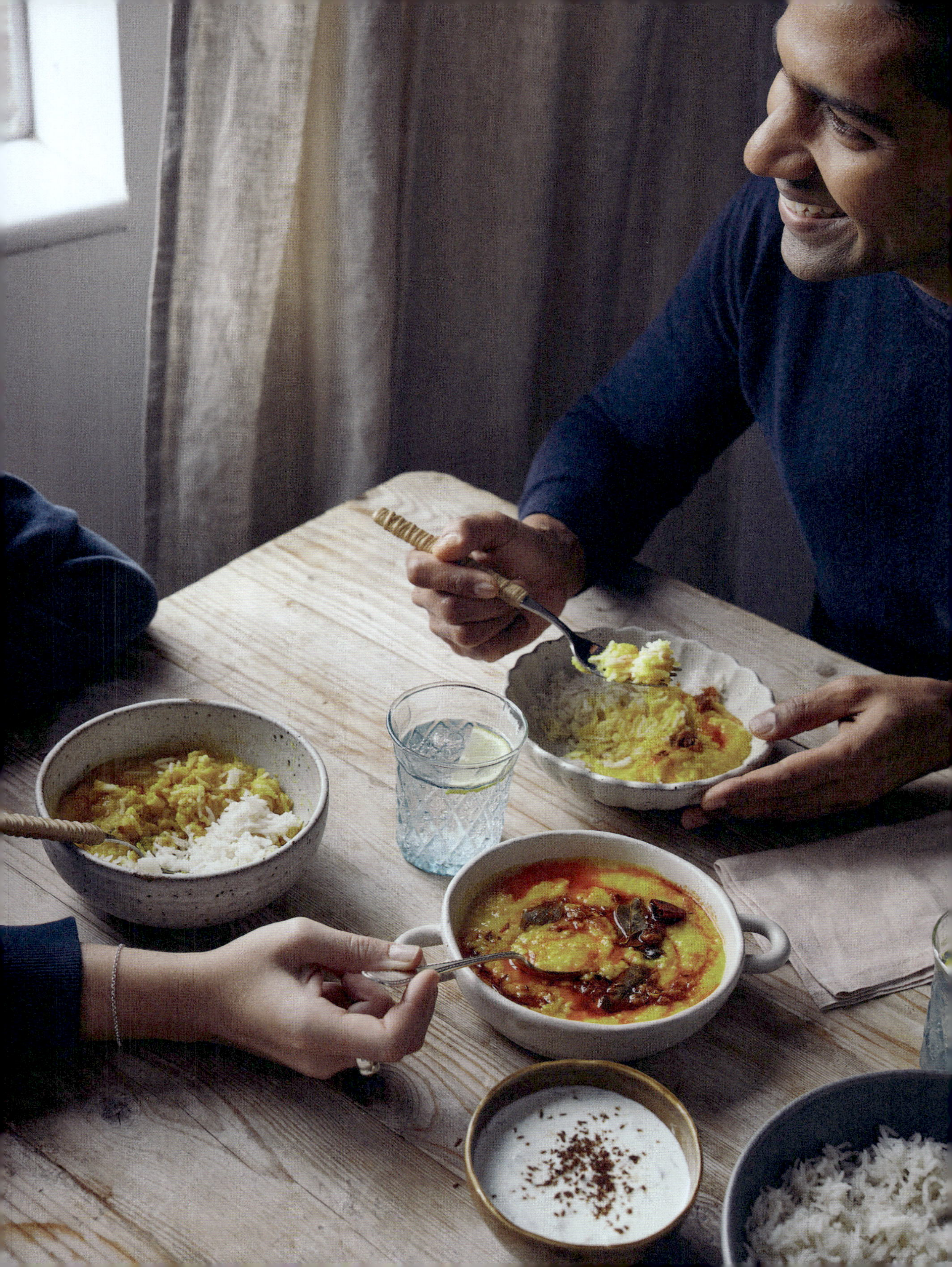

TADKA DAAL

This dish is for when you are craving something very simple, hearty and warm. Tadka daal with rice, some side vegetable dish and cooling natural yoghurt is the perfect answer to that feeling. It doesn't contain any onions and tomatoes, which can make the dish a bit heavy. It tastes so satisfying and is a great way to incorporate protein and fibre into a vegetarian diet. Due to its soupy consistency, you can eat it with all kinds of carbs, or even on its own as a soup. I am sure by now you will be fully convinced to give it a go!

Serves 3–4

180g (6¼oz) dried yellow lentils (moong), washed

1 tsp salt, or to taste

½ tsp ground turmeric

1 tbsp lime juice

2 tbsp chopped fresh coriander (cilantro), to garnish

For the tempering (tadka), or see page 160

2 tbsp ghee

½ tsp cumin seeds

A pinch of asafoetida (hing)

1 dried red chilli

1 tbsp grated fresh peeled ginger

1 tbsp (8–10) curry leaves

¼ tsp red chilli powder

½ tsp ground coriander

¼ tsp Garam Masala (see page 155)

To serve

Plain boiled rice, Jeera (Cumin) Rice (see page 105) or toasted sourdough

Mixed Salad (see page 59)

Cucumber Raita (see page 59)

In a deep pan (with a lid), combine the lentils and 900ml (31fl oz) of water and bring to the boil. Add the salt and turmeric and mix well. Cover the pan and simmer for about 20 minutes, or until the lentils are tender. Keep an eye on it as the lentils produce a lot of froth, so you might need to stir a few times to prevent any spills. If you like, you can blend the lentils for a smoother consistency.

Meanwhile, to make the tempering, heat the ghee in a small pan over a medium heat, the add the cumin seeds and asafoetida. Once they start browning, break the whole chilli into a few pieces and add. A few seconds later, add the ginger and curry leaves. Now you can increase the heat and cook for 1 minute or so until the ginger starts to get some colour.

Remove from the heat and add the red chilli powder, ground coriander and Garam Masala. The tempering is now ready. Keep it aside until you are ready to serve.

Stir the boiled lentils, add the lime juice and taste. Adjust with extra salt if you want to.

Tip the lentils into a serving bowl and drizzle over the tempering. Swirl it gently, so that it is partially mixed in, but so you can still see the vibrant ghee.

Garnish with the fresh coriander and serve with plain rice, Jeera Rice or toasted sourdough, Mixed Salad and Cucumber Raita.

Easy swap
Substitute the yellow lentils for dried split red lentils.

VEGETABLE CURRIES & LENTILS

CHICKPEA CURRY

(CHOLE)

This curry can be made in a similar style to Rajma (see page 46), however this recipe goes very well with bhatura (deep-fried naan) or regular naan bread. It's thick, very dark brown in colour and fragrant with whole spices. Chole bhatura, chole kulcha and chole samosa are also very famous Indian dishes. So, you can always pair this differently to get some variety.

Serves 6

2 x 400g (14oz) cans of chickpeas (garbanzo beans), undrained

3 black tea bags

1 tsp Garam Masala (see page 155)

2 tbsp lime juice

For the tempering
4 tbsp ghee or oil

½ tsp cumin seeds

4 cloves

2 dried bay leaves

3 black cardamom pods

1 tsp black peppercorns

5cm (2in) piece of fresh ginger, peeled and cut into thin matchsticks/julienne

2 garlic cloves, crushed

2 tsp salt

1 tsp ground turmeric

2 tsp ground coriander

2 tbsp tomato purée (paste)

To serve
2 tbsp chopped fresh coriander (cilantro)

1 tbsp sliced green chillies

Naan Bread (see page 98) or bhatura, to serve

Put the chickpeas and their brine/liquid into a large pan and bring to the boil over a high heat, then add the tea bags and keep this boiling while you make the tempering.

Using a small pan, heat the ghee or oil over a medium heat, then add all the whole spices (cumin, cloves, bay, cardamom and peppercorns). Once they start sputtering, add the ginger and garlic and cook for another minute until the garlic takes on some colour. Now add the salt, turmeric and ground coriander, mix well and then remove from the heat. Stir in the tomato purée.

Tip this ghee tempering into the pan of simmering chickpeas and mix well. Keep cooking over a high heat, without a lid, for around 30 minutes, until the curry becomes very thick.

Carefully remove the tea bags and large whole spices (as far as you can – don't worry about the cloves and peppercorns!).

Stir in the Garam Masala and lime juice and cook for 2 minutes. Taste and adjust the seasoning with salt or spices to taste.

Serve garnished with the fresh coriander and sliced green chillies and, with Naan Bread or bhatura. For a different but delicious combination, pair this with onion rings with Chaat Masala (see page 153) and lime juice, fried or roasted potatoes covered in Mint and Coriander Chutney (see page 162), plus the Naan or bhatura.

Easy swap
Replace the yellow chickpeas with canned black chickpeas or any robust canned beans of your choice.

VEGETABLE CURRIES & LENTILS

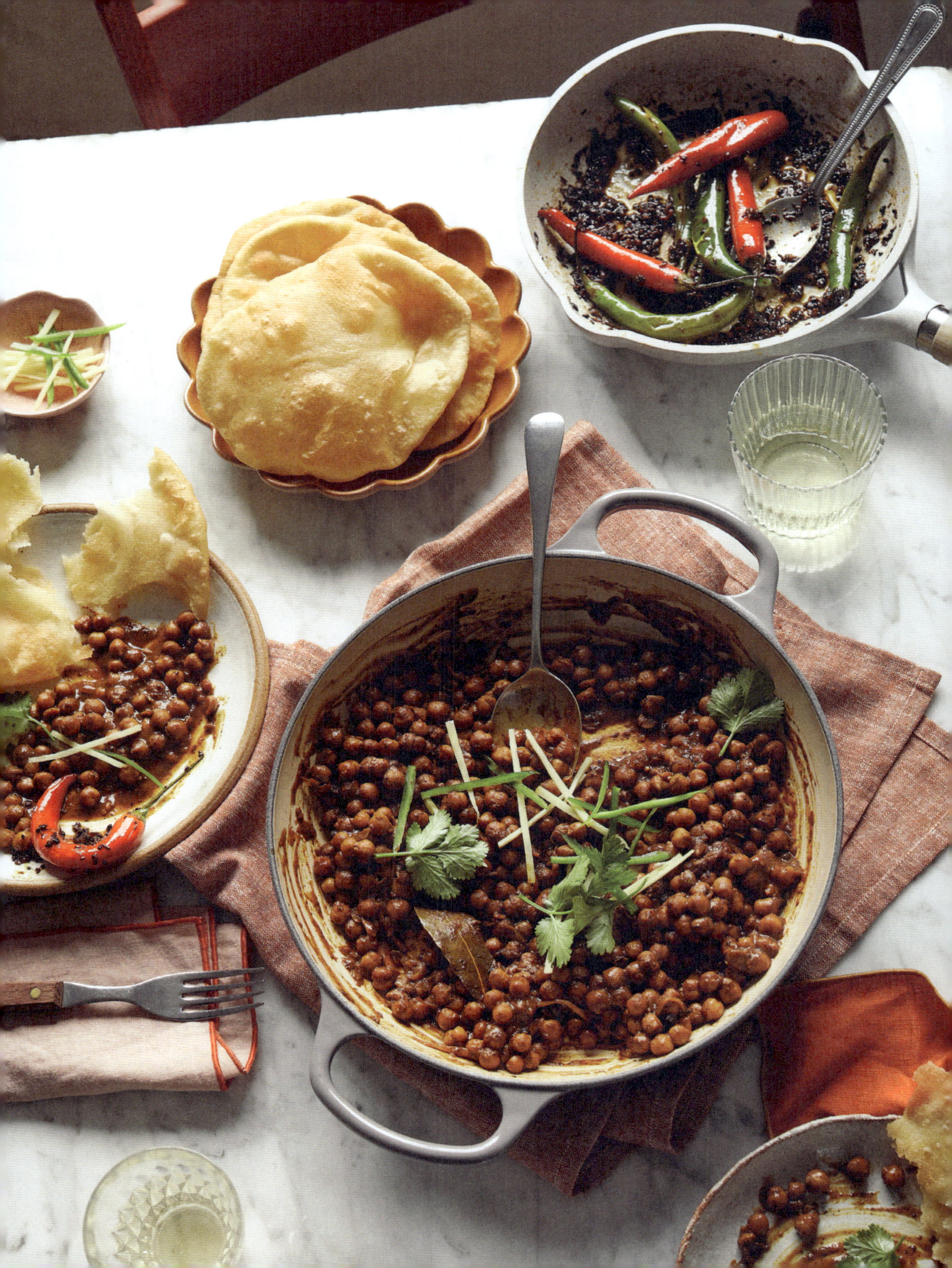

COURGETTE CURRY

(TURIYA)

Courgette (zucchini) was a new vegetable for me when I moved to the UK. It's very similar to a regional vegetable, turiya (ridge gourd), which grows in the summer in north India. Because of its high water content, it's perfect for the hotter months. Simple vegetables like turiya and courgettes are very delicate in texture as well as in flavour, so just a hint of spice can elevate them to another level (rather than overpowering them with lots of spices, onion and the strong flavour of garlic). This recipe does just that, and is an amalgamation of a dry and a wet curry.

Serves 4

1 tbsp ghee
½ tsp cumin seeds
A pinch of asafoetida (hing)
100g (3½oz) tomatoes, chopped
1 tsp salt
½ tsp ground turmeric
¼ tsp red chilli powder
½ tsp ground coriander
600g (1lb 5oz) green or yellow courgettes (zucchini), or crookneck (yellow) squash, when in season, diced
A pinch of Garam Masala (see page 155)
1 tbsp chopped fresh coriander (cilantro), to garnish

To serve
Any combination of lentils and rice, or Roti (see page 88) and Cucumber Raita (see opposite)

Heat the ghee in a deep, heavy-based, non-stick pan (with a lid) over a medium heat, then add the cumin seeds and asafoetida. Once they start browning, add the chopped tomatoes over a high heat. Add the salt, turmeric, red chilli powder and ground coriander and cook for a minute.

Now tip in the courgettes and mix well to ensure the tomato masala coats them evenly.

Cover the pan, reduce the heat and simmer for 15 minutes. Halfway through the cooking time, stir once to ensure there is enough moisture; if not, add a tablespoon of water.

Stir in the Garam Masala, then garnish with the fresh coriander and serve as a side with lentils and rice or even with Roti and Raita.

Tip
Using a heavy-based, non-stick pan is important as we are cooking this dish in its own juices. If you are using a normal pan, add a splash of water to ensure it doesn't get burnt on the bottom.

Pictured overleaf.

MUST-HAVE SIDES

CUCUMBER RAITA

Yoghurt dishes play the important role of offsetting both the heat of spices and the heaviness of curries. In a vegetarian diet, it also provides a great source of protein and calcium. Though there are countless yoghurt sides, this raita is very simple, refreshing and delicious. Creamy yoghurt, cooling cucumber, smoky cumin and refreshing mint are a killer combination.

Serves 6

500ml (17fl oz) Greek-style or natural (plain) set yoghurt
250g (9oz) cucumber (peel on), coarsely grated
½ tsp salt
2 tbsp chopped fresh mint leaves
1 tsp Roasted Ground Cumin (see page 152)

Simply mix together the yoghurt, cucumber and salt in a bowl, adding a little water to adjust the consistency, if you like.

Garnish with the chopped mint leaves and Roasted Ground Cumin. Serve chilled with any curries, as a dip with fried snacks, or eat a small pot on its own to cool down!

Tips
While grating cucumber, catch and use all the liquid it produces as that's where all the fresh flavours are.

If you want to make a dip instead, then strain the yoghurt overnight in the fridge in a muslin cloth (cheesecloth) set over a bowl. Discard the liquid, use the strained yoghurt and continue as above.

MIXED SALAD

In Indian culture, salads have a very different connotation compared to the Western world, where salads can be a whole meal, with added protein and carbs. Generally, Indian salads are an assortment of slices of fresh red onion, cucumber, tomatoes, radishes and green chillies with salt and lime juice. Here is my take on that combination, made a bit more interesting and beautiful.

Serves 6

200g (7oz) small cucumbers (peel on), diced
100g (3½oz) red onions, chopped
200g (7oz) cherry tomatoes, quartered
100g radishes, cut into matchsticks
100g (3½oz) fresh pomegranate seeds
2 tbsp chopped jalapeños
1 tbsp extra virgin olive oil
1 tbsp lime juice
3 tbsp chopped fresh coriander (cilantro)
3 tbsp chopped fresh mint
½ tsp salt

Simply mix all the ingredients together in a large bowl. Serve immediately with almost anything edible (maybe not with cakes!).

Tip
To make this in advance, mix the salad ingredients in a bowl (and keep chilled), but do not mix in the olive oil, lime juice, herbs and salt until just before serving — the salt draws liquid out of the vegetables, meaning the salad won't be crunchy if left to sit in it.

VEGETABLE CURRIES & LENTILS

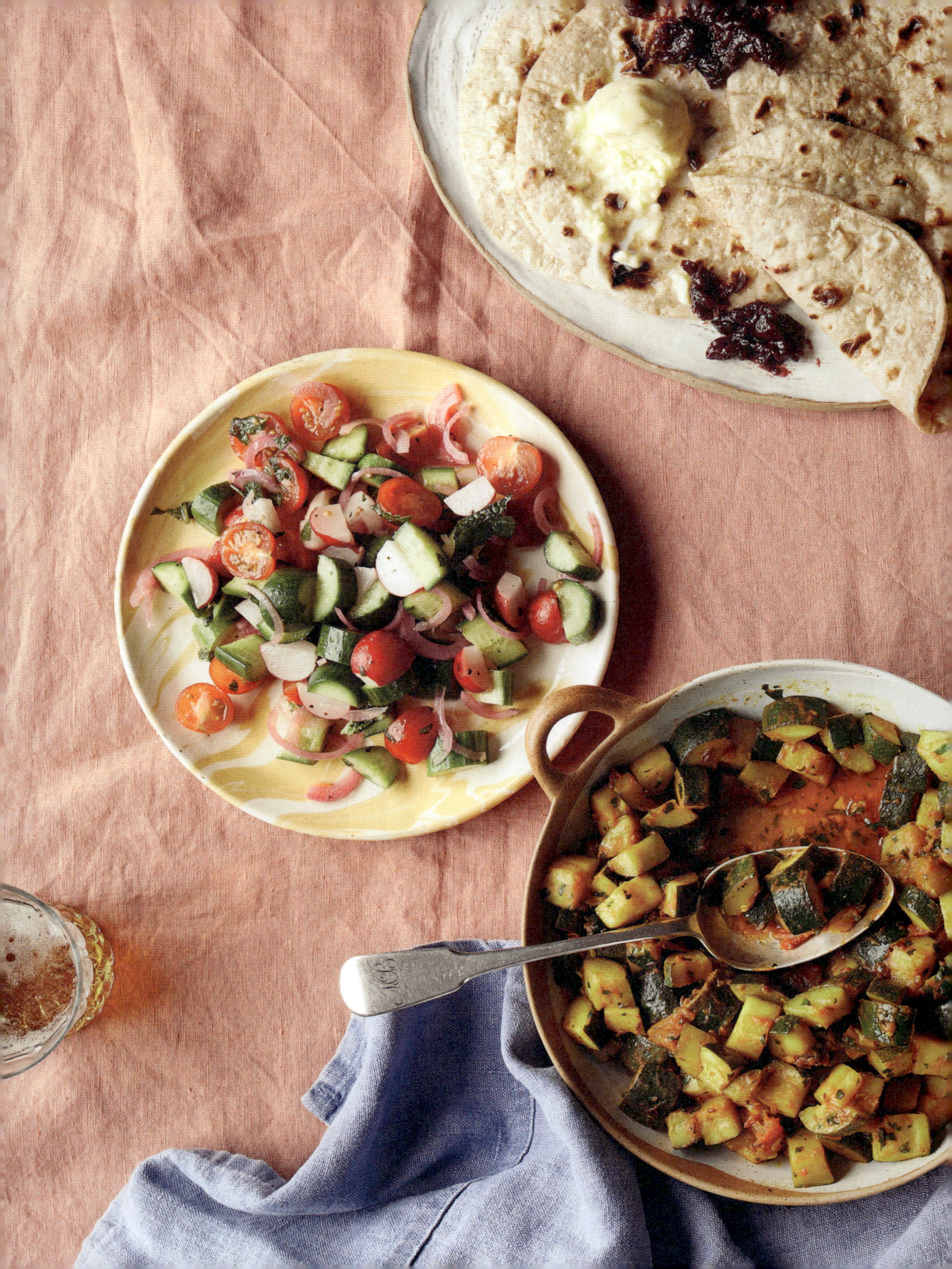

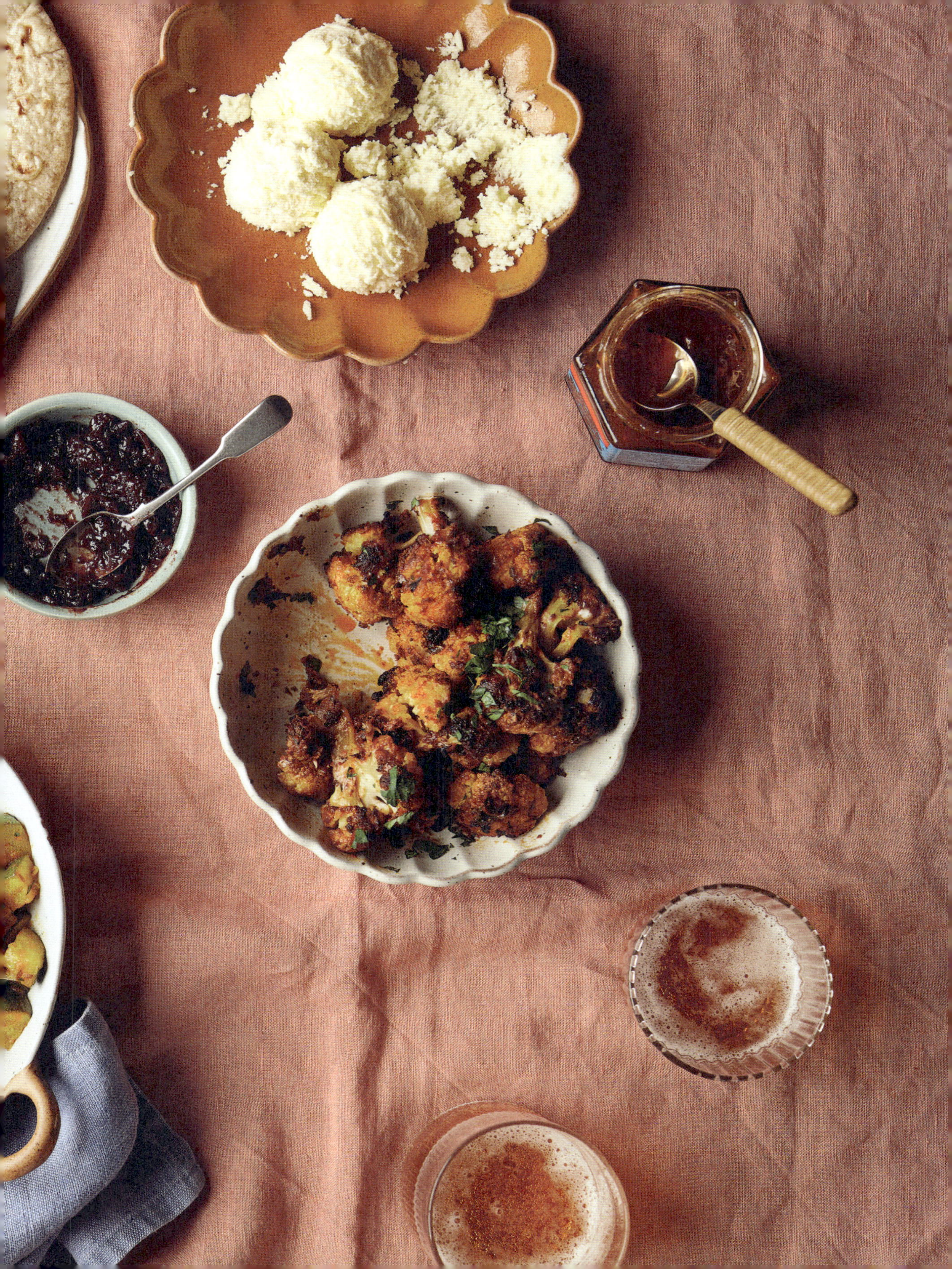

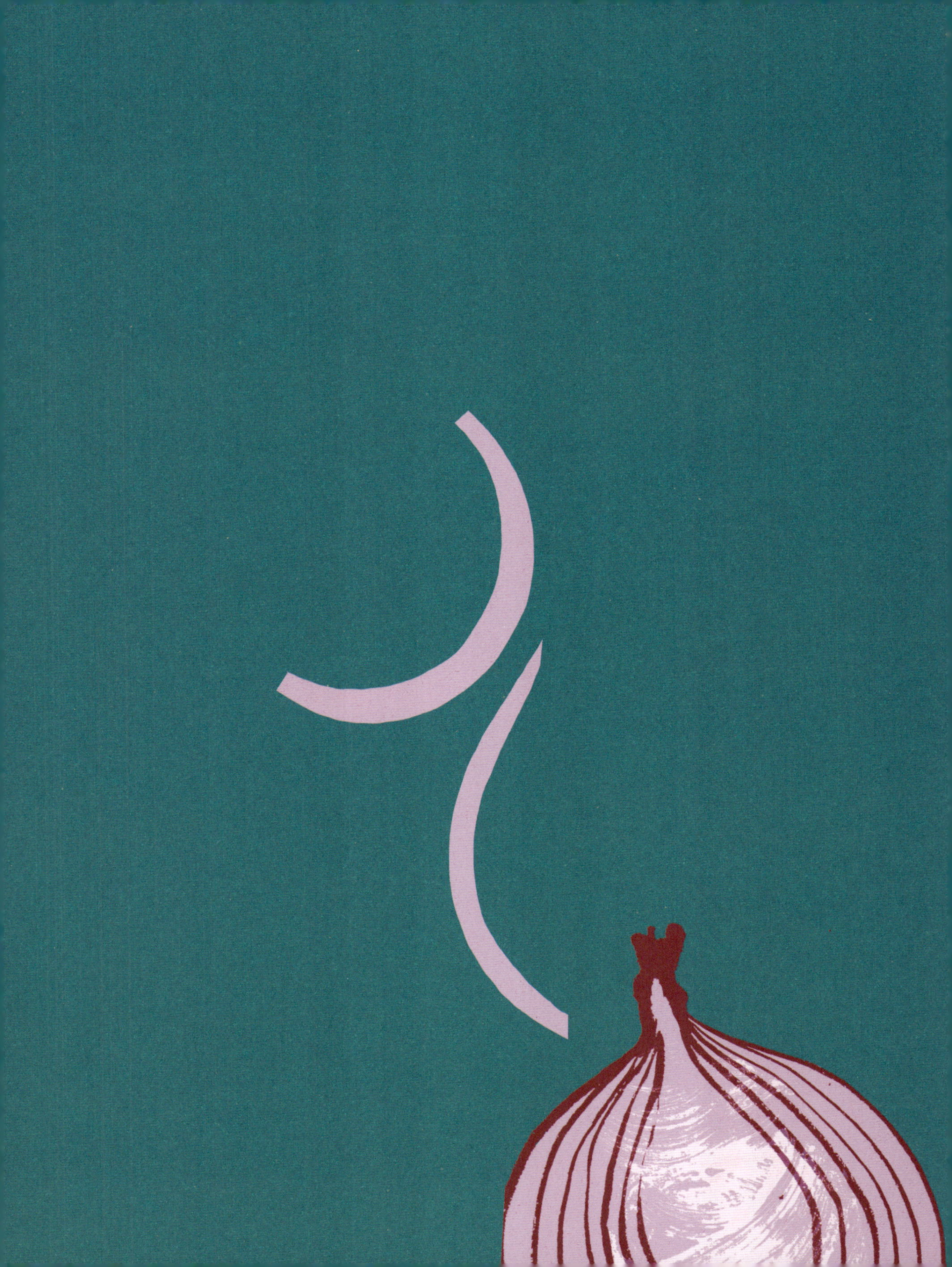

meat-based DISHES

Inaccessibility creates curiosity! That's the theme of my story of Indian meat-based dishes. Born and brought up in a purely vegetarian household does create a certain perception about food in general. Our thoughts can only be influenced by the information that we are exposed to. Therefore, as a child, any animal product (other than dairy) was never part of my food awareness. I feel blessed that in the 1980s and 1990s there was no or little internet, so most of the time we were content with what we had.

Printed media advertisements and restaurant menus did create some curiosity in my mind about non-vegetarian food. Although my family was vegetarian, they were very open-minded about me exploring this side of the cuisine. I vaguely remember that I was around 10 years old when I took the very first bite of a lamb dish while dining with family friends. Speaking honestly, as a vegetarian, I struggled to enjoy the meat. But I kept trying different meat dishes over a period and gradually developed a taste for them.

This chapter captures some of the simple and easy meat-based recipes that I enjoy cooking and eating, as a not-too-hardcore vegetarian. I find my background of choosing meat versus vegetables very useful, as they are just different options of food, rather than seeing meat as the main dishes and vegetables as the side dishes. I am sure you will notice a difference when you cook these recipes, in terms of freshness and the light feel of them, rather than the heavy and processed feel you may get when you eat Indian meat-based dishes in a restaurant or from your favourite takeaway.

HOME-STYLE CHICKEN CURRY

(DESI CHICKEN)

Serves 4

600g (1lb 5oz) skinless, boneless chicken thighs, each cut into 4 pieces

For the marinade

2 tbsp Greek-style yoghurt

2 tbsp lime juice

1 tbsp Ginger Garlic Paste (see page 159)

1 tsp salt

For the base sauce

2 tbsp oil

4 black cloves

6 green cardamom pods

200g (7oz) white onions, sliced

1 tsp salt

2 tbsp Curry Masala (see page 154)

1 x 400g (14oz) can of chopped tomatoes

100 (3½fl oz) double (heavy) cream, plus extra to garnish

½ tsp Garam Masala (see page 155)

1 tbsp dried fenugreek leaves (kasoori methi)

2 tbsp chopped fresh coriander (cilantro), to garnish

Naan Bread (see page 98) or Jeera (Cumin) Rice (see page 105) and some sliced raw red onion, to serve

There are many popular chicken curries, such as kadahi chicken, butter chicken and the British classic chicken tikka masala. My personal favourite is this very simple home-style chicken curry, which uses only a few ingredients. It's creamy, subtly spiced and bursting with flavour. Please excuse me in advance, because after trying this dish, you may no longer want to eat chicken curry in any other form!

In a bowl, mix together all the marinade ingredients, then add the chicken and stir to coat. Cover and leave to marinate at room temperature for 15–30 minutes, or refrigerate overnight.

When you are ready to cook, heat the oil for the base sauce in a deep pan (with a lid), add the cloves and green cardamom pods and cook over a medium heat for 1 minute. Now add the onion and salt, mix well, then put the lid on and cook over a low heat for 5 minutes.

Increase the heat to high, add the Curry Masala and tomatoes and cook for another 5–10 minutes, until the masala becomes dry. Now add the marinated chicken and the cream and mix well. Reduce the heat, cover and simmer for 15 minutes, or until the chicken is fully cooked.

To finish, stir in the Garam Masala and dried fenugreek leaves, crushing them between your palms as you add them, and cook for another 2–3 minutes.

Serve hot, garnished with extra cream and the fresh coriander. Enjoy with crispy Naan or Jeera Rice and a zingy onion salad.

Easy swaps

You can replace the chicken thighs with breasts, but keep an eye on the chicken during cooking as chicken breast meat can go dry very quickly.

Swap the dried fenugreek for 1 teaspoon of dried mint leaves.

Choose dairy-free yoghurt and cream, if you prefer.

MEAT-BASED DISHES

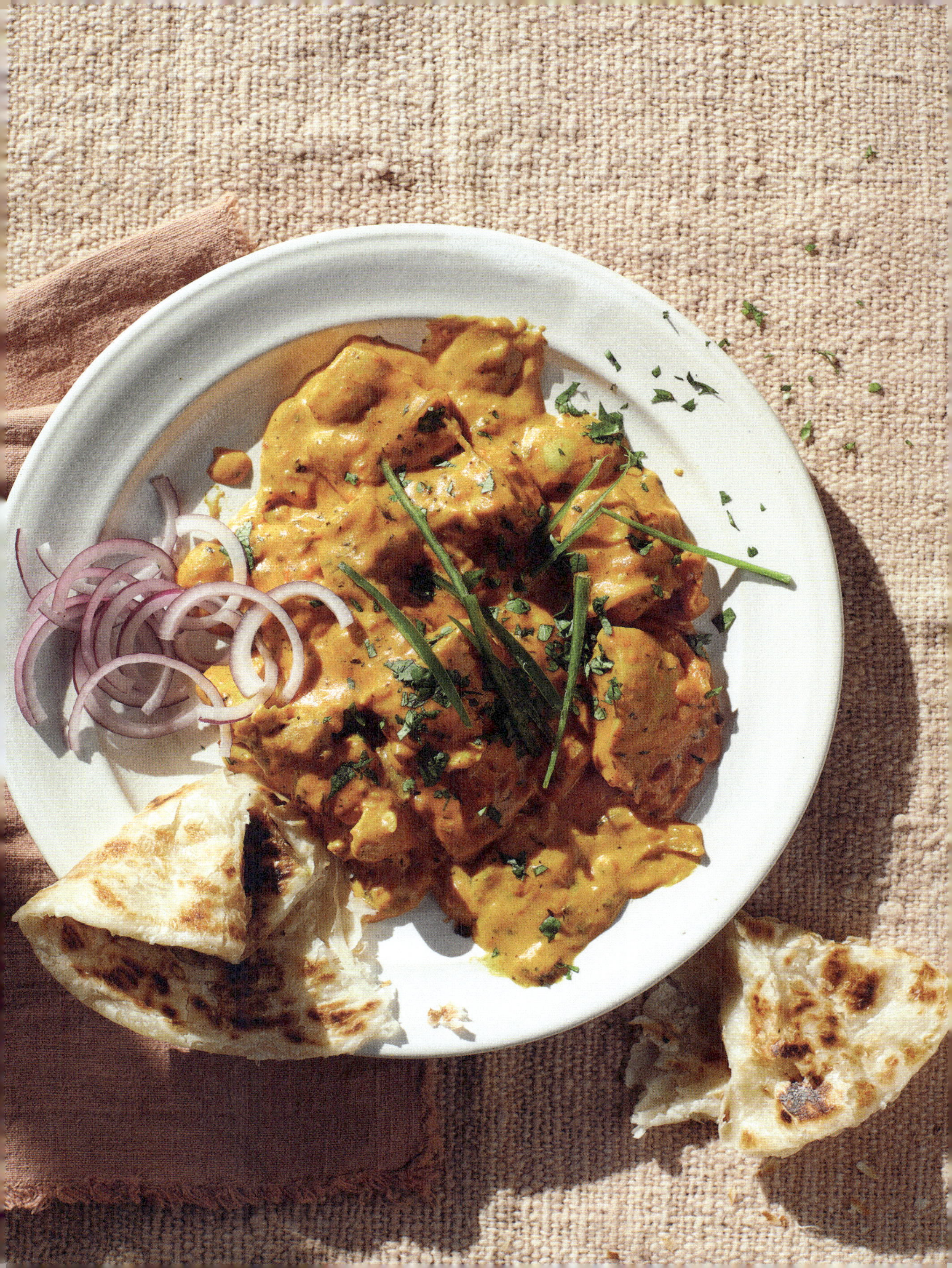

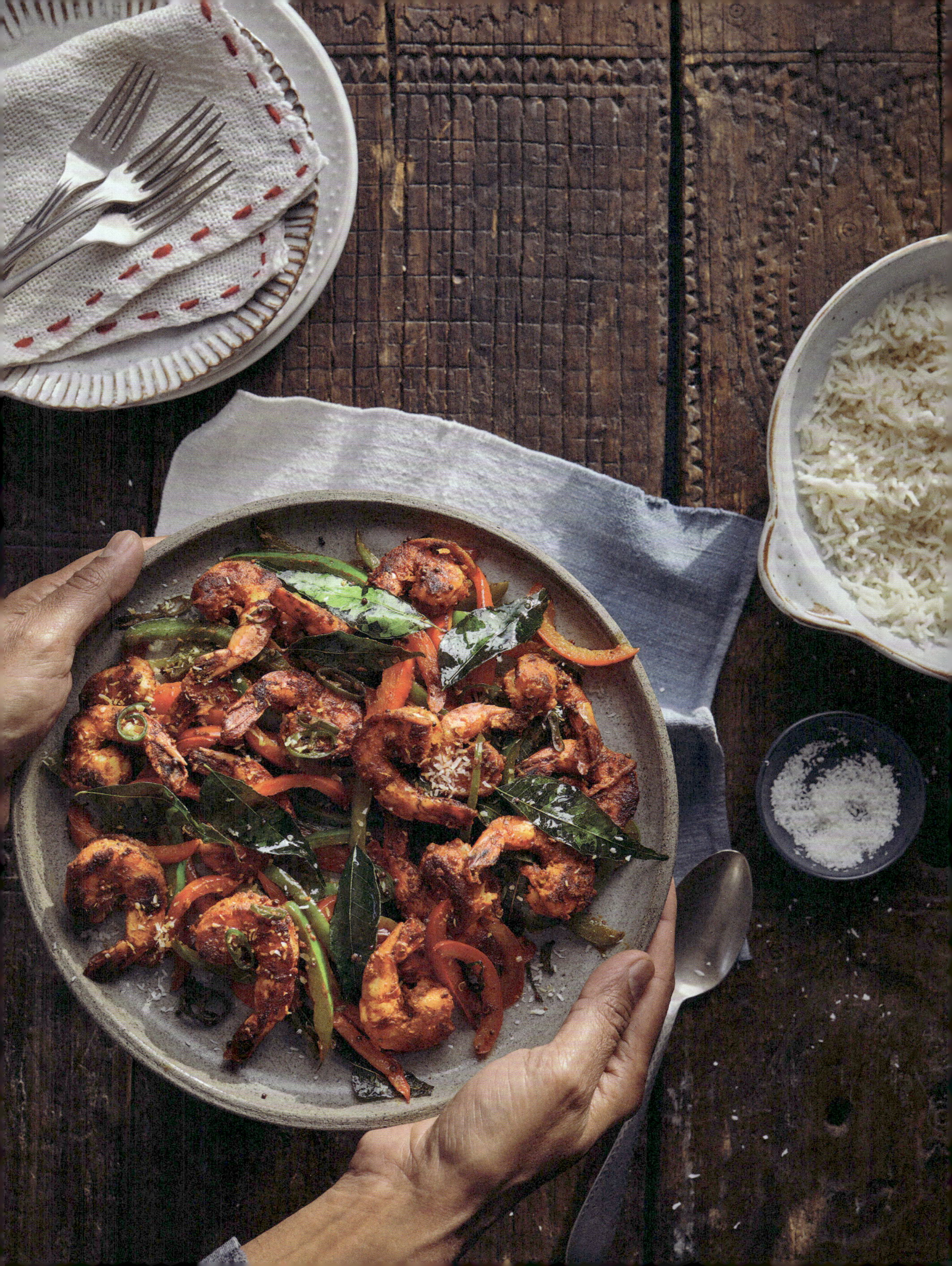

SMOKED PAPRIKA TIGER PRAWNS WITH RED AND GREEN PEPPERS

(LAL JHEENGA)

This recipe elevates the natural flavour and inherent sweetness of the tiger prawns with smokiness from the paprika, the aroma of the coconut oil and fragrant curry leaves, all complemented by the vibrant peppers.

Serves 4

16–20 fresh or frozen raw tiger prawns (shrimp), in shells or at least tail-on, defrosted if frozen

1 tbsp ground turmeric

2 tbsp smoked paprika

2 tbsp coconut oil

1 tbsp neutral oil (optional)

½ tsp black mustard seeds

2–3 green chillies, finely sliced

2 tbsp curry leaves

½ tsp salt

250g (9oz) deseeded red (bell) peppers, sliced

250g (9oz) deseeded green (bell) peppers, sliced

150g (5½oz) tomatoes, sliced (optional)

1 tbsp lime juice

1 tbsp desiccated (dried shredded) coconut, to garnish

To serve

Boiled rice or Lemon Rice (see page 106)

Peanut and Chilli Salsa (see page 169)

To prepare the prawns, if in shells, first remove and reserve the shells and heads (leave the tails on), then devein them. Dry the tail-on prawns using paper towels, place in a bowl, then sprinkle over the turmeric and smoked paprika. Mix well.

Heat the coconut oil in a frying pan (skillet). Once it starts smoking, add the reserved prawn shells and heads, if using. Cook over a high heat for 3–5 minutes, or until fully caramelized. Remove and discard the shells and heads, leaving the residual oil in the pan.

Using the same pan and oil, fry the prawns over a medium heat. This should take 2–3 minutes, depending on size. When fully cooked, they will be pink and not translucent, but do not overcook them or they will become chewy. Remove to a plate and set aside.

Using the same pan again, add the neutral oil if the residual oil is not enough and place over a high heat. Once it's hot, add the black mustard seeds. As soon as they start sputtering, add the green chillies, curry leaves and salt and cook for another minute.

Keeping the heat high, tip in the peppers and toss to coat in oil. Lower the heat to medium and cook for 5 minutes, then add the tomatoes, if using, and lime juice. You want fully cooked peppers with a slight bite and blistered skin. Remove from the heat, mix in half the cooked prawns, then scatter over the remaining prawns.

Serve hot, garnished with the desiccated coconut. Enjoy with plain or Lemon Rice and Peanut and Chilli Salsa.

Easy swap
Replace the curry leaves with lime leaves.

MEAT-BASED DISHES

MASALA LAMB CHOPS WITH MUSTARD POTATOES

(LAMB MASALA)

Serves 4

8 lamb rib chops from a rack of lamb (see method), each about 2cm (¾in) thick, or 8 ready-prepared chops of even thickness

2 tbsp oil

For the marinade
1 tbsp Greek-style yoghurt
1 tbsp lime juice
1 tbsp Ginger Garlic Paste (see page 159)
1 tbsp gram flour (besan) or cornflour (cornstarch)
1 tsp salt
1 tbsp ground cumin
½ tsp Garam Masala (see page 155)
½ tsp smoked paprika
1 tsp salt

For the mustard potatoes
2 tbsp oil
1 tsp black mustard seeds
1 tbsp dried yellow lentils (moong)
1 tbsp curry leaves
2 green chillies, finely sliced
200g (7oz) tomatoes, sliced
1 tsp salt
½ tsp ground turmeric
1 tbsp lime juice
500g (1lb 2oz) boiled and cooled starchy potatoes, cubed

To garnish
50g (1¾oz) fresh mint, chopped
Juice of 1 lime

To serve
Mustard Garlic Yoghurt (see page 59) and salad of your choice

Lamb is such an earthy meat and goes so well with fragrant spices and a comforting mustard potato mash. Many Indian lamb dishes require long cooking times to achieve a tender and melt-in-the-mouth texture. However, this easy lamb dish is relatively quick to make and very delicious to eat.

To prepare the lamb chops, clean the rack of lamb, pat it dry, trim off any excess fat and slice between the ribs to separate the chops, cutting them into even chops, each about 2cm (¾in) thick.

Combine all the marinade ingredients in a large bowl to make a thick marinade, then evenly coat the chops with it. Cover and leave to marinate for at least 1 hour or overnight in the fridge.

Heat the oil in a large frying pan (skillet) and cook the chops, fat-side down, over a high heat until the fat has rendered, then cook for 3–5 minutes on each side until they develop a nice crust. Continue cooking until you reach the desired doneness – the time will vary depending on the thickness of the lamb. Use a meat thermometer inserted into the thickest part of each chop (avoiding the bone) and cook until 50°C (120°F) for very rare, 55°C (130°F) for medium-rare, 60°C (140°F) for medium, 65°C (150°F) for medium-well or 72°C (160°F) for well done. Alternatively, use a griddle or BBQ and adjust the cooking time according to the temperature guide above.

For the mustard potatoes, heat the oil in a large pan over a high heat, add the mustard seeds and dried lentils. Once they start sputtering, add the curry leaves, chillies and tomatoes. Continue cooking for 1 minute, then add the salt, turmeric and lime juice. Add the cubed cooked potatoes and mix well. Finally, use a large spoon to break the potatoes down into a very chunky mash.

To serve, scoop out some potatoes onto each serving plate, place two lamb chops on top and garnish with the chopped fresh mint and a squeeze of lime juice. Add the Mustard Garlic Yoghurt and salad of your choice.

MEAT-BASED DISHES

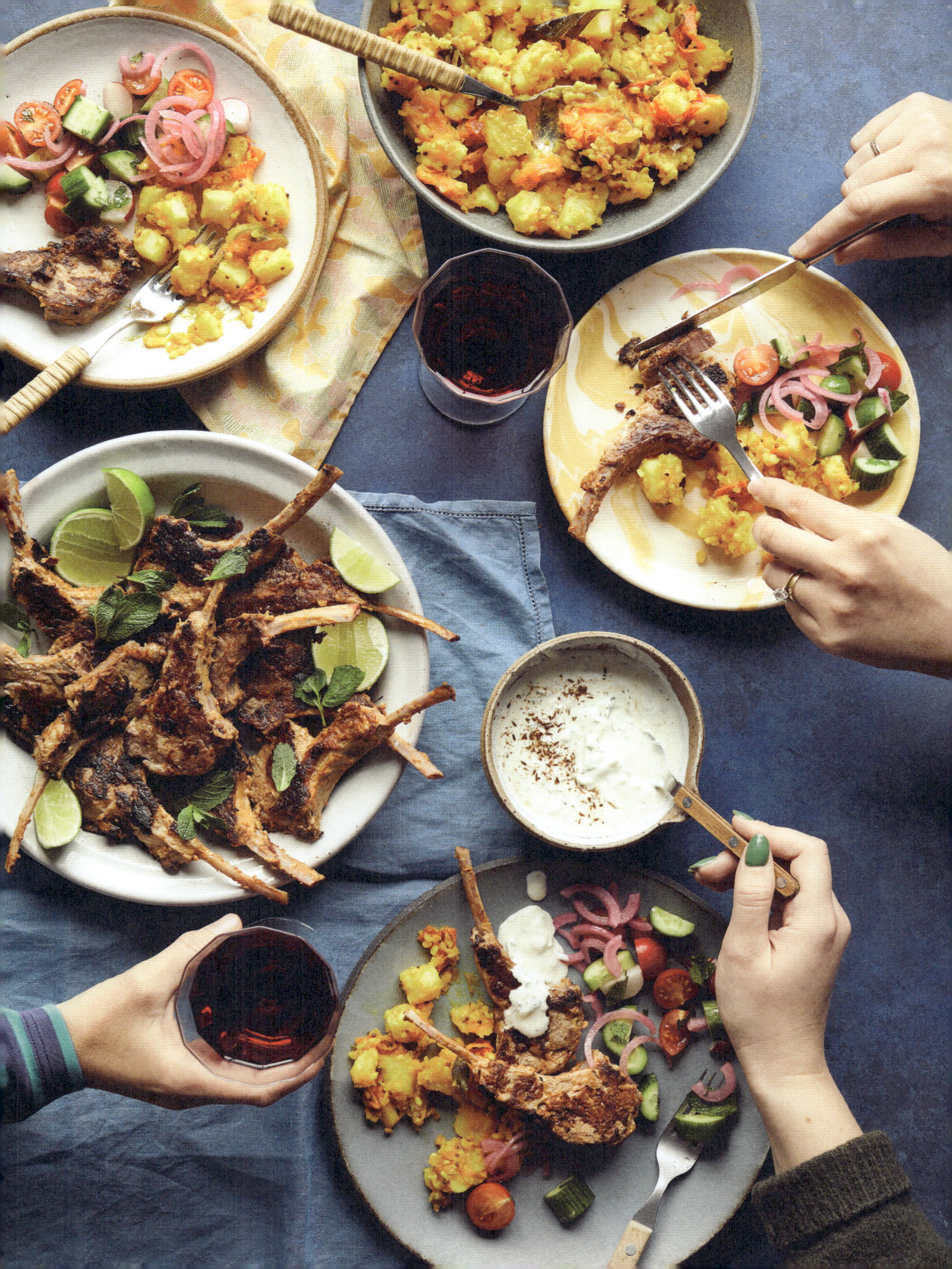

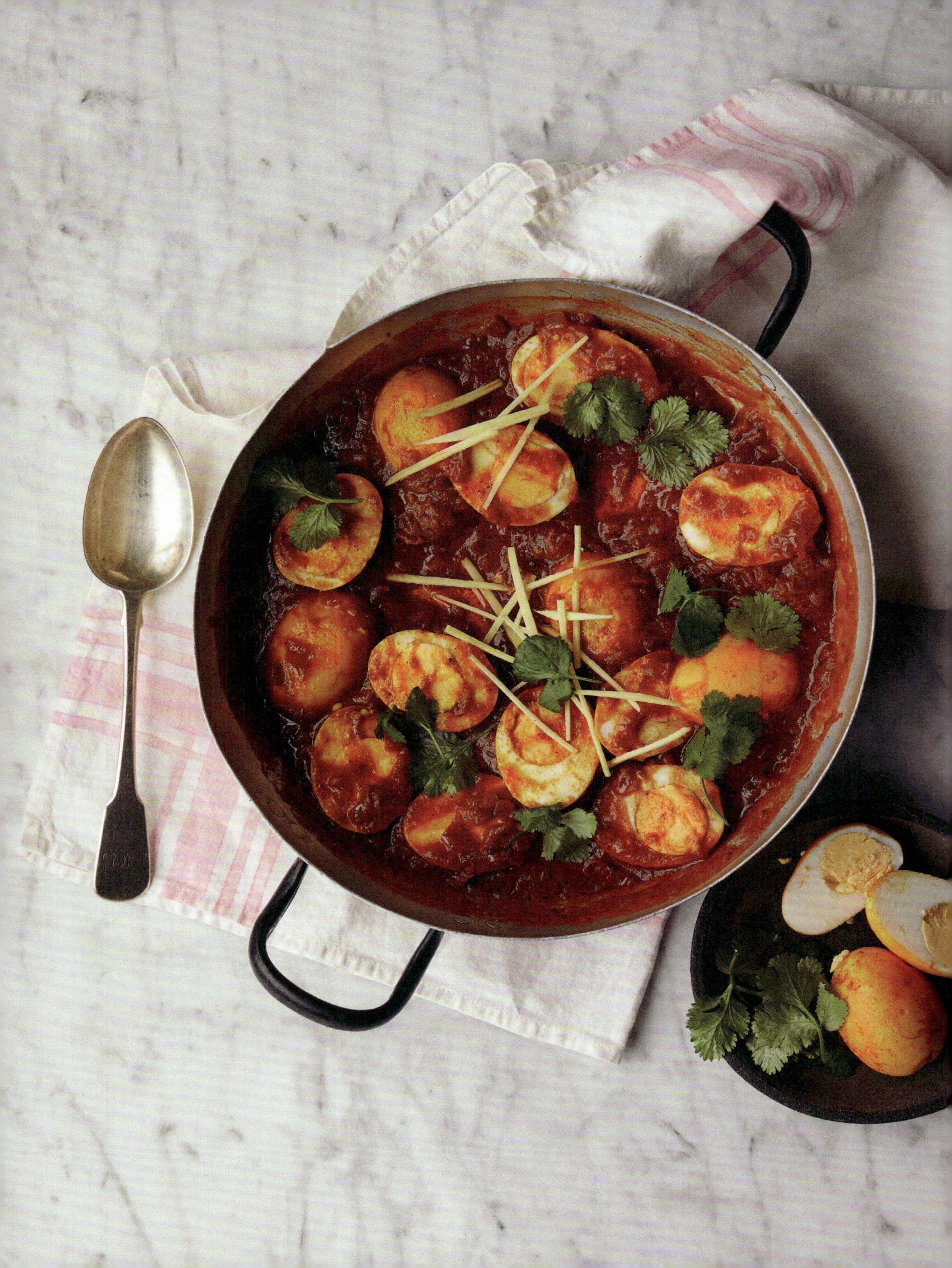

EGG CURRY

(ANDA CURRY)

In the Western world, eggs are considered to be vegetarian, however, in Indian cuisine, they are not. That's why I am sharing this delightful recipe in this section. It wouldn't be wrong to call this a bachelor's curry – if you can do some basic cooking, it's almost impossible to not get this right. The sauce keeps well in an airtight container in the fridge for up to five days: follow the method up until the oil is separating from the masala but do not add the water. Then simply reheat, add the water and continue following the instructions.

Serves 4

10 large eggs, hard-boiled and cooled
2 tbsp oil
1 tsp ground turmeric
200g (7oz) red onions, finely chopped
1 tsp Ginger Garlic Paste (see page 159)
1 tsp salt
1 tbsp Curry Masala (see page 154)
200g (7oz) tomato passata (strained tomatoes)

To garnish
5cm (2in) piece of fresh ginger, peeled and cut into thin matchsticks/julienne
2 tbsp chopped fresh coriander (cilantro)

To serve
Plain steamed rice or Roti (see page 88) or Mixed Salad and Cucumber Raita (see page 59)

Peel the hard-boiled eggs, keep them whole and gently pierce each one a few times with a knife.

To fry the eggs (this is optional), heat the oil in a deep pan over a medium heat. Add the eggs and sprinkle over the turmeric. Keep stirring. In a minute or so, the eggs will have a nice golden crust. Remove to a plate.

Using the same pan and residual oil, add the red onions and Ginger Garlic Paste. Cook over a medium heat until the onion becomes soft and is starting to brown slightly.

Add the salt and Curry Masala, mix well, then stir in the tomato passata. Keep cooking over a medium heat for another 8–10 minutes, until the oil starts separating from the masala. It's important to cook until this happens, otherwise the sauce will remain watery.

Now add 200ml (7fl oz) of water and bring it to the boil – it should be soupy in consistency. If not, let it simmer for few more minutes.

Slice the eggs in half lengthways, then carefully add into the simmering sauce without letting the yolks fall out. Gently mix and then remove from the heat.

Serve hot, garnished with the ginger and fresh coriander. This dish goes so well with plain steamed rice or Roti. You can also pair this with a Mixed Salad and Cucumber Raita.

Easy swap
Swap out the eggs for 500g (1lb 2oz) of cubed paneer or firm tofu.

COCONUT TROUT CURRY
(NARIYAL MACHHI JHOL)

The nostalgia and inspiration for this curry comes from southern India, where I spent some time during my first job in the early 2000s. Fresh oily fish with fiery chillies, balanced with fragrant coconut milk sauce; I feel like drowning in this beauty. The regional aspect of Indian cuisine always fascinates me – by changing a few ingredients here and there, you end up making a completely new dish. Well, do message me via my social media after trying this recipe if you have ever tried such a delicious fish curry.

Serves 4

2 tbsp coconut oil
1 tsp black mustard seeds
1 tbsp dried yellow lentils (moong)
3–4 dried hot red chillies, or to taste
2 tbsp curry leaves
1 tbsp grated fresh peeled ginger
1 tsp finely chopped garlic
200g (7oz) white onions, sliced
200g (7oz) tomatoes, chopped
1½ tsp salt, or to taste
1 tsp ground turmeric
1 tsp smoked paprika
1 tbsp lime juice, or to taste
1 x 400ml (14fl oz) can of coconut milk
400g (14oz) skin-on trout fillets, cut into 4cm (1½in) pieces

To serve
Lemon Rice (see page 106) or Idlis (see page 22)
Your choice of salad

Heat the coconut oil in a deep pan (with a lid) over a medium heat, then add the black mustard seeds and dried lentils. As soon as they start sputtering, add the red chillies (break each one in half first), curry leaves, ginger and garlic and cook for another minute.

Add the onion and sauté over a medium heat for 2–3 minutes, then add the tomatoes and turn the heat to high.

Add the salt, turmeric and smoked paprika and keep cooking over a high heat until the oil starts separating.

Stir in the lime juice and coconut milk, then bring to the boil.

Add the trout pieces to the boiling liquid. Mix well, then cover the pan, reduce the heat and simmer for 5 minutes. It's really important to reduce the heat here, otherwise it will become dry.

Remove from the heat and let it rest for 5 minutes before removing the lid. The fish should be nicely cooked and soft. Mix gently and adjust the seasoning with salt and lime juice, if needed.

Serve hot with Lemon Rice or Idlis and pair with a salad.

Easy swaps
Swap out the coconut oil for vegetable oil, and the coconut milk for single (light) cream.

Salmon fillets work well instead of trout, and lime leaves are a good substitute for the curry leaves.

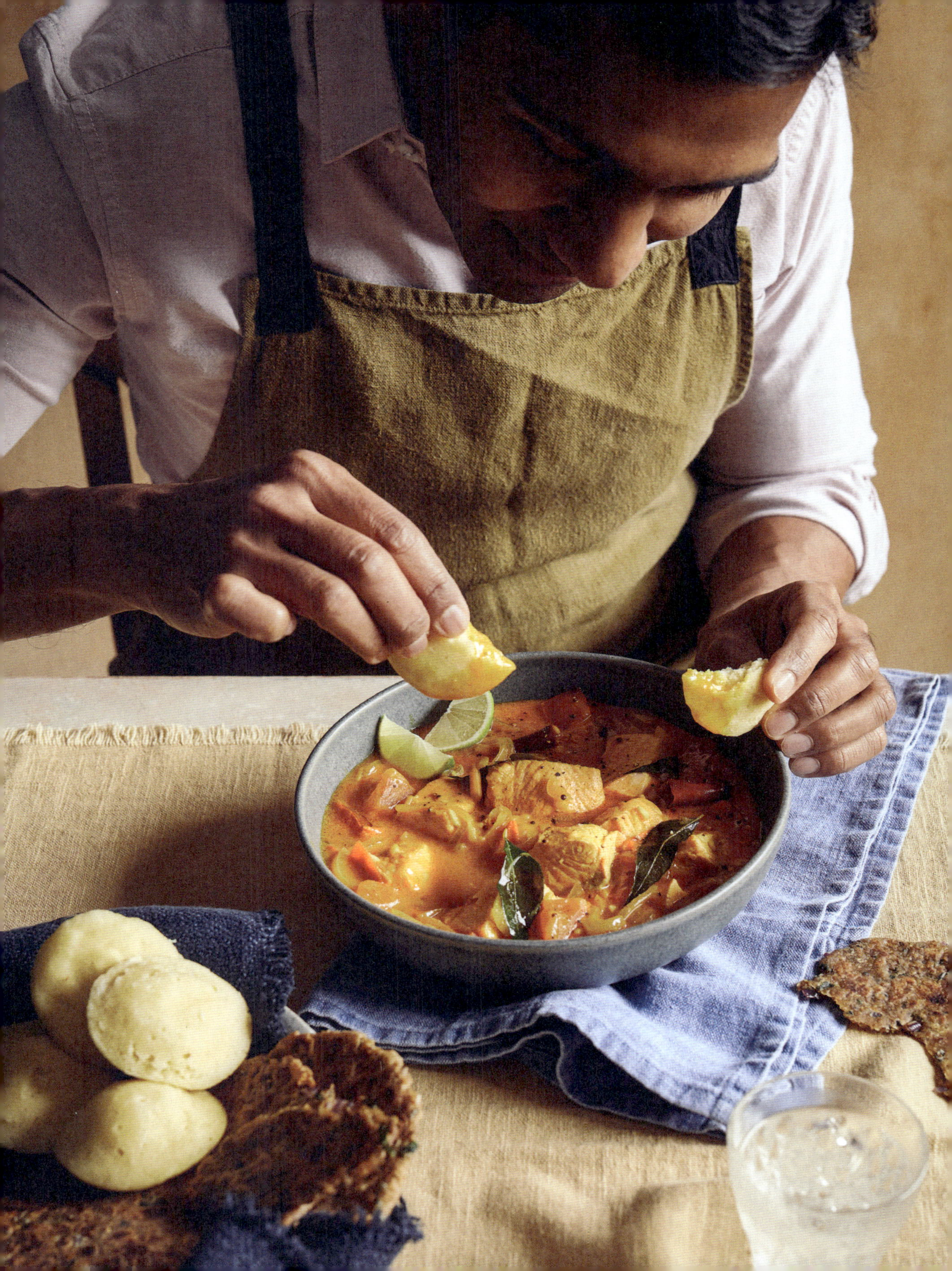

SLOW-COOKED LAMB SHOULDER IN ROGAN JOSH SAUCE

(LAAL MAAS)

This dish is very special to me as it is based on a recipe I used in the final of *MasterChef UK*. It brings back many fond memories! Rogan josh sauce is very famous in the north of India. Rogan means colour, and traditionally the recipe uses the vibrant colour of kashmiri mirch (very close to smoked paprika) and dried red-hot chillies instead of using tomatoes or onion. Therefore, I won't call my recipe authentic by any means, but I can say for sure that it did get me some very good comments from the judges. Let's see what your verdict is when you cook this recipe!

Serves 4

- 1.5–2kg (3lb 5oz–4lb 8oz) bone-in lamb shoulder joint (at room temperature)
- 3 tbsp ghee
- 2 black cardamom pods, crushed
- 2 cinnamon sticks
- ½ tbsp black peppercorns
- 500g (1lb 2oz) white onions, finely chopped
- 2 tsp salt
- 2 tbsp Ginger Garlic Paste (see page 159)
- 2 tbsp smoked paprika
- 1 tsp ground coriander
- 1 tsp ground cumin
- 200ml (7fl oz) Greek-style yoghurt
- 600ml (21fl oz) lamb or chicken stock

Preheat the oven to 200°C/180°C fan/400°F/Gas 6.

Using a paring knife, make deep incisions in the lamb shoulder joint and trim off any excess fat.

Heat the ghee in a large, ovenproof casserole (with a lid) and add the cardamom, cinnamon sticks and peppercorns. Then add the lamb shoulder and sear on all sides over a high heat for about 10 minutes. Remove the seared lamb to a plate and set aside.

In the same casserole, in the residual fat, cook the onions and salt over a medium heat for about 3–5 minutes, or until golden brown, then add the Ginger Garlic Paste and cook for 2 minutes.

Return the lamb to the casserole, along with the smoked paprika, coriander and cumin and cook for another 2–3 minutes. Then turn the heat to low and gradually whisk in the yoghurt. Do not add all the yoghurt at once over a high heat, otherwise it will split.

Stir in the stock and cover with the lid or seal tightly with foil. Cook in the oven for 2½ hours.

ingredients and method continued overleaf

MEAT-BASED DISHES

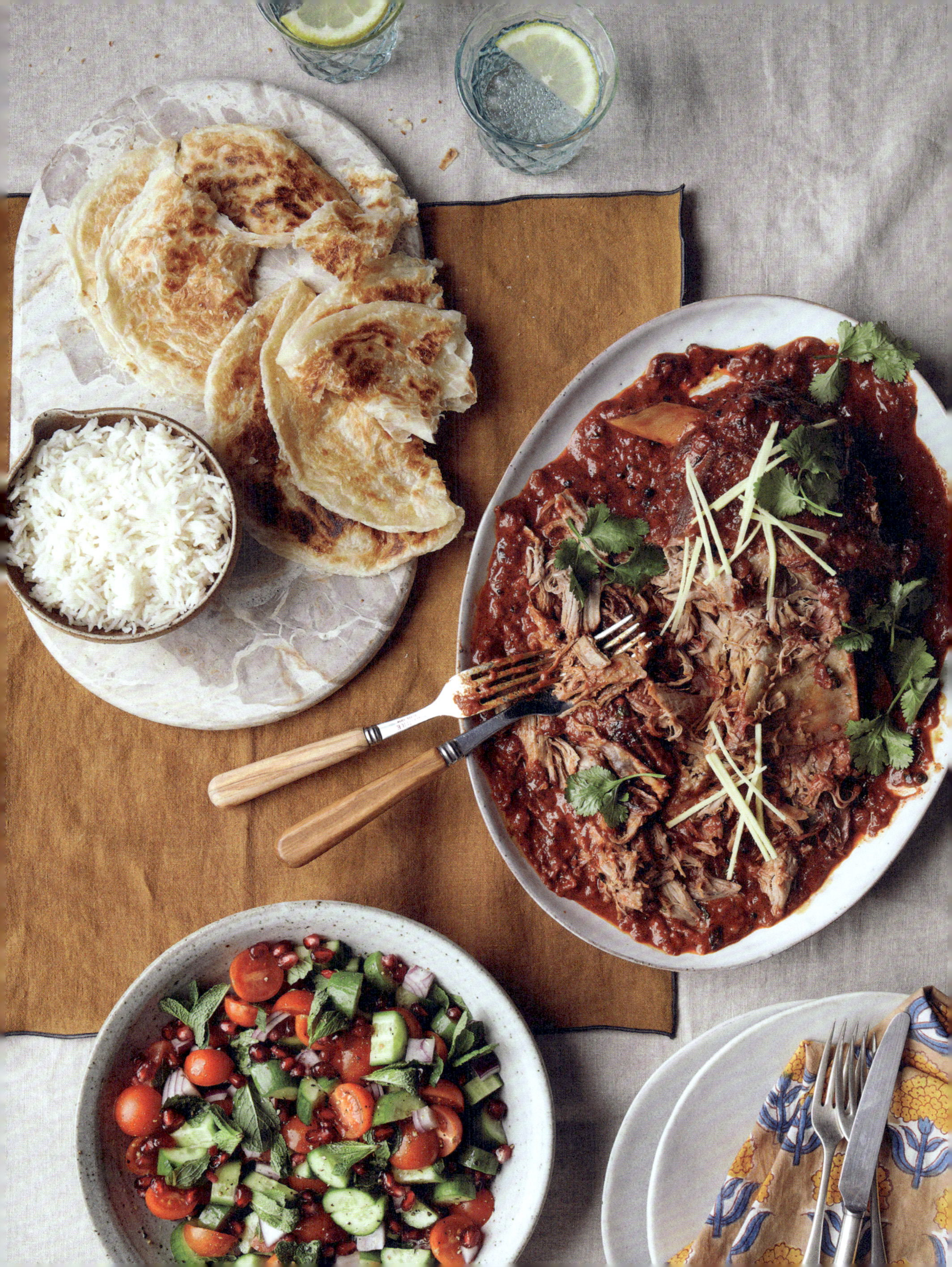

2 tbsp double (heavy) cream

1 tsp ground fennel seeds

½ tsp Garam Masala (see page 155)

1 tsp finely chopped fresh peeled ginger

1 tbsp chopped fresh coriander (cilantro)

100ml (3½fl oz) beetroot (beet) juice

To garnish
2 tbsp chopped fresh coriander (cilantro)

5cm (2in) piece of fresh ginger, peeled and cut into thin matchsticks/julienne

To serve
Plain or Jeera (Cumin) Rice (see page 105), or Naan Bread (see page 98)

Mixed Salad and Cucumber Raita (see page 59)

Remove the casserole from the oven, carefully remove the lid/foil and mix well. At this stage, the sauce will be nice and smooth as the onions will have totally disintegrated. Taste the sauce, adjust the seasoning and place the casserole on the hob (stove) over a low heat.

Stir in the cream, ground fennel seeds, Garam Masala, ginger, fresh coriander and beetroot juice. Let it simmer for another 10 minutes, occasionally basting the lamb while it simmers. Remove from the heat and allow to rest for 15–20 minutes.

Serve warm, garnished with fresh coriander and fresh ginger julienne. This goes so well with plain rice or Jeera Rice, or Naan Bread. Remember to pair it with Mixed Salad and Raita.

Easy tip
You can cook this dish in a pressure cooker (in half the time – refer to your model's manual) or in a covered pan over a low heat on the hob (cover and cook for the same time as the oven method, over the lowest heat, adding a splash of water as the cooking time goes on, so it doesn't dry out).

Easy swaps
Swap out the lamb for a fatty pork or venison joint such as shoulder.

You can skip the beetroot juice or add a little red food colouring instead, if you like.

LAMB AND POTATO CURRY
(MUTTON ALOO)

Serves: 4–6

800g (1lb 12oz) boneless lamb shoulder, cut into 5cm (2in) pieces

For the marinade

3 tbsp Greek-style yoghurt

2 tbsp lime juice

2 tsp salt

2 tbsp Curry Masala (see page 154)

1 tbsp smoked paprika

1 tsp ground cumin

1 tsp Garam Masala (see page 155)

For the sauce

2 tbsp oil

5 cloves

5 green cardamom pods

1 cinnamon stick

1 tbsp finely chopped fresh peeled ginger

1 tbsp finely chopped garlic

400g (14oz) white onions, finely chopped

400g (14oz) chopped tomatoes

400g (14oz) large potatoes, peeled and cut into chunks (slightly bigger than the lamb pieces)

200ml (7fl oz) boiling water

Lamb is one of those meats that can carry loads of flavours. Traditional vindaloo or takeaway lamb curries are too spicy and oily for me, so here I take inspiration from those dishes, but in a more everyday way. This recipe is the best of both worlds – it has the flavours of a takeaway, without being too rich or hot.

Mix all the marinade ingredients together in a bowl, add the lamb and stir to coat all over. Cover and leave to marinate in the fridge for at least 1 hour or overnight. Bring it back to room temperature before cooking.

For the sauce, in a heavy-based pan (with a lid), heat the oil over a medium heat, then add the cloves, cardamom pods and cinnamon stick and cook for 1 minute.

Now turn the heat to medium and add the ginger and garlic, then cook for 2–3 minutes until starting to colour. Add the onions and keep cooking until they become caramelized, about 5 minutes.

Once the mixture starts sticking to the pan, add the lamb, then deglaze the pan with the marinade over a medium heat, stirring to seal the meat all over. Add the tomatoes and cook over high for another 5 minutes – by this stage, the masala will be thickened.

Add the potatoes to the pan together with the boiling water. Bring to the boil, then cover the pan, reduce the heat and simmer for 35–40 minutes, without stirring or removing the lid.

ingredients and method continued overleaf

MEAT-BASED DISHES

To serve

2 tbsp chopped fresh coriander (cilantro), to garnish

Plain or Jeera (Cumin) Rice (see page 105) or Roti (see page 88)

Mixed Salad and Cucumber Raita (see page 59)

Remove from the heat. Carefully remove the lid, then gently mix well without breaking the soft potatoes. Taste and adjust the seasoning.

Serve hot, garnished with the fresh coriander. This goes very well with plain or Jeera Rice or Roti, paired with Mixed Salad and Raita.

Easy swaps
You can use bone-in lamb, if you prefer – increase the simmering time by 10–15 minutes, until the meat is falling off the bone.

Beef or pork would work well here – use a fatty joint like shoulder for best results.

CHICKEN KEEMA WITH PEAS

(MURG MATAR KEEMA)

This dish reminds me of the late-night hustle and bustle of Mumbai streets. After working late in offices, people rush back home and, on their way, eat this delicacy packed inside a soft bun. You can pretty much compare it with getting a kebab or burger on your way home after a late night (party or work, up to you!). You can also enjoy this as a wrap by using a tortilla or Roti (see page 88) instead of a roll or bun.

Serves 4

- 2 tbsp butter or oil, plus a little extra for frying the rolls/buns
- 1 green chilli, chopped
- 1 tbsp grated fresh peeled ginger
- 200g (7oz) white onions, finely chopped
- 2 tsp salt
- 1 tsp ground cumin
- ½ tsp ground turmeric
- 1 tsp red chilli powder
- ¼ tsp Garam Masala (see page 155)
- 2 tbsp tomato purée (paste)
- 500g (1lb 2oz) minced (ground) chicken
- 200g (7oz) frozen peas
- 2 tbsp chopped fresh coriander (cilantro)
- 4 soft bread rolls/buns, cut in half
- Mint and Coriander Chutney (see page 162), to serve

In a deep pan, heat the butter or oil over a medium heat, then add the green chilli and ginger and cook until the ginger beings to colour.

Tip in the onion and sauté over a medium heat until soft. Now add the salt, all the spices and the tomato purée, mix well and turn the heat to high.

Stir in the minced chicken and cook for 6–8 minutes, or until the moisture evaporates, the mince is fully cooked and beginning to caramelize.

Add the peas and mix well. Allow to cook through for a couple of minutes, then taste, adjust for seasoning and then mix in the chopped coriander.

In a separate pan, melt a little butter and pan-fry the sliced rolls/buns over a medium heat until lightly toasted on both sides.

Spread some chutney on one half of each roll/bun, then spoon in a generous amount of chicken keema, cover it with the top half of each roll/bun and press gently. Tuck in!

Easy swap
Replace the minced chicken with minced lamb or turkey or soya mince.

Pictured overleaf.

MEAT-BASED DISHES

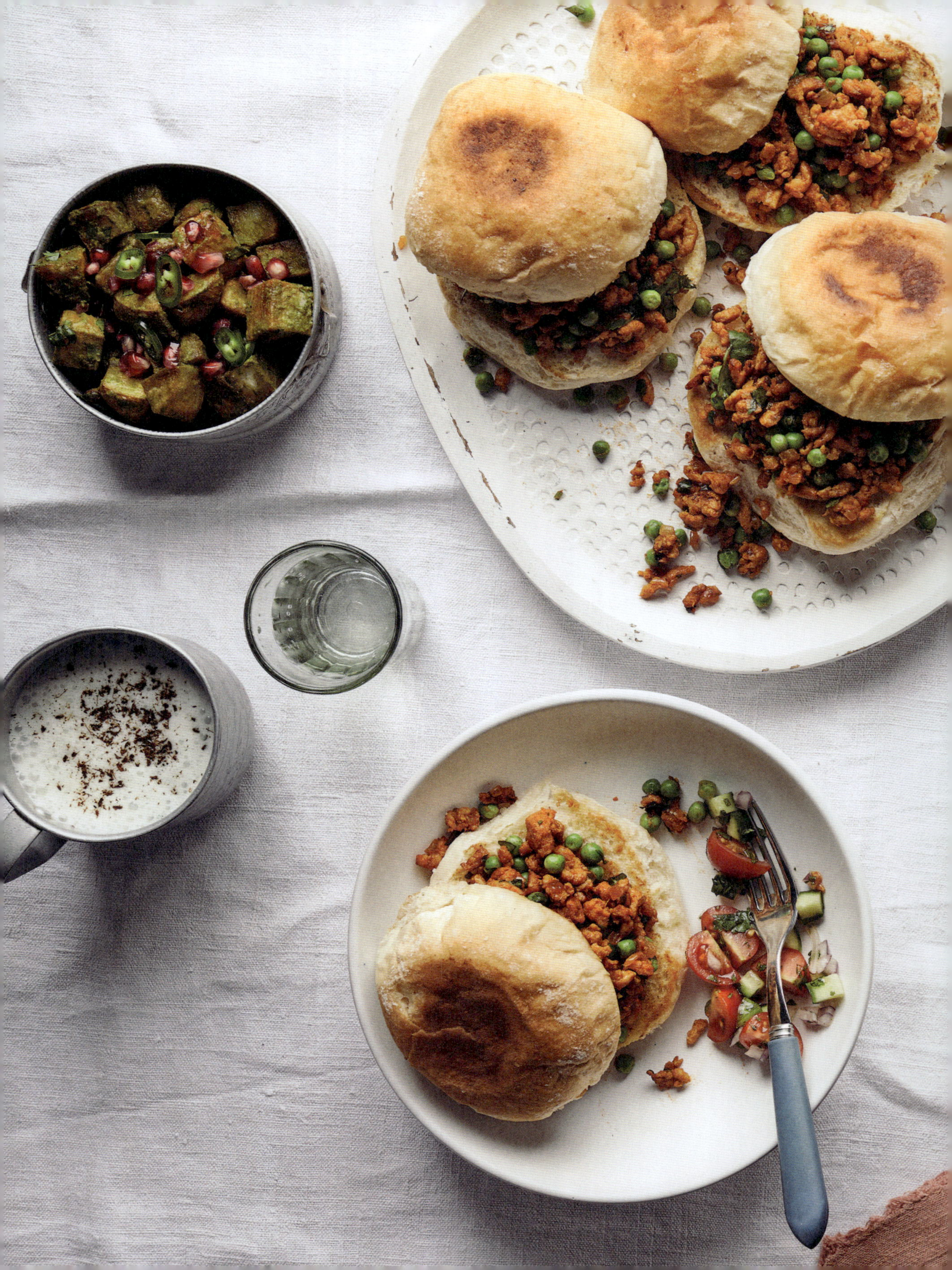

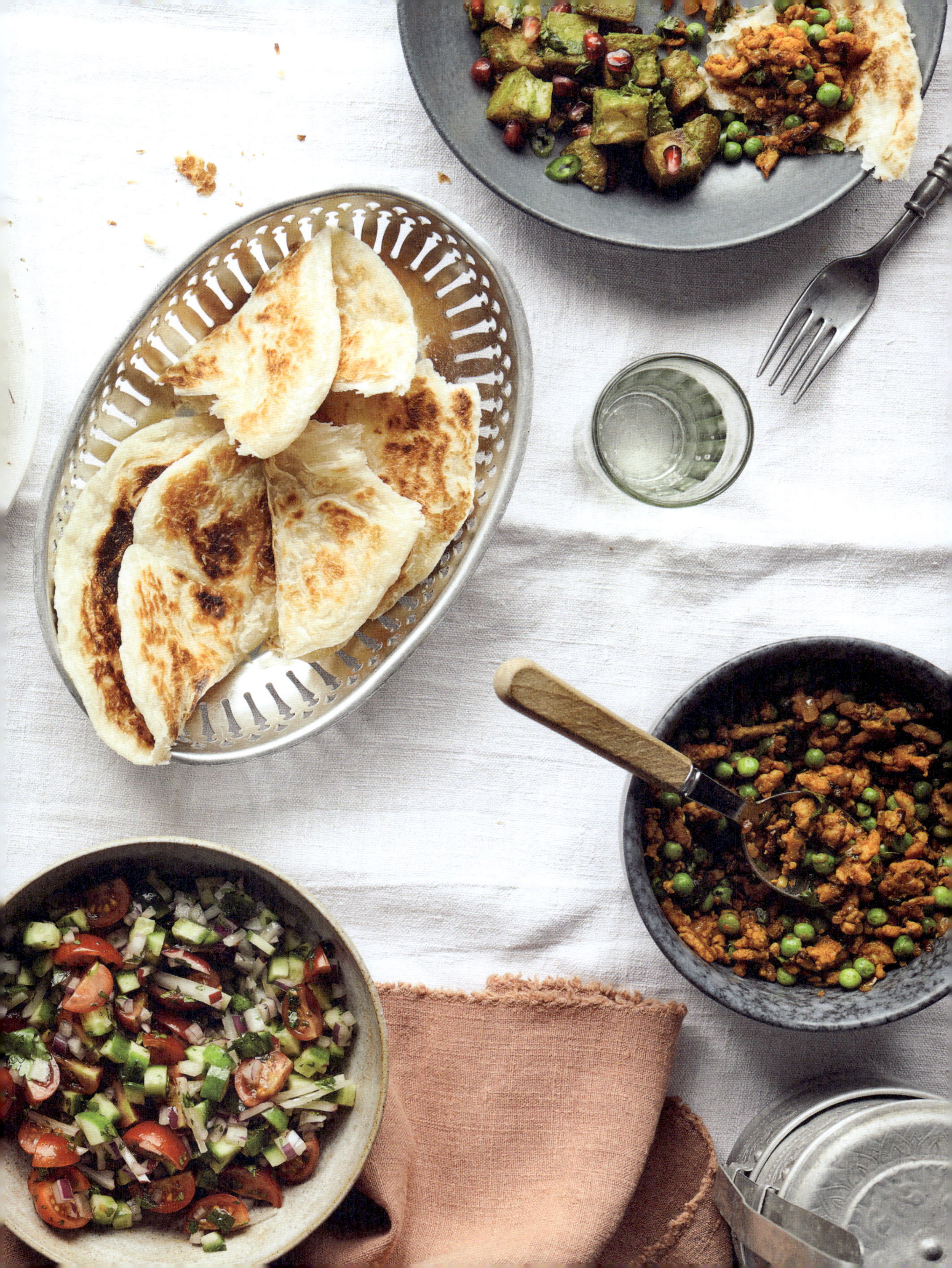

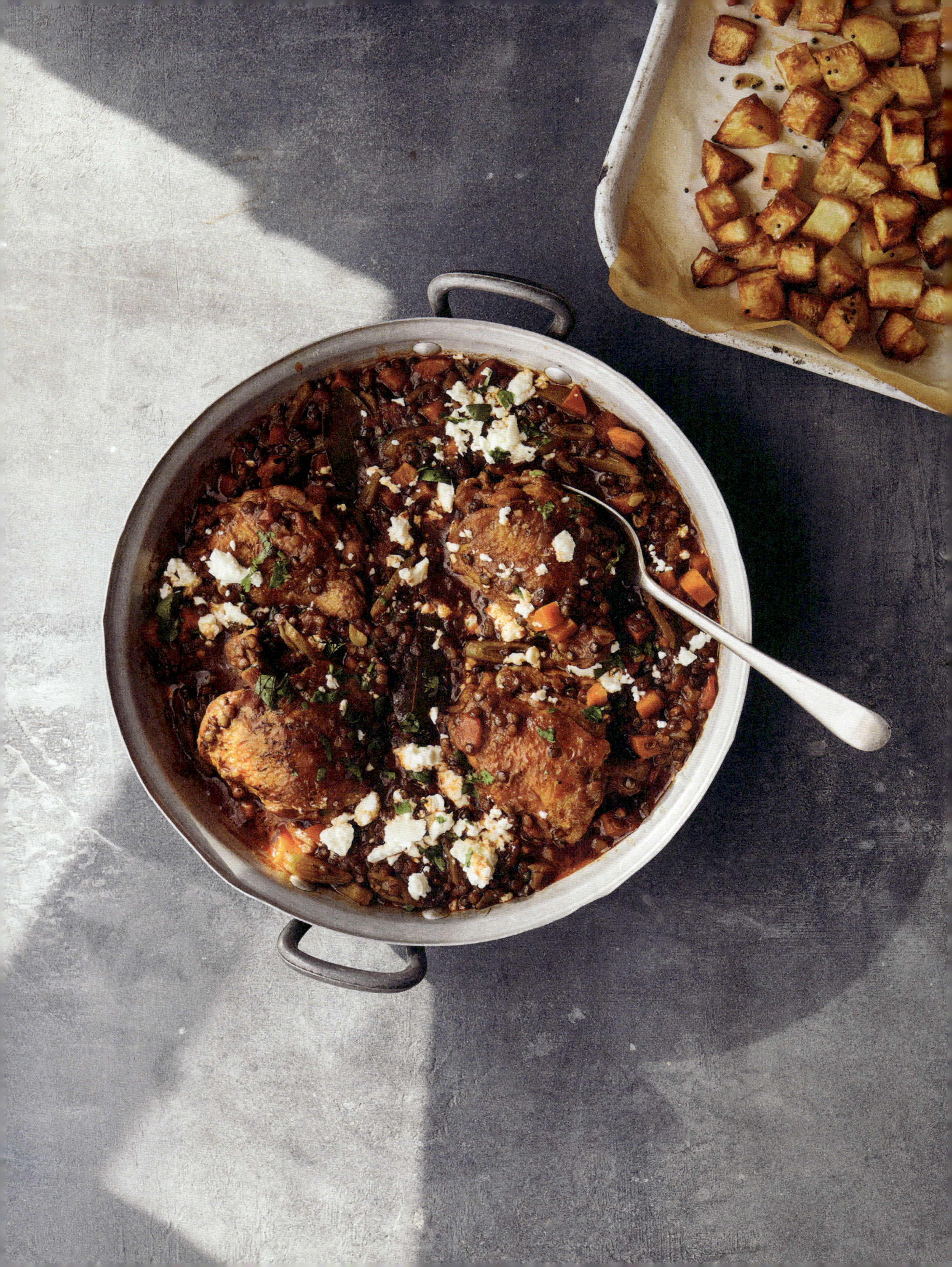

CHICKEN THIGHS WITH VEGETABLES AND BLACK LENTILS

(MURG DAAL)

Serves 6

2 tbsp oil

2 dried bay leaves

3 garlic cloves, crushed

600g (1lb 5oz) skin-on, bone-in chicken thighs

200g (7oz) red onions, finely chopped

200g (7oz) carrots, peeled and diced

200g (7oz) runner (string) beans, trimmed and sliced into 2cm (1in) pieces

200g (7oz) dried black (Puy) lentils, washed

1 tsp salt

2 chicken stock (bouillon) cubes

1 tbsp Curry Masala (see page 154)

1 x 400g (14oz) can of chopped tomatoes

500ml (17fl oz) boiling water

Juice of 1 lime

To serve

400g (14oz) hot roasted diced potatoes (optional)

100g (3½oz) feta cheese, crumbled

2 tbsp chopped fresh coriander (cilantro)

Generally speaking, Indian dishes need some sides or pairing to turn them into a complete meal. The method of one-pot cooking inspired me to come up with this recipe, which is a complete meal requiring very little effort. This is full of flavours, multiple textures and is very nutritious indeed.

In a heavy-based pan (with a lid), heat the oil over a medium heat, then add the bay leaves and crushed garlic and cook for 1 minute.

Now turn the heat to high, add the chicken thighs and get some colour on them by cooking for another 2–3 minutes.

Add the red onion, carrots, runner (string) beans, lentils, salt, crumbled stock cubes and Curry Masala and mix well. Cook over a medium heat for 5 minutes.

Once it starts sticking to the pan, tip in the chopped tomatoes. Mix well, turn the heat to high and pour in the boiling water (or more or less, to get the consistency you prefer – I like this to have the consistency of a very thick soup). Bring to the boil, then cover the pan, reduce the heat and simmer for 25–30 minutes, stirring once or twice.

Once the chicken and lentils are fully cooked, remove from the heat. Stir in the lime juice and adjust the seasoning to taste.

Serve hot in soup bowls with the roasted potatoes and garnished with the crumbled feta and fresh coriander.

Easy swaps

You can play with different spices and vegetables to create your own version of this one-pot meal.

Swap out the chicken thighs for turkey legs.

MEAT-BASED DISHES

SPICED CRUST SEA BASS WITH CHICKPEA SALAD
(MASALA FISH FRY)

Serves 4

4 sea bass fillets, skin on, total weight 500–600g (1lb 2oz–1lb 5oz)
2 tbsp olive oil
Juice of 1 lime

For the rub
1 tsp ground cumin
1 tsp ground coriander
1 tsp smoked paprika
1 tsp garlic powder
½ tsp freshly ground black pepper
½ tsp mustard powder
½ tsp salt

For the chickpea salad
1 x 400g (14oz) can chickpeas (garbanzo beans), drained and rinsed
100g (3½oz) red onions, finely chopped
100g (3½oz) cherry tomatoes, chopped
100g (3½oz) cold boiled potatoes, diced
1 green chilli, finely chopped
50g (1¾oz) chopped fresh coriander (cilantro)
1 tbsp extra virgin olive oil
1 tbsp lime juice
½ tsp Chaat Masala (see page 153)
½ tsp salt

This dish is inspired by my Mediterranean travels. I find that dishes from this part of the world are always very light and fresh, so this recipe has a Mediterranean ethos with Indian flavours. I believe that food stretches beyond recipes and cuisine. It should make us happy and healthy – geographical borders are man-made, after all!

Start by making a dry spice rub by mixing all the rub ingredients together in a bowl, then rub the mixture on both sides of the sea bass fillets. Set them aside on a plate for pan-frying at the end – but don't leave them longer than that, or they will start to dry out.

To make the chickpea salad, simply mix all the ingredients together in salad bowl. Using a potato masher, crush the salad in a few places to bind the ingredients together.

To cook the fish, heat the olive oil in a frying pan (skillet) over a medium heat and place the dry-rubbed fish fillets, skin-side down, in the pan. Gently press them down so they don't curl up. Sea bass is a very delicate fish, therefore cooking the fish for 1–2 minutes on each side should be enough (although the cooking time will depend on the thickness of the fillets).

Scoop some crushed chickpea salad into the centre of each serving plate, place a pan-fried fish fillet on top and squeeze over a little lime juice, then serve. You can pair this with some warm soup and crusty bread, if you like.

Easy swaps
Swap the sea bass for any other white fish.

Butter (lima) beans make a good alternative to the chickpeas.

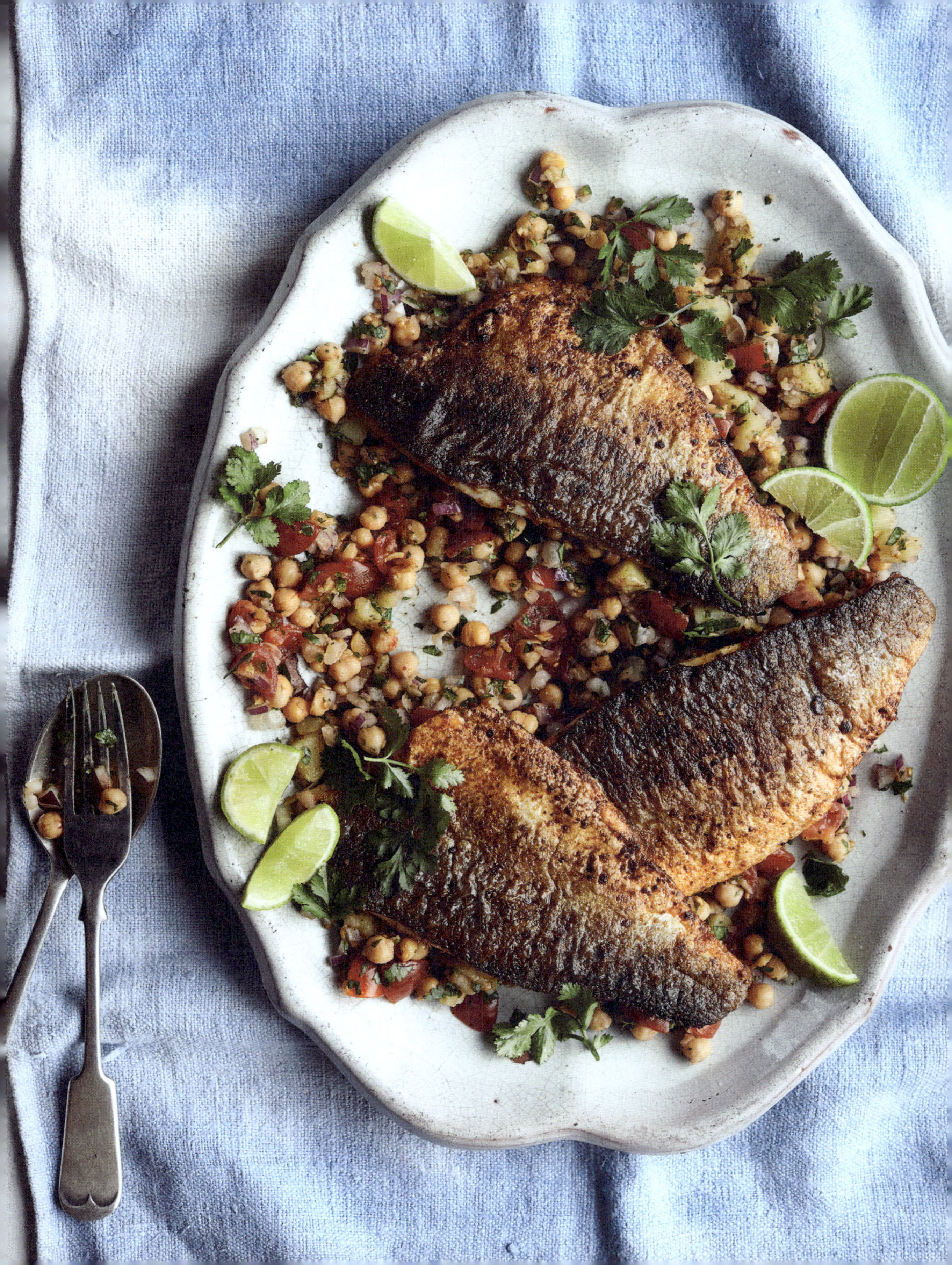

rice dishes & BREADS

Even the largest ocean's water cannot quench your thirst if you don't have a cup to drink it from. That's the relationship rice and breads share with Indian dishes and curries. They play such an important role and act as a medium for us to appreciate the beauty of Indian cuisine. These sides are the key to unlocking the mesmerizing world of flavours and textures.

Indian cuisine is all about balance and sharing. In any typical meal, there will be one or two main dishes and two or three sides such as salads, yoghurt and rice or breads. If all these components are rich, full of flavour and spicy, then they may end up competing with each other.

Therefore, rice and breads maintain their character due to their simplicity, neutral flavours and by providing a great source of carbohydrate to perfectly complement the protein- and fat-rich dishes they are served with.

In this chapter, I am focusing on the ease of cooking, simple flavours and a very homely feel. It doesn't matter whether you can roll a roti as a perfect round disc or so it might look like a map of Europe, or if your rice becomes a bit sticky and mushy. At the end of the day, both will taste good and will do their job as an accompaniment. So please keep up your confidence and start your journey in the very comforting world of rice dishes and Indian breads.

THIN FLATBREAD

(ROTI)

Roti is the blood of north Indian cuisine. Sometimes, in rural areas, people refer to the overall meal as 'roti'. Being the simplest yet most essential part of a meal, roti has earned first place in my eyes when it comes to Indian breads. Amazingly, it uses only two ingredients: flour and water. The taste and texture will differ from person to person, so I will be curious to know how your roti tastes when you try this recipe. You can easily adjust the basic dough with some salt, herbs or a little oil.

Makes 8

250g (9oz) roti/chapati flour, plus extra for dusting

Optional extras (add these to the dough!)

Salt, to taste

Chopped/dried herbs of your choice

Melted ghee or butter (optional), to serve

First, make the dough by combining the flour with 125ml (4fl oz) of water in a bowl, following the instructions on page 14. Cover the dough with a damp dish towel and let it rest at room temperature for 15 minutes. (The dough can be stored in an airtight container for 2–3 days – just bring it back to room temperature before use.)

Knead the dough once again for 1–2 minutes and divide it into 8 equal-sized balls.

On a clean, flat surface, sprinkle some flour, then press one dough ball into a thick disc using your hands. Now flip over the small disc and sprinkle it with some more flour, so that it doesn't stick to the surface. Using a rolling pin, roll it evenly to make a thin, round disc with a thickness of around 2mm ($\frac{1}{16}$in).

Preheat a large, flat pan over a medium heat, then carefully place the rolled roti into the pan. Cook it for a minute on each side. You will notice small brown blisters developing.

Using a folded kitchen towel, start pressing the roti gently in the middle while spinning it at the same time. Once it starts to puff up, almost into a balloon disc, flip it and do this again. Be careful not to burn your fingers on the hot steam.

Using a flat spatula, lift the roti out of the pan and keep it warm in a dish towel or foil-lined plate. Repeat with the remaining dough.

You can enjoy roti with any curry as it is, or spoon over or brush the roti with a little melted ghee or butter before serving to make it extra special. To store the roti for later, wrap them in foil or a clean dish towel to keep them soft and moist, or freeze them in an airtight bag. Then just reheat from frozen in a hot pan.

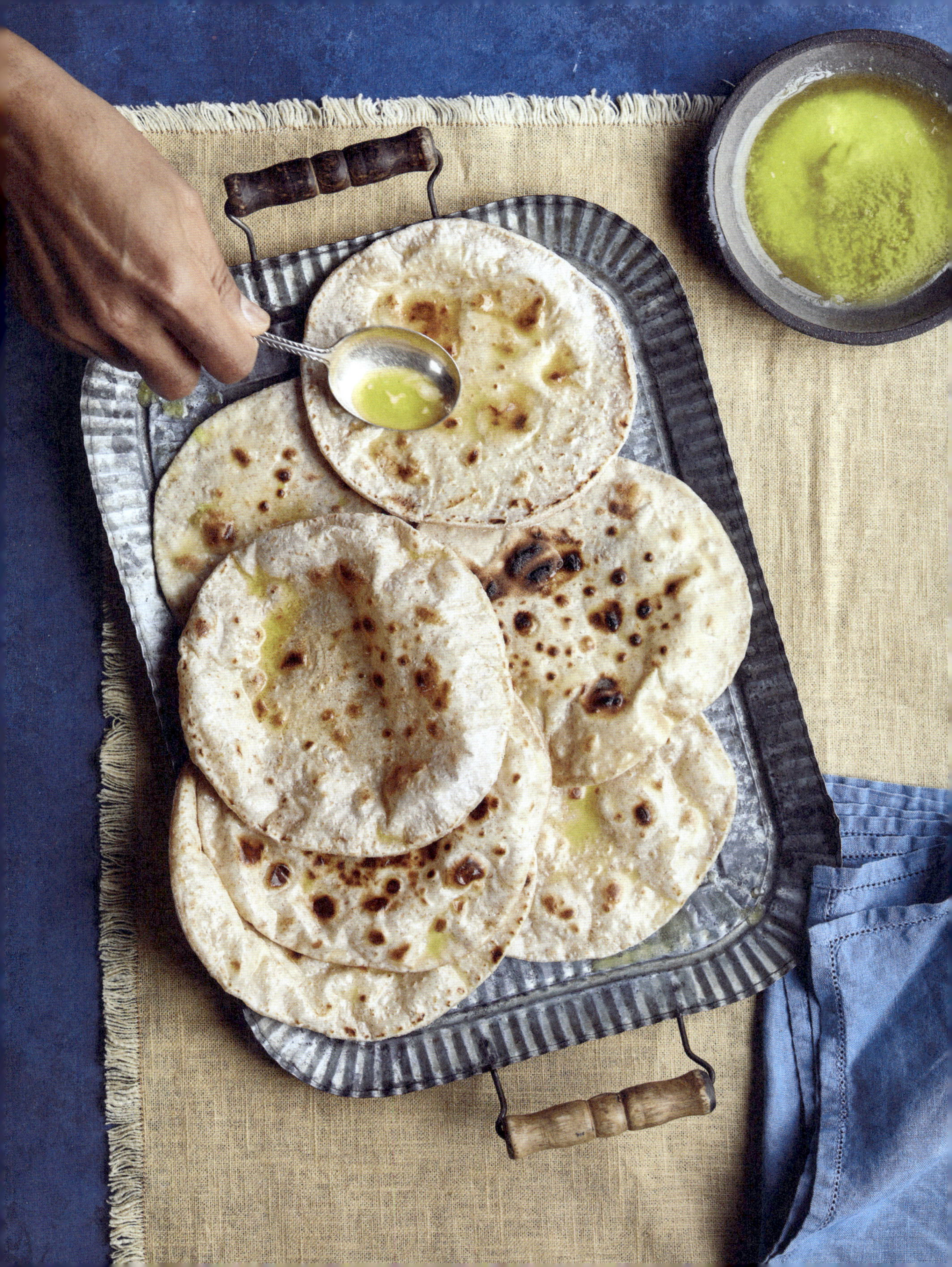

PAN-FRIED PLAIN PARATHA
(SADA PARATHA)

Plain parathas are like upgraded versions of roti – they are pan-fried and contain fat and some flavourings, plus they are slightly thicker, meaning they stay fresh for longer. They're perfect for scooping up creamy curries and are an ideal partner for dishes such as mutton curry or tandoori chicken, or they can be used as a wrap. Stuffed parathas are often eaten as at breakfast (see page 25) – it's all up to how and when you enjoy eating them!

Serves 6

250g (9oz) plain (all-purpose) or roti/chapati flour, plus extra for dusting

¼ tsp salt

½ tsp ajwain (carom seeds) or crushed fennel seeds

1 tbsp ghee or oil, plus extra for frying

To make the dough, combine the flour, salt and ajwain with 100ml (3½fl oz) of water in a bowl, following the instructions on page 14. Cover the dough with a damp dish towel and let it rest at room temperature for 30 minutes.

Knead the dough once again for 1–2 minutes and divide it into 6 equal-sized balls.

On a clean, flat surface, sprinkle some flour, then press one dough ball into a thick disc using your hands. Spread ½ teaspoon of the ghee or oil in the middle of the disc and reseal the edges together to make a flat ball so that all the ghee/oil stays inside.

Lightly press to make a small disc and dust it well with flour before rolling it into a wide circular shape using a rolling pin. The size is up to you, but make sure the thickness is around 3–4mm (⅛in).

Preheat a large, flat, non-stick pan or tava (see page 15) over a medium heat and cook the paratha for about 2 minutes on each side. Now apply ⅓ teaspoon of ghee on each side and fry over a low heat until the paratha puffs up and turns golden brown and flaky.

Using a flat spatula, lift the paratha out of the pan and keep it warm in a dish towel or foil-lined plate. Repeat with the remaining dough.

Serve the parathas warm with a curry of your choice. If you have any left over, you can freeze them in an airtight freezer bag for later use. Then just heat directly from frozen with a little or no oil on a hot pan, turning once.

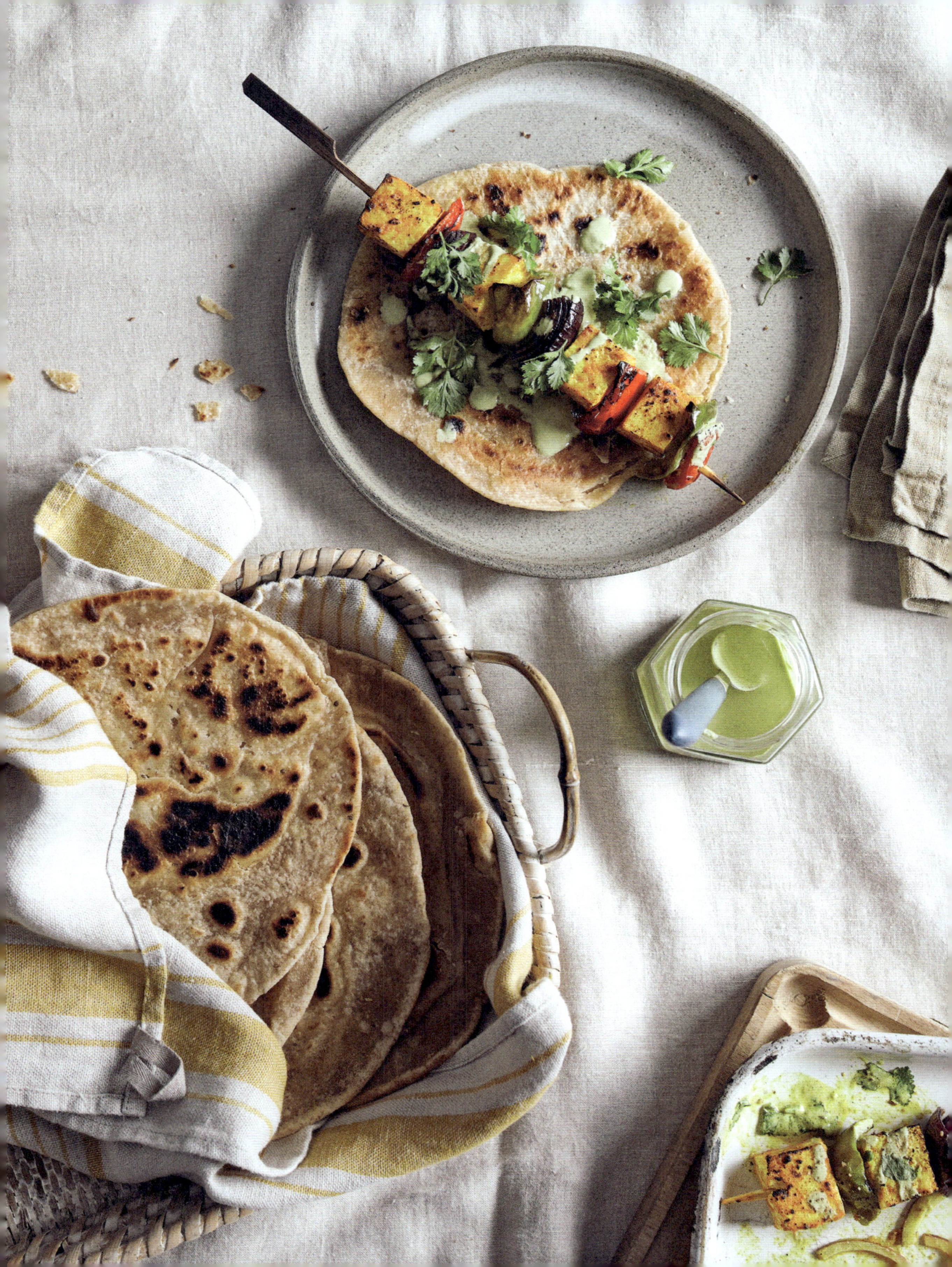

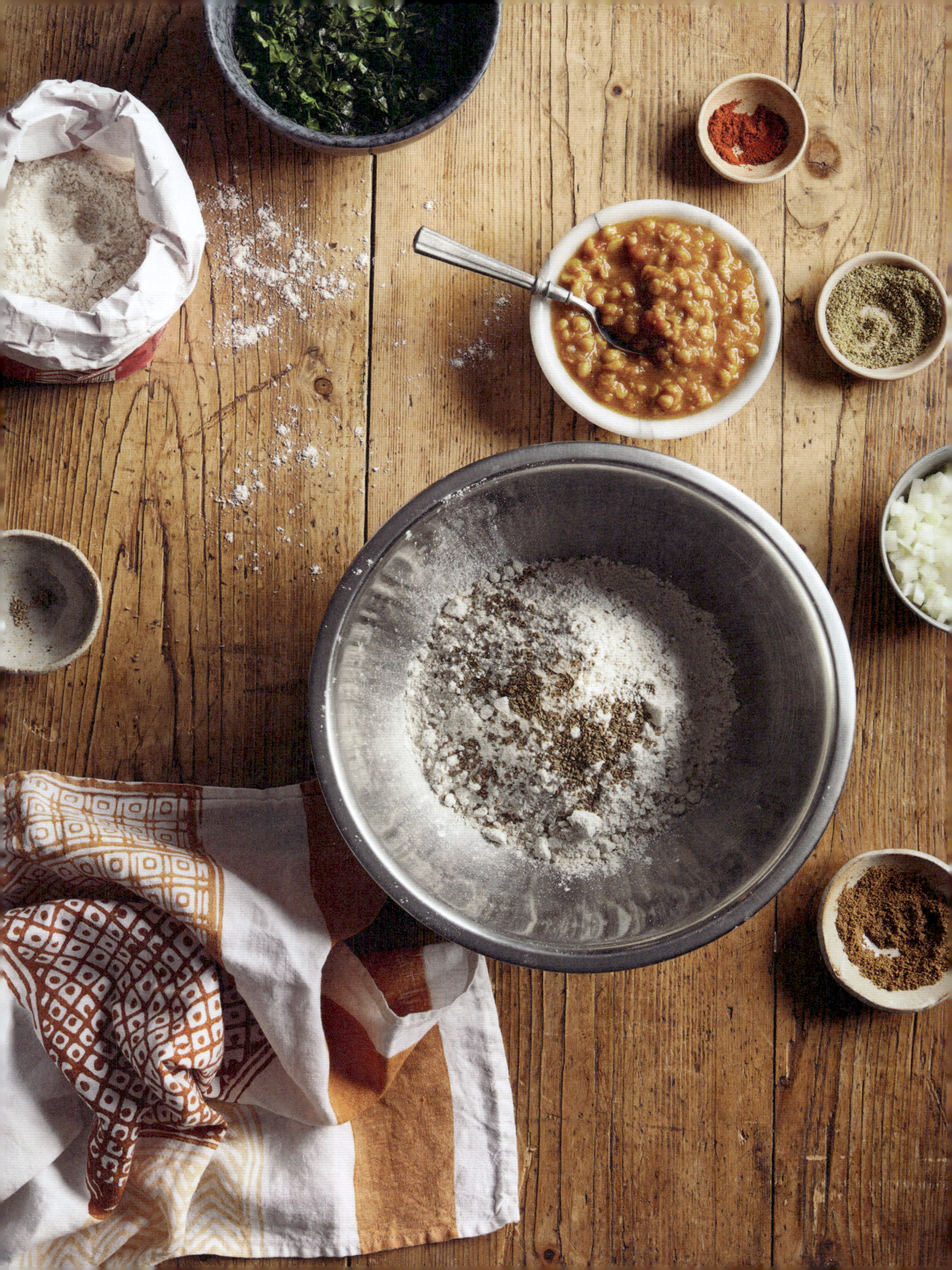

LENTIL FLATBREAD

(DAAL PARATHA)

It's hard to put this dish in a category of breakfasts, main meals or even snacks. It's very versatile and can be enjoyed at any time of day. This recipe is the best way to use up any leftover lentils or veggies to create something delicious. Although it is a variant of plain parathas, I find it the easiest to make as you can mix and match any ingredients.

Makes 6

250g (9oz) roti/chapati flour or plain wholemeal (wholewheat) flour, plus extra for sprinkling

1 tsp ajwain (carom seeds)

1 tsp ground fennel seeds

1 tsp salt

½ tsp red chilli powder

½ tsp Garam Masala (see page 155)

150g (5½oz) white onions, finely chopped

50g (1¾oz) spinach, finely chopped

200g (7oz) cold cooked yellow daal (lentils)

2 tbsp ghee or vegetable oil, plus extra for frying

In a mixing bowl, combine all the ingredients to make a dough (see page 14). At first do not add any water as the cooked lentils and chopped vegetables contain a lot of water. Once the dough starts to come together, add a little water at a time (to a maximum of 100ml/3½fl oz) to get a very tight structure.

Cover the dough with a damp dish towel and let it rest at room temperature for 30 minutes.

Knead the dough once again for 1–2 minutes and divide it into 6 equal-sized balls.

On a clean, flat surface, sprinkle some flour, then press one dough ball into a thick disc using your hands. Dust it well with flour before rolling it into a wide circular shape using a rolling pin. The size depends on your preference and dough hydration, but make sure the thickness is even and around 3mm (⅛in).

Preheat a large, flat, non-stick pan or tava (see page 15) over a medium heat and cook the paratha for about 3–4 minutes on each side. Now apply ⅓ teaspoon of ghee on each side and fry over a low heat until it puffs up and turns golden brown and flaky. This will take longer to cook than plain paratha as it has lot of moisture from the lentils and veg. Therefore, keep the heat level to medium and don't rush.

Using a flat spatula or something similar, lift the paratha out of the pan and keep it warm in a dish towel or on a foil-lined and covered plate. Repeat with the remaining balls of dough.

Serve the parathas warm with a curry of your choice. If you have any left over, see page 90 for how to freeze and reheat.

RICE DISHES & BREADS

PUFFED FRIED BREAD

(POORI)

Poori is a sphere-shaped bread reminiscent of many Indian festive celebrations. I am not sure if it makes the occasion special or if the occasion is special and that's why we make it! It goes well with so many vegetarian curries. As a child, I had a lot of fun with this by poking it in its crispy shell. Now my kids follow that same tradition!

Makes 12–16

200g (7oz) medium semolina (cream of wheat)

100g (3½oz) plain (all-purpose) flour

100g (3½oz) chapati flour

1 tbsp ghee

½ tsp salt

½ tsp ajwain (carom seeds) or crushed fennel seeds

Oil, for brushing and deep-frying

First, make a dough by combining all the ingredients except the oil with 180ml (6fl oz) of water in a bowl, following the instructions on page 14.

Cover the dough with a damp dish towel and let it rest at room temperature for 30 minutes.

Knead the dough again for 2 minutes and then shape it into a thick log. Now cut the log into 12–16 equal portions and roll each portion into an individual ball.

If the dough sticks, brush some oil on the dough balls and on your hands as well. Do not dust them with flour. Now, using a rolling pin, roll each ball into a flat, thin round disc, about 2mm (1/16in) thick.

In a large pan, wok or deep-fat fryer, heat enough oil for deep-frying (don't fill the pan more than two-thirds full) over a medium heat to 150°C (300°F). Test if the oil is hot enough (see page 113).

Carefully slide the rolled poori (one at a time) into the hot oil. In few seconds, it will start coming to the surface. Now, using a slotted spoon, gently tap or turn it until the poori puffs up. It should only take 1 minute on each side. Then remove the puffed poori to some paper towels to drain off any excess oil and repeat to cook the remaining dough.

Serve the poori hot, with your choice of curry and a side dish or two, some spicy pickles, yoghurt, salads and desserts, or see my suggestions for a full Indian celebratory meal on page 179.

Tip
Try stuffing the dough balls with some filling (something dry, like grated paneer, spices or pan-fried peas) before rolling out. They won't puff up like plain poori, but they will taste amazing.

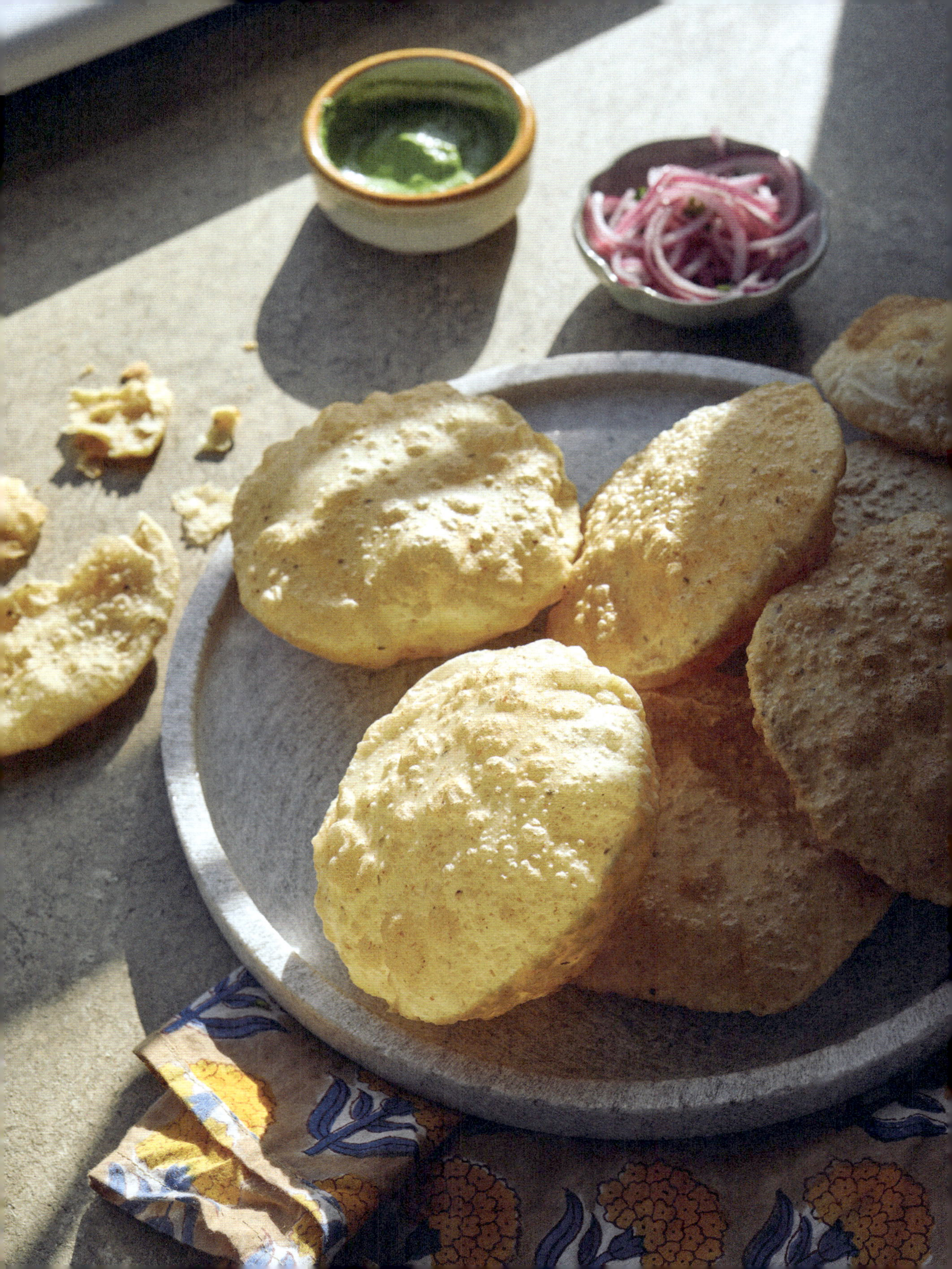

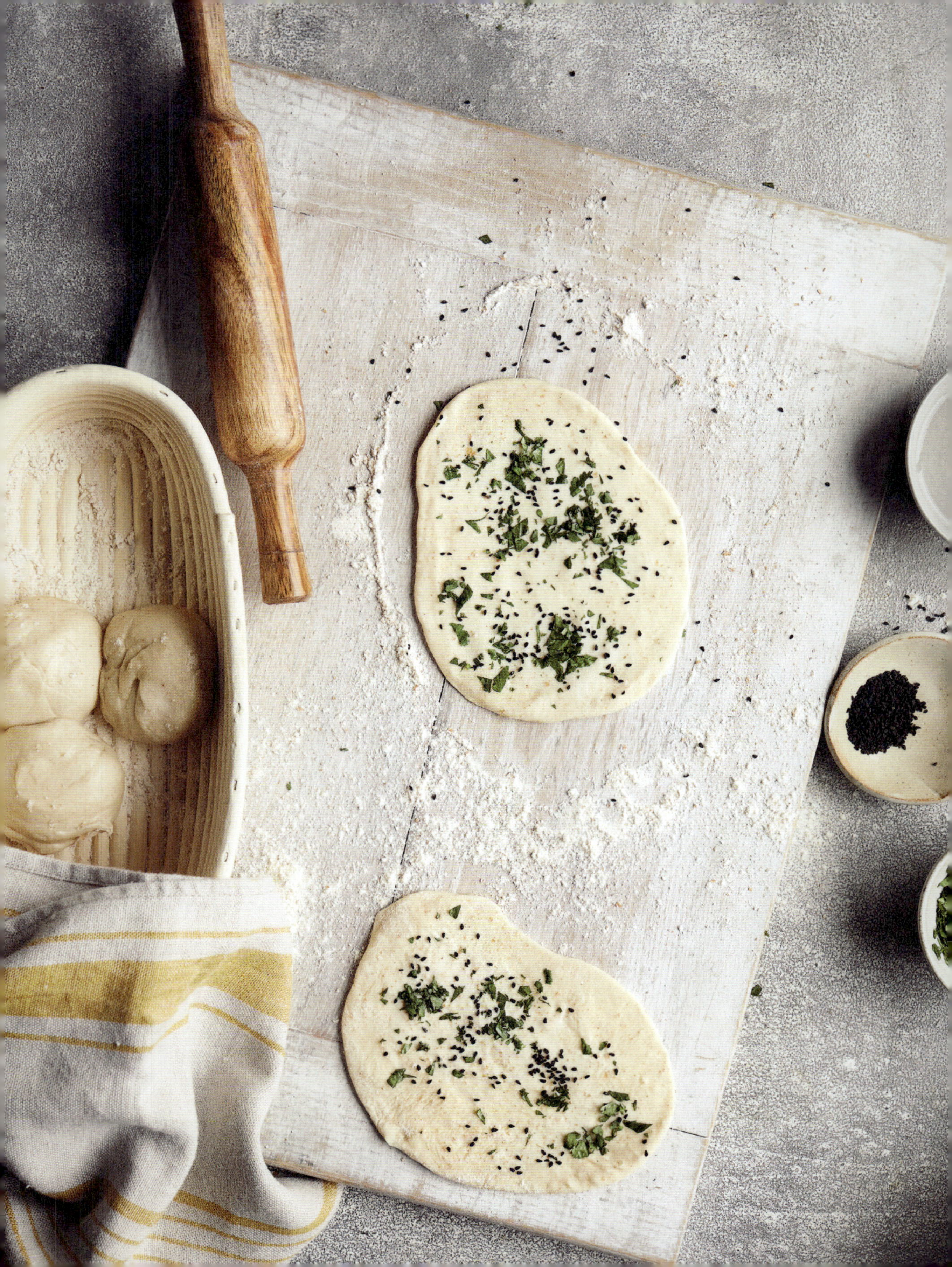

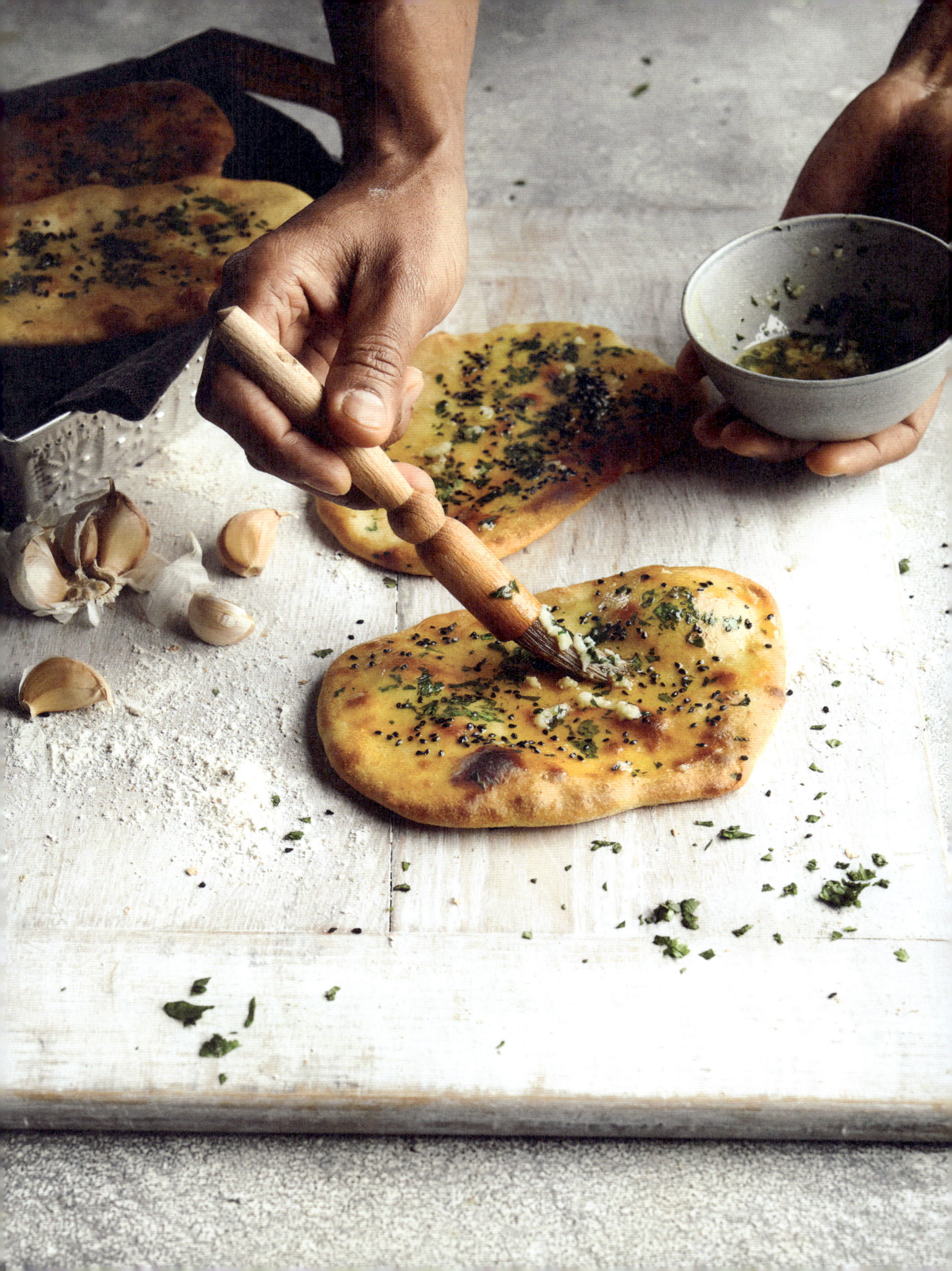

NAAN BREAD

This is one of those dishes that doesn't need any introduction. Traditionally, naan bread is cooked in a tandoor (clay oven) and the dough is fermented with yoghurt. Rather than being fluffy and bready, like supermarket naan, it should be a bit chewy and crispy. After moving to the UK, I created this recipe, which is as close to what I remember as possible. I hope you enjoy it!

Makes 6

250g (9oz) plain (all-purpose) flour, plus extra for dusting

¼ tsp bicarbonate of soda (baking soda)

1 tsp baking powder

¾ tsp salt

½ tsp granulated sugar

2 tbsp oil, plus extra for brushing

50g (1¾oz) natural (plain) yoghurt

3 tbsp butter

2 garlic cloves, finely grated or crushed

2 tbsp nigella seeds (kalongi)

2 tbsp chopped fresh coriander (cilantro)

To serve

Any curry of your choice!

or

Tandoori chicken or Paneer Tikka (see page 52)

Mint and Coriander Chutney (see page 162)

Mustard Garlic Yoghurt (see page 168)

Sliced red onions

In a large bowl, mix the flour, bicarbonate of soda, baking powder, salt, sugar, oil and yoghurt. Bring it together and then gradually add 100ml (3½fl oz) of water, a little at a time.

Knead for at least 5 minutes until you reach a very smooth consistency. The dough will be sticky and wet. Place in a bowl, brush with oil, cover and leave to rest in a warm place for 2 hours. In a small pan, melt the butter, stir in the garlic and set aside.

Remove the dough from the bowl, dust it with a little flour and divide and shape it into 6 equal-sized balls.

Dust some flour over a flat surface, then, one at a time, roll out each dough ball using a rolling pin into an oval shape. Aim for 5mm (¼in) thickness. Brush a little water on top of each one and sprinkle over a few nigella seeds and some fresh coriander. Press the naans down gently with your hand.

Preheat a grill (broiler) to high, or preheat an oven grill to 240°C/475°F/Gas 9. Then preheat a pizza stone or hot, flat ovenproof pan until very hot. Place a naan (with the nigella seed and coriander side facing up) on the hot stone/pan and cook for 2–3 minutes under the grill. It should puff up and will be golden brown on the edges. (Alternatively, cook them in a hot pan over a gas hob/stove, nigella seed-up, then, using tongs, cook the other side over the open flame.)

Carefully take the naan out from the grill, generously brush some of the garlic butter on top and repeat with the remaining dough. Serve with curry, or make a wrap with some Tandoori Chicken or Paneer Tikka, topped with a drizzle of Mint and Coriander Chutney, Mustard Garlic Yoghurt and some sliced red onions.

Tip
You can make one extra large naan then slice it up like a pizza!

Pictured on pages 96–97.

RICE DISHES & BREADS

EGG RICE

Egg rice is a very famous dish in many cuisines, and, needless to say, the Indian version is full of flavour and many surprises. I like it very much as it's a complete meal with rice, vegetables and eggs, which provide a great source of protein, plus subtle spicing lifts the dish to the next level. This recipe uses leftover boiled rice, so on a busy evening you can make this in under 15 minutes. If I have to list some of the key words about it, then they will be: one-pot, quick to cook, a balanced meal and delicious!

Serves 4–5

3 tbsp oil

2 green chillies, finely sliced

100g (3½oz) onions, chopped

100g (3½oz) deseeded red (bell) pepper, sliced

100g (3½oz) frozen peas

1 tsp salt

1 tsp Curry Masala (see page 154)

¼ tsp Garam Masala (see page 155)

4 large eggs, beaten

500g (1lb 5oz) cooked plain white rice, cooled

4 tbsp chopped fresh coriander (cilantro), to garnish

Mint and Coriander Chutney (see page 162), to serve

In a pan, heat the oil over a high heat, then add the green chillies, onion and red pepper and sauté for 2 minutes. Stir in the peas.

Turn the heat down to low, add the salt, Curry Masala and Garam Masala and mix well, then pour in the beaten eggs.

Once the eggs start cooking, increase the heat and stir occasionally to get a chunky scramble.

Mix in the fluffed-up cooked rice, add a splash of water and mix well over a high heat. Cover the pan, reduce the heat and let it cook over a very low heat for 2–3 minutes.

Remove from the heat and let it rest for another 5 minutes, so all the flavours are absorbed by the rice.

Garnish with the fresh coriander and serve hot with the chutney.

Easy swaps

Swap out the white rice for cooked cooled couscous or bulgur wheat.

Scrambled paneer or shredded cooked chicken are good swaps for the eggs.

RICE DISHES & BREADS

VEG RICE

(MIXED VEG AND PANEER PULAV)

Serves 6

For the veg rice
300g (10½oz) basmati rice
1 tbsp ghee or oil
4 green cardamom pods
5 cloves
1 star anise
200g (7oz) white onions, chopped
100g (3½oz) potatoes, peeled and diced
100g (3½oz) carrots, peeled and diced
1½ tsp salt
½ tsp Garam Masala (see page 155)
1 tsp ground coriander
½ tsp red chilli powder
200g (7oz) deseeded red (bell) pepper, diced
600ml (21fl oz) boiling water
200g (7oz) frozen peas, defrosted

For the paneer
2 tbsp ghee or oil
1 tsp ground turmeric
1 tsp salt
1 tsp Chaat Masala (see page 152)
200g (7oz) paneer, cut into 2cm (¾in) cubes

To serve
Cumin yoghurt (see page 102), papadams and Mint and Coriander Chutney (see page 162)

Mixed veg pulav is a perfect one-pot family dish – it's easy to make and full of nutrients and protein. This was one of our family favourites for Sunday lunch back in India, especially during winter, due to the availability of seasonal sweet carrots and peas, making this extra delicious and healthy.

To make the veg rice, first, soak the rice in a bowl of cold water for 30 minutes.

Meanwhile, for the paneer, combine the ghee or oil with the turmeric, salt and Chaat Masala in a bowl. Add the paneer cubes and toss to coat them all over.

Heat a frying pan (skillet) over a medium heat until hot, then add the paneer cubes and lightly pan-fry them for about 2–3 minutes until starting to colour. Remove to a plate and set aside.

For the veg rice, heat the ghee or oil in a pan (with a lid) over a medium heat, then add the whole spices. Once fragrant, add the onion, potatoes, carrots, salt and all the ground spices.

Drain and wash the soaked rice, then drain well in a sieve (strainer). Add it to the pan and mix well to coat every single grain in the oil masala. Stir in the red pepper and boiling water. Bring to the boil, cover with a lid, then reduce the heat. Simmer for 8–10 minutes.

Remove from the heat and keep the pan covered for another 10 minutes. Now add in the fried paneer and peas. Mix well and cover again with the lid to allow all the flavours to infuse thoroughly for another 5 minutes. The residual heat and steam will continue cooking everything.

Serve hot with sides of cumin yoghurt, papadams and Chutney.

Tip
For perfectly cooked rice, the rule of thumb is to use double the amount of water to the volume/weight of raw rice.

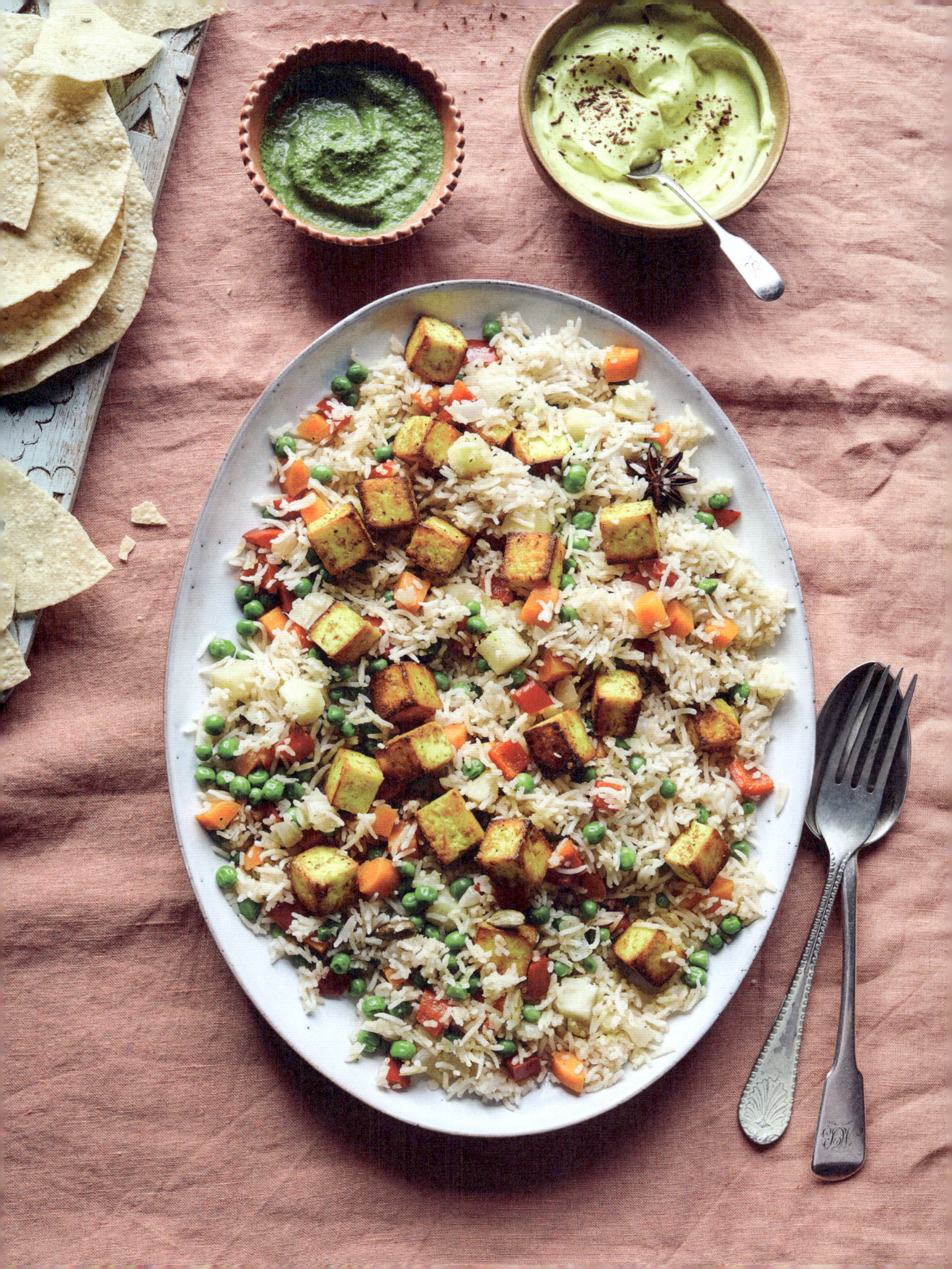

SIMPLE CHICKEN BIRYANI

Biryani is a delicacy in Indian cuisine, with a long list of ingredients and processes, and multiple layers. It can take hours to prep and cook – which is why I came up with this simplified version. It's delicious and easy to cook *without* spending hours in the kitchen. If anyone objects to its authenticity, just tell them it's Anurag's cheat biryani!

Serves 6–8

600g (1lb 5oz) skinless, boneless chicken thighs, each cut in half
300g (10½oz) basmati rice
4 tbsp ghee
1 tsp cumin seeds
6–8 cloves
6–8 green cardamom pods
3–5 dried bay leaves
50g (1¾oz) cashew nuts
50g (1¾oz) golden sultanas
200g (7oz) red onions, chopped
200g (7oz) tomatoes, chopped
1 tsp salt
1 tsp ground turmeric
¼ tsp saffron threads
500ml (17fl oz) boiling water

For the marinade

1 tbsp Ginger Garlic Paste (see page 159)
2 tbsp (shop-bought) peri-peri hot marinade
2 tbsp lemon juice
1 tsp salt
2 tsp Curry Masala (see page 154)
1 tsp Garam Masala (see page 155)

To serve

Cumin yoghurt (stir some of the Roasted Ground Cumin on page 152 into plain yoghurt), papadams, Chilli Pickle (see page 166) and Mint and Coriander Chutney (see page 162)

In a bowl, combine all the marinade ingredients, then add the chicken thigh pieces and turn to coat all over in the marinade. Cover and marinate for 15–30 minutes or overnight in the fridge. Bring back to room temperature before cooking.

Soak the rice in a bowl of cold water for 30 minutes. Drain and wash the soaked rice, then drain well in a sieve (strainer). Set aside.

Preheat the oven to 200°C/180°C fan/400°F/Gas 6.

In a heavy-based pan (with a lid), heat 2 tablespoons of the ghee over a medium heat, then add all the whole spices, the nuts and sultanas and cook until the cashews take on some colour. Now add the onion, tomatoes, salt and turmeric. Mix well, then cover and cook over a low heat for 10–15 minutes.

Once the masala starts to dry, add the marinated chicken and cook over a high heat for another 5 minutes without the lid.

Spread the dry chicken mixture in an even layer in a 30 x 20cm (12 x 8in) ovenproof dish. Then spread the soaked, drained rice in an even layer on top and press gently with a large spatula.

Sprinkle over the saffron, drizzle over the remaining 2 tablespoons of melted ghee, then very gently pour over the boiling water, without spoiling the chicken and rice layers. Cover and seal the dish with foil, then bake for 35–40 minutes, until the chicken is cooked through and the rice has absorbed all the liquid.

Remove from the oven and leave to rest for 10–15 minutes, before removing the foil. Don't mix it – serve it hot, in small blocks, almost like you would serve lasagne, with all the sides.

Easy swap

You can use boneless lamb shoulder instead of the chicken – just make sure it's at least half-cooked before you layer it.

RICE DISHES & BREADS

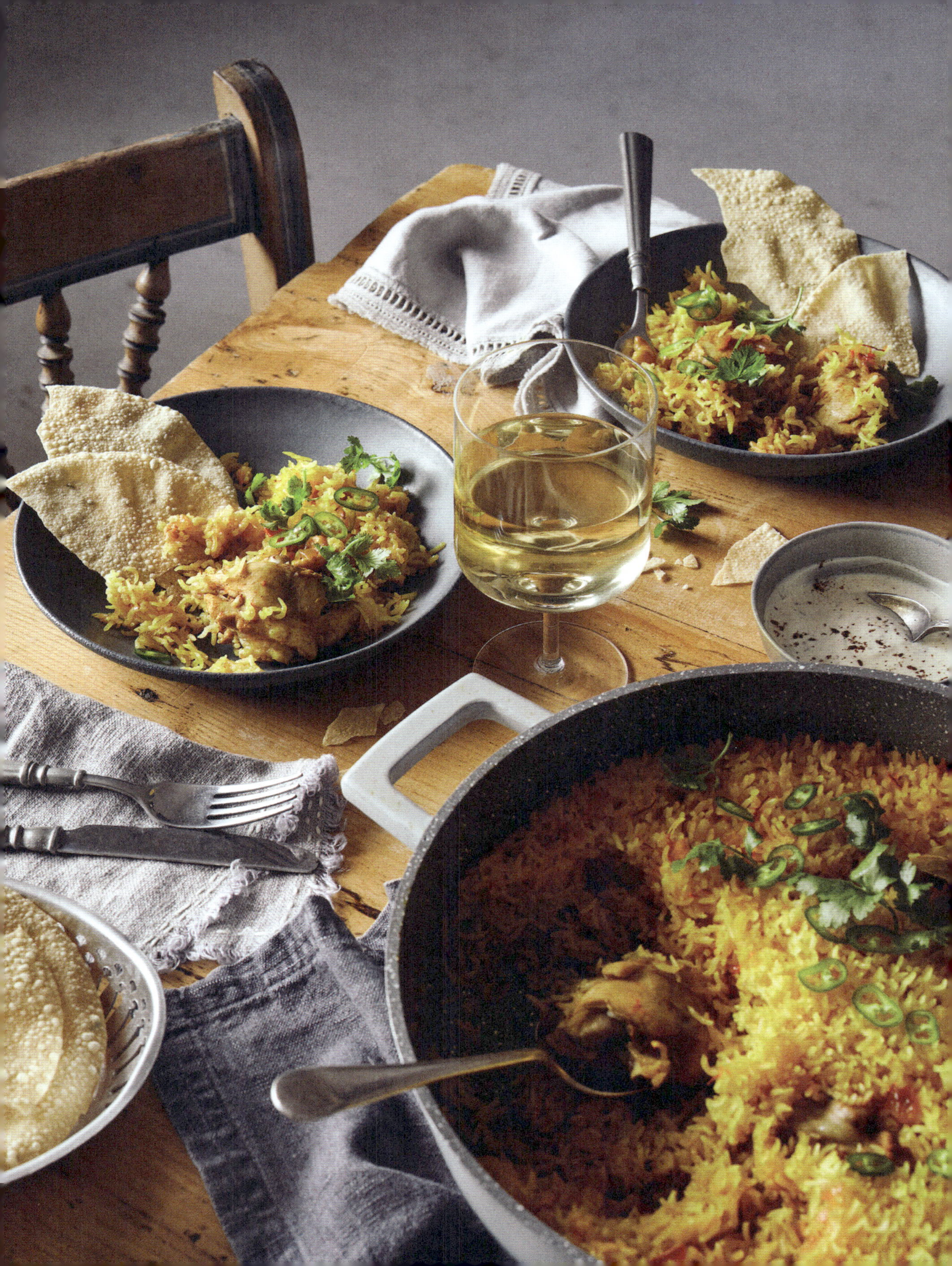

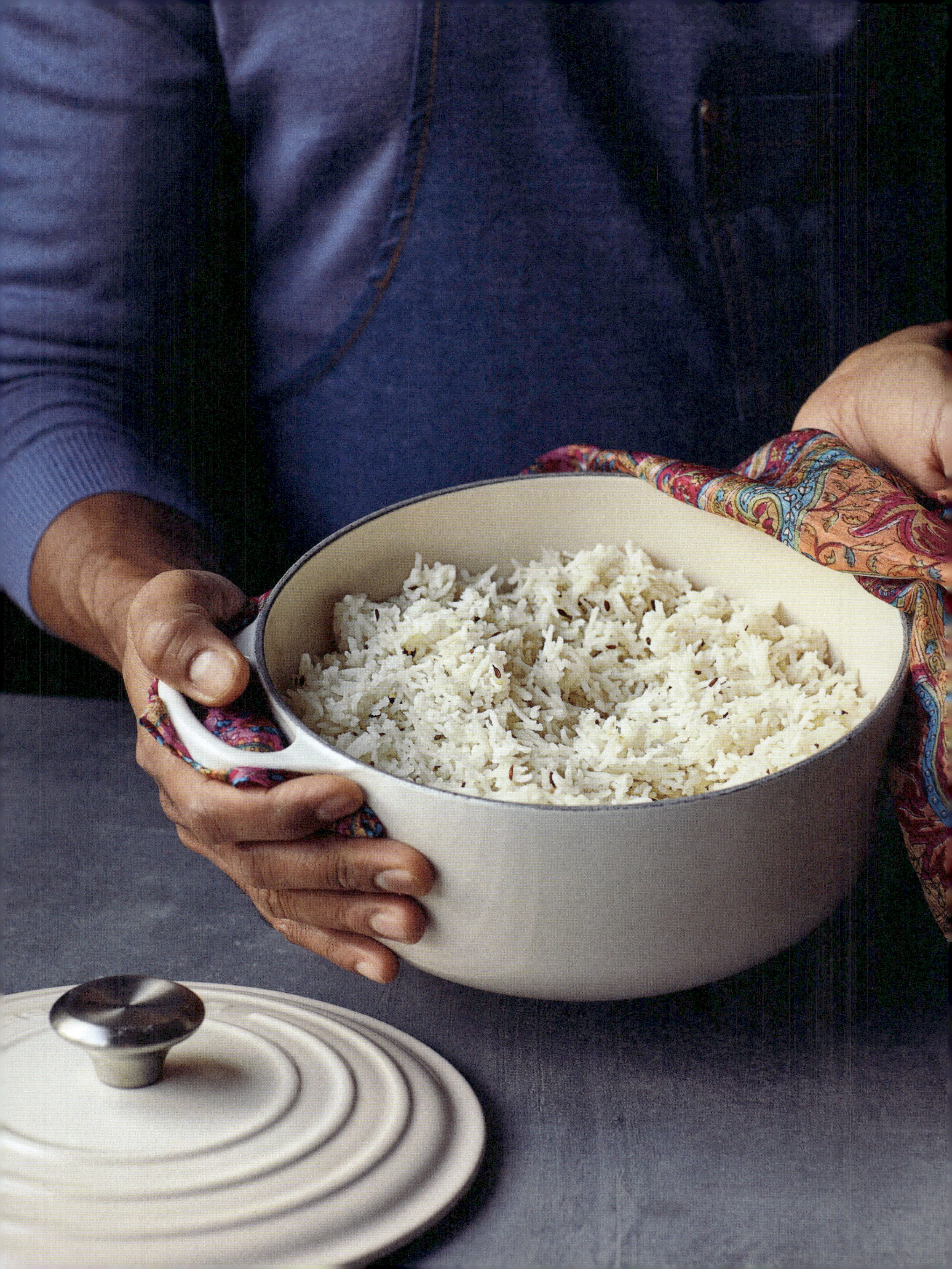

CUMIN RICE
(JEERA RICE)

Jeera rice is a very popular variant of plain steamed rice, which comes with the additions of cumin seeds and ghee or oil. The aroma of cumin seeds adds an earthy feel and the ghee/oil helps to keep the rice fluffy and prevents the grains from sticking together. This variant goes so well with special lentil preparations such as Rajma (see page 46), Chole (see page 56) and with heavier curries like Home-style Chicken Curry (see page 64) and Palak Paneer (see page 45).

Serves 4

200g (7oz) basmati rice
1 tbsp ghee or oil
½ tsp cumin seeds
400ml (14fl oz) boiling water

Using a bowl, soak the rice in cold water for 30 minutes. Now transfer the soaked rice to a large sieve (strainer), wash under cold running water and then allow all the water to drain out.

In a pan (with a lid), heat the ghee or oil over a medium heat, then add the cumin seeds and cook until brown, about 1 minute.

Immediately add the soaked and drained rice and the boiling water, then bring to the boil.

Now cover the pan, reduce the heat and simmer for 8–10 minutes, or until you can't see any bubbles, then remove from the heat. Let it rest with the lid on for at least 15 minutes (this is critical – the residual heat and steam means the cooking process continues even after the pan is removed from the heat), then carefully remove the lid and gently fluff up the rice using a fork.

Serve hot with any curry or lentil dishes of your choice.

Tip
The rule of thumb is to use double the amount of water to the volume/weight of raw rice.

Easy swap
Swap the cumin seeds for cloves, cardamom pods or star anise.

LEMON RICE

The use of a few ingredients like mustard seeds and curry leaves can instantly transport you from north India to south India. That's the power and magic of this recipe. You end up making something very light and refreshing, which can be enjoyed with any curry or lentil dishes or even on its own.

The nuttiness from the peanuts with the tang of lemon works wonderfully with fluffy rice. Well, if we can drizzle lemon juice over cakes, then why not rice? But I know it may sound a bit strange if you have never heard of this before!

Serves 4

3 tbsp oil
1 tsp yellow mustard seeds
A pinch of asafoetida (hing)
1 tbsp dried yellow lentils (moong)
4 tbsp raw peanuts (with red skin on)
3 dried red chillies
2 tbsp curry leaves
1 tsp salt
½ tsp ground turmeric
2 tbsp lemon juice
500g (1lb 2oz) cooked plain white rice, cooled

In a saucepan (with a lid), heat the oil over a medium heat, then add the mustard seeds and asafoetida. Once the seeds start sputtering, add the dried lentils and cook for a minute until they become light brown in colour.

Add the peanuts and whole red chillies and cook over a low heat for 3–4 minutes, until the peanuts are crispy.

Now add in the curry leaves, let them sizzle for a few seconds, then add the salt and turmeric and mix well.

Tip in the lemon juice, mix well and then immediately add the fluffed-up cooked rice. Mix well and add a splash of water. Make sure that the peanut masala is thoroughly mixed with the rice.

Cover the pan and let it cook over a very low heat for 5 minutes. Remove from the heat and let it rest for another 5–10 minutes.

Serve hot with any curry or lentil dishes, or just serve on its own. Onion Tomato Chutney (see page 163) or coconut chutney goes really well with this rice.

Easy swap
Swap out the white rice for cooked couscous or bulgur wheat.

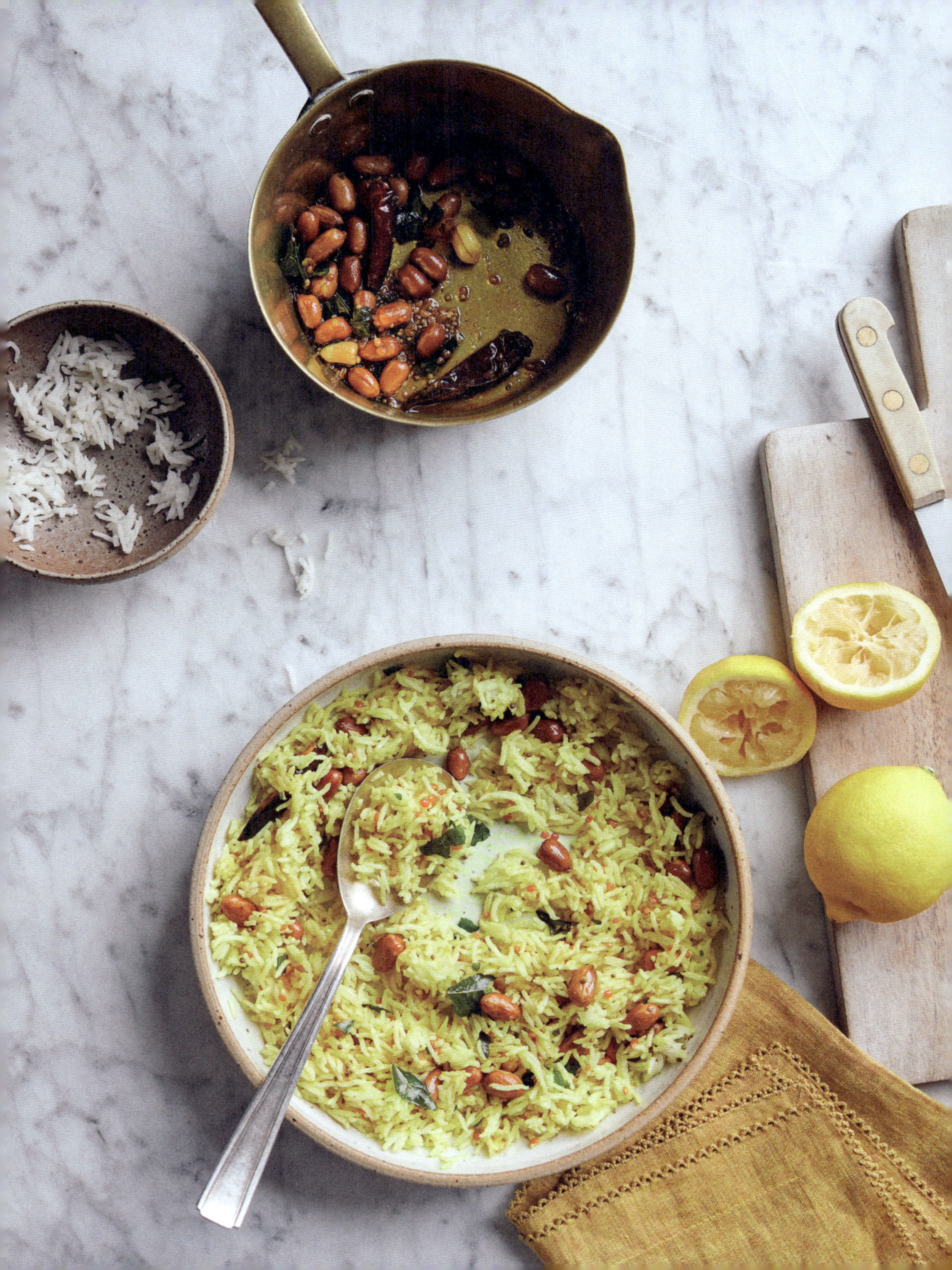

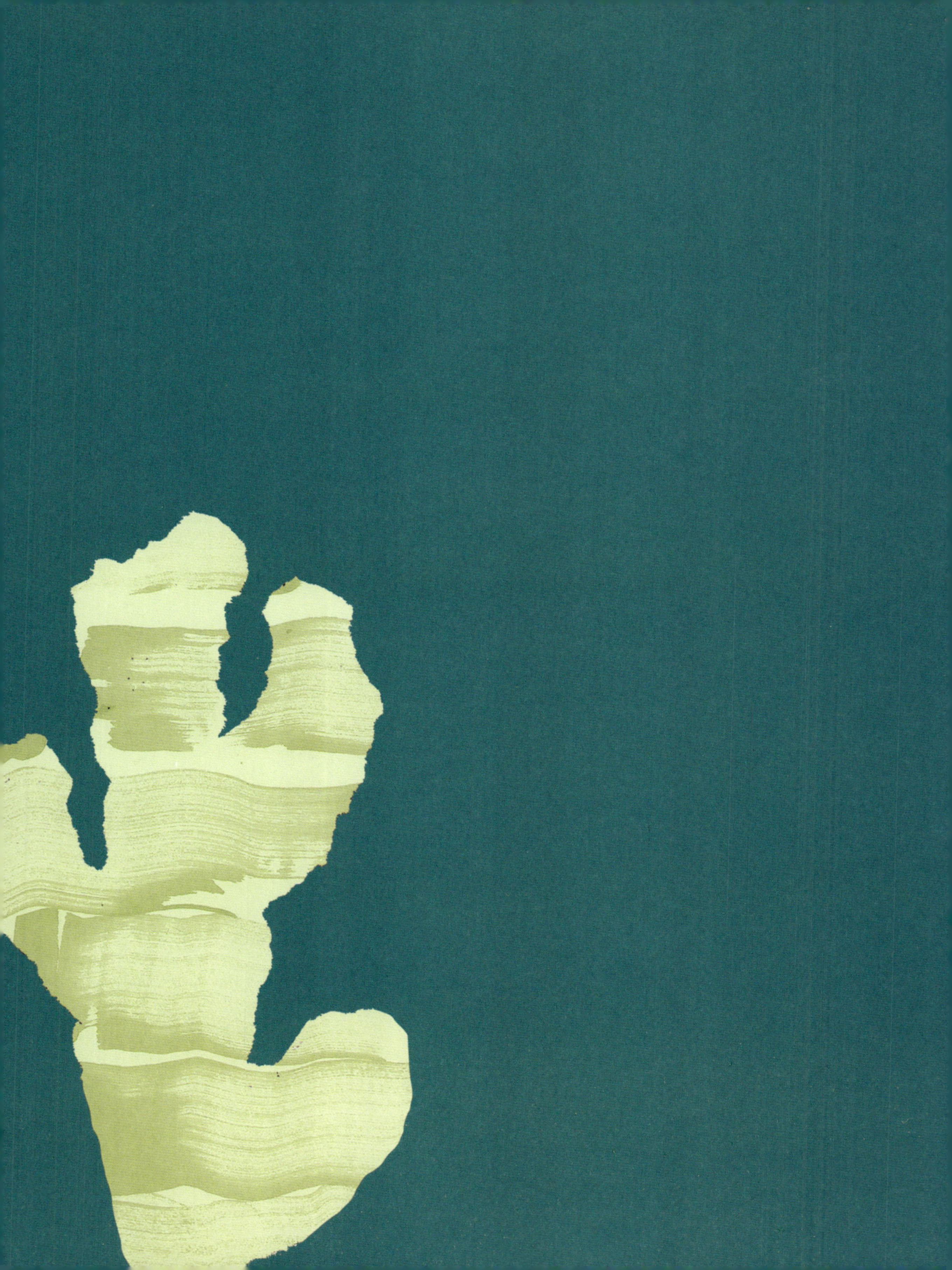

snacks, soups & SALADS

Diversity and variety in Indian cuisine are intrinsic to its nature. That's why it is very hard to classify many dishes into specific chapters. This chapter focuses on all the wonderful Indian delicacies that deserve an exclusive classification.

We all experience that feeling when we are a little hungry, but don't want to indulge in a full meal. We crave something delicious, yet we don't want to spoil our appetite for the main meal. If this sounds familiar, then you have come to the right chapter.

The dishes I have included here are some of my favourites and can be cooked very easily using readily available ingredients. They go so well as in-between snacks or even as part of a high tea. You may even enjoy them as main meals as well, tapas-style (serving two or three dishes per person).

I like to stay fit, so I like to eat a healthy and balanced diet throughout the day. With busy and demanding lifestyles, our bodies do need some refueling here and there. Rather than relying on a packet of crisps or a chocolate bar, I prefer to eat something more wholesome. The recipes included in this section provide a good mix of different nutrients. When it comes to food, it's all about the balance after all!

BLACK CHICKPEA AND SPINACH SALAD

(PALAK CHANA CHAAT)

Black chickpeas are a bit smaller than regular yellow chickpeas and have a thicker skin. They are easily available in Indian stores or can be bought online dried or in cans. They taste very earthy and nutty and are a great source of iron, protein and fibre. Black chickpeas are mostly used in Indian street food, or sometimes in curries.

The idea behind this salad was to bring together the tang of street food, the nutrients of chickpeas and the freshness of salad in one dish. It can be enjoyed on its own or as a side. I like eating this with my afternoon tea. I wonder what time of the day you will enjoy it!

Serves 4

- 400g (14oz) boiled, drained and cooled black chickpeas (garbanzo beans), or 180g (6¼oz) dried
- 200g (7oz) boiled cold potatoes, cut into small cubes
- 100g (3½oz) red onions, finely chopped
- 100g (3½oz) cherry tomatoes, quartered
- 100g (3½oz) baby spinach
- ½ tsp chopped green chilli (optional)
- 50g (1¾oz) chopped fresh coriander (cilantro)
- 2 tbsp lime juice
- 2 tbsp extra virgin olive oil
- ½ tsp salt
- 1 tsp Chaat Masala (see page 153)

If using dried chickpeas, soak them in cold water overnight, then drain and boil in plenty of fresh water the next day, until soft. Drain and cool. If using canned chickpeas, rinse the drained and cooled chickpeas.

In a large mixing bowl, combine the chickpeas, potatoes, red onion, cherry tomatoes, baby spinach and green chilli (if using). Keep chilled in the fridge until you are ready to serve.

Just before serving, add the fresh coriander, lime juice, olive oil, salt and Chaat Masala and mix well. Do wait until just before serving, otherwise the salad will become watery rather than crisp. Serve cold or at room temperature.

Easy swap
Swap the black chickpeas for black beans or regular yellow chickpeas.

SNACKS, SOUPS & SALADS

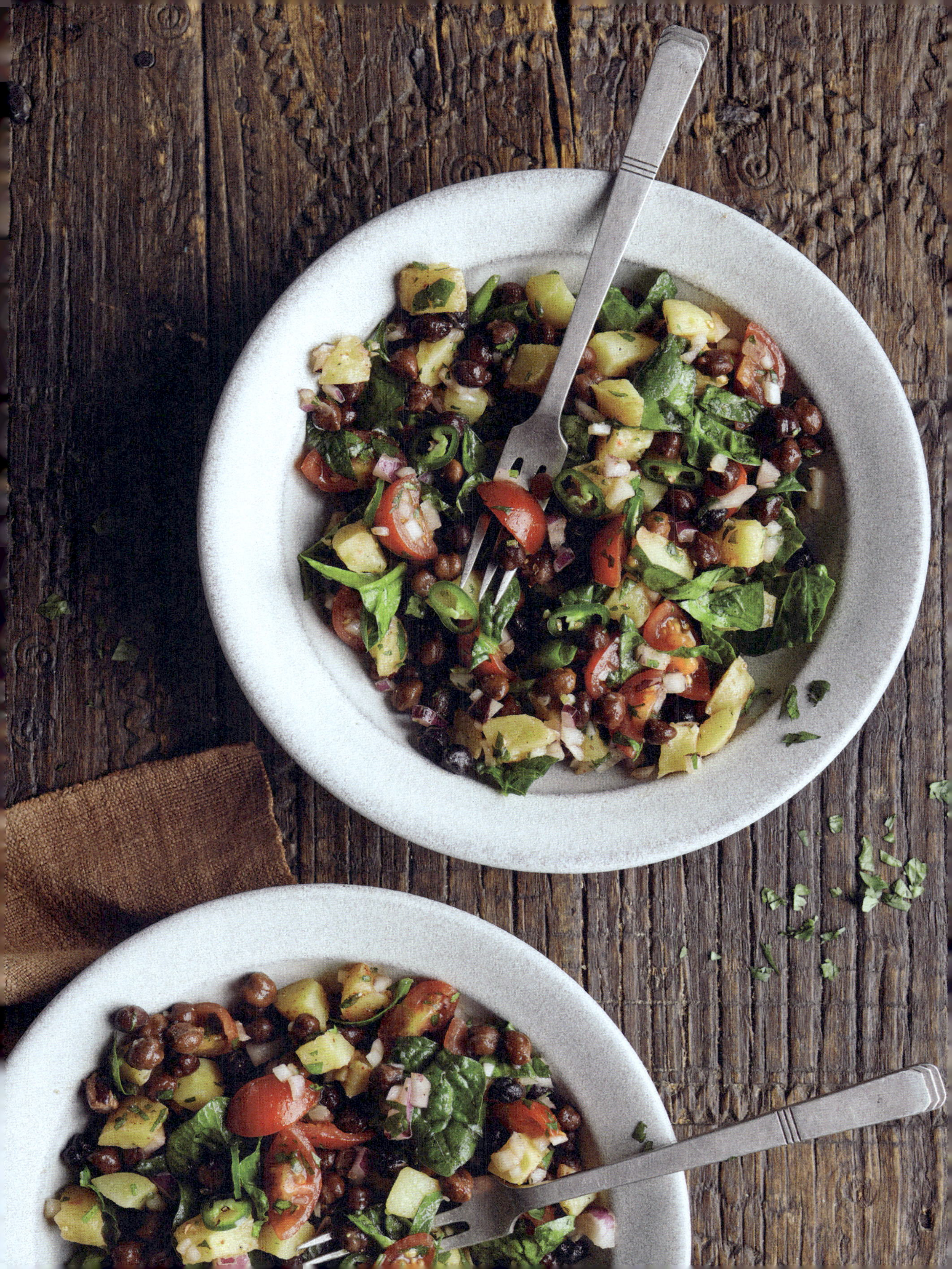

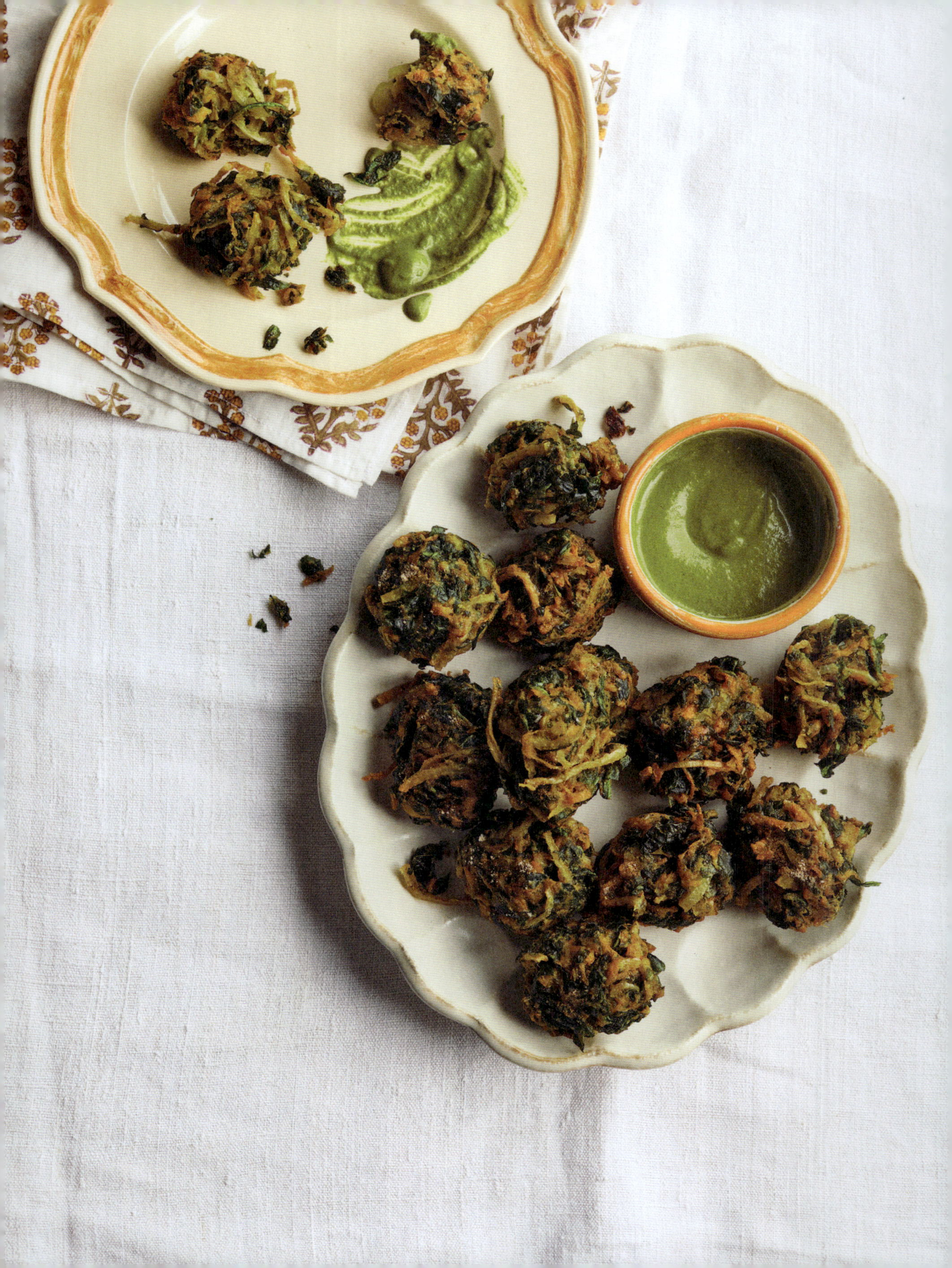

MIXED VEG PAKORA

Pakoras are a nice way to incorporate lots of veg into your snacks. The nuttiness of the gram flour with the crunch of the veg tastes amazing. Back in India, pakoras are very popular during monsoon season, especially when served with masala chai. After moving to the UK, I had to consciously suppress this craving, otherwise I would have ended up eating them almost every day in the lovely wet and windy English weather!

Makes 12–15

200g (7oz) spinach, chopped

200g (7oz) onions, sliced

200g (7oz) carrots, peeled and grated

50g (1¾oz) fresh mint, chopped

8 tbsp gram flour (besan)

4 tbsp rice flour or 1 tbsp cornflour (cornstarch)

1 tsp salt

A pinch of asafoetida (hing)

½ tsp ground turmeric

½ tsp red chilli powder

1 tsp ground coriander

½ tsp Garam Masala (see page 155)

Oil, for deep-frying

To serve
Tomato ketchup

Mint and Coriander Chutney (see page 162)

Mustard Garlic Yoghurt (see page 168)

Masala Chai (see page 34) or black tea

In a large bowl, combine the spinach, onion, carrots, mint, both flours, the salt, asafoetida and all the spices, mixing well. Gradually add about 60ml (2fl oz) of water, a little at a time, until the mixture binds well and holds itself together. You may not need all the water, and be careful to not add too much, otherwise the fritters won't be crispy once cooked.

Using wet hands, divide and shape into 12–15 small patties.

In a large pan, wok or deep-fat fryer, heat enough oil for deep-frying (remember not to fill the pan more than two-thirds full) over a medium heat to 160°C/320°F. To test if the oil is hot enough, drop a small piece of the mixture into the hot oil; it should start bubbling and float to the surface in a few seconds.

Carefully slide the patties, a few at a time, into the hot oil and deep-fry until they become golden brown on both sides, about 4–5 minutes.

Remove the pakoras from the hot oil using a slotted spoon and place on a plate lined with paper towels to drain off any excess oil. Repeat to cook the remaining pakoras.

Serve the pakoras hot and enjoy with tomato ketchup, Mint and Coriander Chutney and Mustard Garlic Yoghurt. For me, they are incomplete without a cup of masala chai or regular tea.

Tip
You can use any vegetables in this recipe, just make sure they are chopped to a medium size and choose vegetables that won't release too much water during cooking.

SNACKS, SOUPS & SALADS

RED LENTIL SOUP
(DAAL SHORBA)

This is the perfect recipe for when you feel a bit under the weather. It's earthy and so warm and comforting, almost like a mother's hug in a bowl. Irrespective of the season, I am sure it will bring some sunshine to your day. It's amazing how simple, humble ingredients can create such magical dishes. In my own experience, the most memorable dishes I have ever tasted were indeed uncomplicated and easy on the pocket!

Serves 4

200g (7oz) dried split red lentils
2 tbsp oil
4 garlic cloves, crushed
200g (7oz) white onions, chopped
200g (7oz) carrots, peeled and diced
2 vegetable stock (bouillon) cubes
1 tsp salt
½ tsp ground cumin
1 tsp dried mixed herbs
½ tsp smoked paprika
1 x 400g (14oz) can of chopped tomatoes
1 litre (35fl oz) boiling water
2 tbsp lime juice

To serve
Extra virgin olive oil
Crumbled feta cheese
Chopped fresh parsley
Toasted sourdough, to serve

Wash the lentils, then leave to soak in a bowl of cold water for 15 minutes and then drain in a sieve (strainer).

Heat the oil in a large pan (with a lid) over a medium heat and add the garlic. Cook for a minute until it begins to colour.

Add the onion, carrots, crumbled stock cubes, salt, cumin, dried herbs and smoked paprika. Increase the heat and keep stirring until the spices start sticking to the bottom of the pan.

Imediately add the tomatoes to deglaze the pan and then tip in the drained lentils and the boiling water.

Bring to the boil, then reduce the heat, cover and simmer for 15–20 minutes. Keep an eye on the pan and stir once or twice as these lentils produce a lot of froth which might cause a spill.

Check if the lentils are fully cooked and feel nice and tender when you touch them. If not, then keep simmering for another few minutes.

Remove the pan from the heat and carefully blitz the mixture with a stick blender for a smooth consistency. Stir in the lime juice and adjust the seasoning to taste.

Serve the soup in bowls. Drizzle each portion with a little olive oil and garnish with some crumbled feta and chopped parsley. Serve warm with toasted sourdough.

Easy swap
Swap out the dried split red lentils for dried yellow lentils.

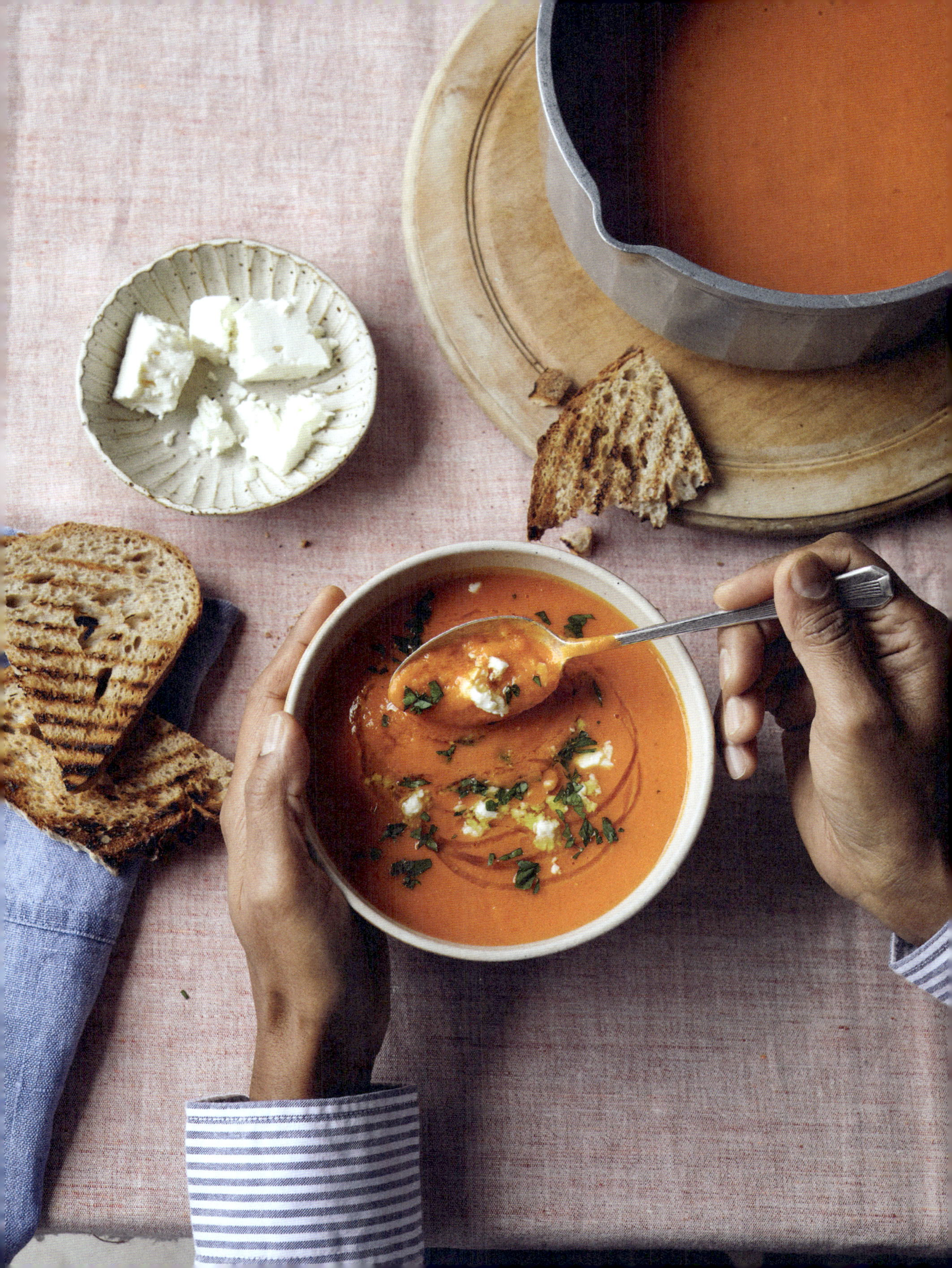

TOMATO SOUP

Soups were not very common while I was growing up in India. Having said that, tomato soup *was* popular, especially at big fat Indian weddings. That was my earliest memory of it, then later in my life I realized there are other kinds of soups as well. But I must say that in north Indian chilly winters, during grand wedding celebrations in open farmhouses (yes, that's right!), this indulgent, steaming, creamy, buttery and tangy soup, floating with fried croutons, tastes divine.

Warmed by those lovely memories, I came up with this recipe. It won't give you the celebratory experience of grand Indian weddings, but it will surely invoke an inner feeling of warmth!

Serves 4

2 tbsp butter

4 garlic cloves, crushed

2 tsp dried mixed herbs

200g (7oz) white onions, roughly chopped

200g (7oz) carrots, peeled and roughly chopped

100g (3½oz) fresh beetroot (beets), peeled and roughly chopped

200g (7oz) celery stalks, roughly chopped

2 x 400g (14oz) cans of plum tomatoes or 1kg (2lb 4oz) fresh tomatoes, chopped

2 vegetable stock (bouillon) cubes

2 tsp granulated sugar

1 tsp salt

½ tsp freshly ground black pepper

240ml (8fl oz) double (heavy) cream, plus extra to garnish

2 tbsp chopped fresh coriander (cilantro), to garnish

Buttered toasted sourdough, to serve (optional)

Melt 1 tablespoon of the butter in a large pan (with a lid) over a medium heat, then add the garlic and dried herbs. Cook for 2 minutes, until the garlic is fully cooked.

Add the onion, carrots, beetroot and celery to the pan and sauté for 1 minute. Cover the pan and simmer for 5 minutes.

Once the veg are soft, add in the tomatoes, crumbled stock cubes and 200ml (7fl oz) of water. Bring to the boil over a high heat, then reduce the heat, cover the pan and simmer for 15 minutes.

Remove the pan from the heat and carefully blitz the soup with a stick blender. You can then pass it through a sieve (strainer) for a smoother texture, if you like. Add the sugar, salt, black pepper and cream and cook gently for another 5 minutes. Add a little water to adjust the consistency, if desired.

Remove from the heat and add the remaining tablespoon of butter. Let it melt with the residual heat and emulsify in the soup.

Serve the soup hot in bowls and garnish each portion with a little extra cream and the fresh coriander. Buttered toasted sourdough goes very well with this.

Easy swap
Choose dairy-free or plant-based alternatives to the butter and cream, if you like.

CHICKEN ROLLS

Chicken rolls in India come in different names and forms. This simplified recipe, ideal for snacking on, is inspired by my nostalgic memories of my participation in *MasterChef UK*.

Makes 4

600g (1lb 5oz) skinless, boneless chicken thighs

400g (14oz) red onions, sliced

100ml (3½fl oz) white wine vinegar

1 tsp salt

4 large (30cm/12in) white flour tortillas or plain Parathas (see page 90)

4 tbsp Mint and Coriander Chutney (see page 162)

For the marinade

2 tbsp Greek-style yoghurt

2 tbsp lime juice

1 tbsp Ginger Garlic Paste (see page 159)

1 tsp salt

2 tsp Curry Masala (see page 154)

To serve (optional)

Palak Chana Chaat (see page 110)

Mint yoghurt dip

Mix all the marinade ingredients together in a bowl, then add the chicken thighs and turn to coat them evenly. Cover and leave to marinate for 30 minutes, or preferably overnight, in the fridge. (If you like, you can do this step in advance, then store in an airtight container in the frdige or freezer until needed.)

Combine the sliced red onions, vinegar and salt in a separate bowl and leave to soak for at least 1 hour. Drain off the excess liquid before serving.

To cook the chicken, heat a griddle pan over a high heat until hot, then add the marinated chicken thighs and cook over a medium–high heat for 7–8 minutes on each side, until fully cooked through. Or cook the chicken under a preheated hot grill (broiler) or over a hot BBQ for about 20 minutes until fully cooked. Remove the chicken from the heat and leave it to rest for 10 minutes, then slice it into strips and set aside.

To assemble, heat the tortillas (or Parathas), one at a time, in a preheated hot large frying pan (skillet) over a medium heat for a few seconds on each side to make them softer and more pliable. Spread a tablespoon of the chutney over the middle of each warmed tortilla, then place a quarter of the sliced chicken on top and finish with some pickled red onions. Flip one side of the tortilla over the filling, then roll it into a tight log. Wrap it in foil or baking paper. Cut in half diagonally to make two equal portions.

Serve at room temperature or cold with Palak Chana Chaat and a mint yoghurt dip.

Tip

You can cook the chicken thighs in advance, then cool and store them in an airtight container in the fridge for 3–5 days, or freeze for later use. Just defrost before using.

Easy swaps

Use any other salad veg with or instead of the pickled onions.

Swap out the chicken for paneer or a diced lean cut of lamb.

SNACKS, SOUPS & SALADS

ROASTED POTATO CHAAT
(ALOO CHAAT)

Aloo chaat is a well-known Indian street food delight. It's so spicy, crispy and warm. Whenever I think about it, I remember the Old Delhi street food vendor's carts. People don't mind queuing for this dish: it tastes amazing, especially when made fresh in front of you. As a street food lover, these hot and crispy potatoes tossed with a special spice mix, as well as Mint and Coriander Chutney and lime drizzle, create a feeling of absolute bliss. I love this dish so much that I may have exaggerated this a bit. Let's see if after cooking and eating this dish, you think my exaggeration is justified!

Serves 4

400g (14oz) unpeeled starchy potatoes
3 tbsp oil
3 tbsp Mint and Coriander Chutney (see page 162)
1 tbsp lime juice
½ tsp chopped green chilli, or to taste (optional)
2 tsp Chaat Masala (see page 153)
½ tsp salt
2 tbsp chopped fresh coriander (cilantro)
Fresh pomegranate seeds, to garnish
Yoghurt, to garnish (optional)

Preheat the oven to 200°C/180°C fan/400°F/Gas 6.

Wash and dry the potatoes and leave the skin on. Cut them into cubes of around 3cm (1¼in).

Spread the cubed potatoes over a baking sheet, drizzle with the oil and toss to coat. Roast in the oven for 30–35 minutes, until golden brown.

Just before serving, tip the hot roasted potatoes into a large heatproof bowl. Add all the remaining ingredients, except the pomegranate seeds, and toss them together nicely. The chutney and spices should coat every bit of the crispy potatoes. Garnish with some pomegranate seeds and serve immediately, before the chutney and lime juice kill the heat.

This dish is going to be a very hot and spicy dish to eat, but please take small bits and resist drinking any water. Little bursts of the sweet pomegranate seeds will balance the heat so well. Only then will you start enjoying the magic. If it is truly too hot for you to handle, drizzle over some cooling yoghurt as a garnish.

Easy swap
You can use leftover roast potatoes: reheat in the oven on a baking sheet for around 8 minutes from chilled, then toss with the rest of the ingredients, as above. Alternatively, oven-roasted or fried celeric (celery root) cubes are a great swap.

SNACKS, SOUPS & SALADS

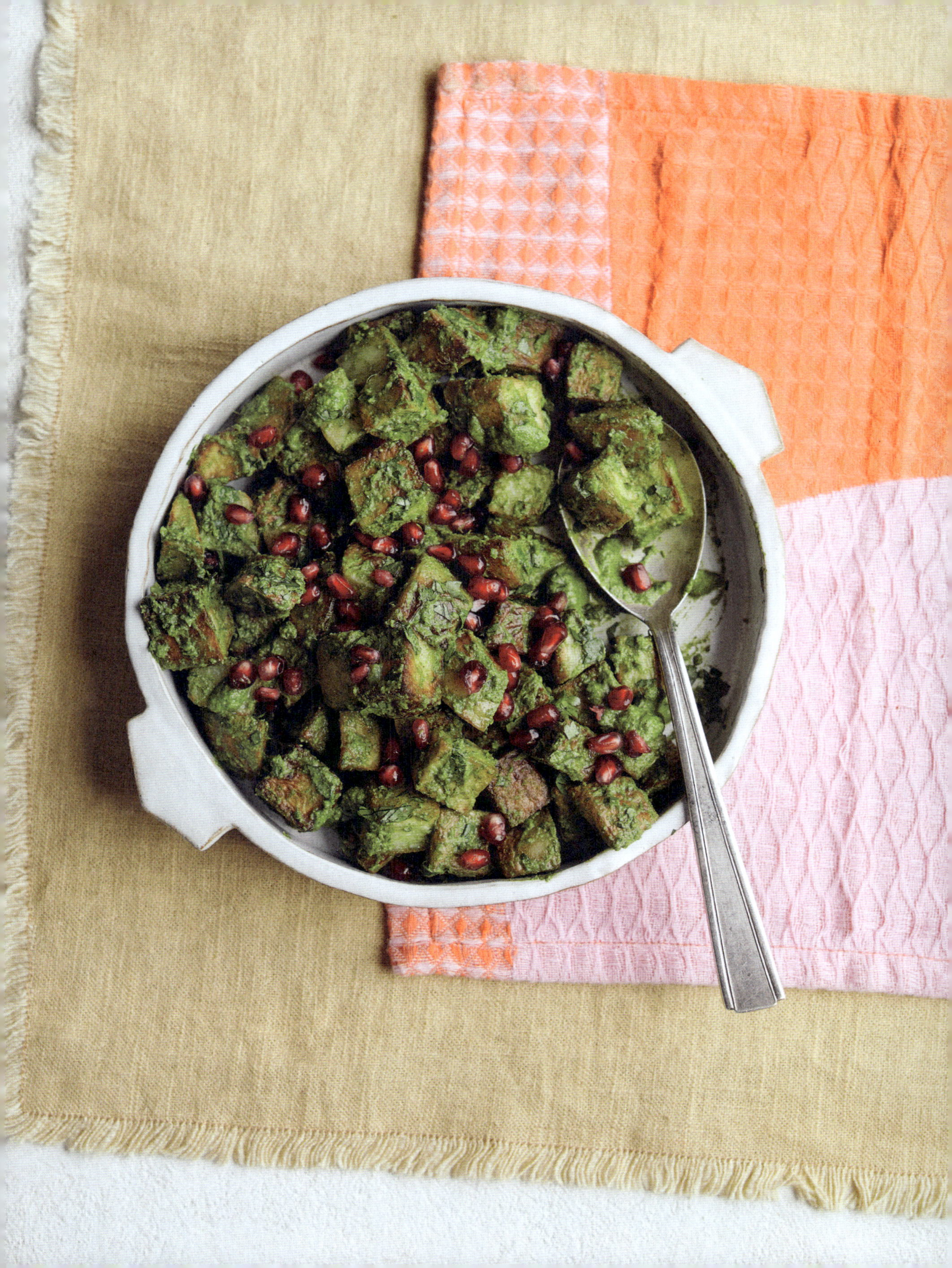

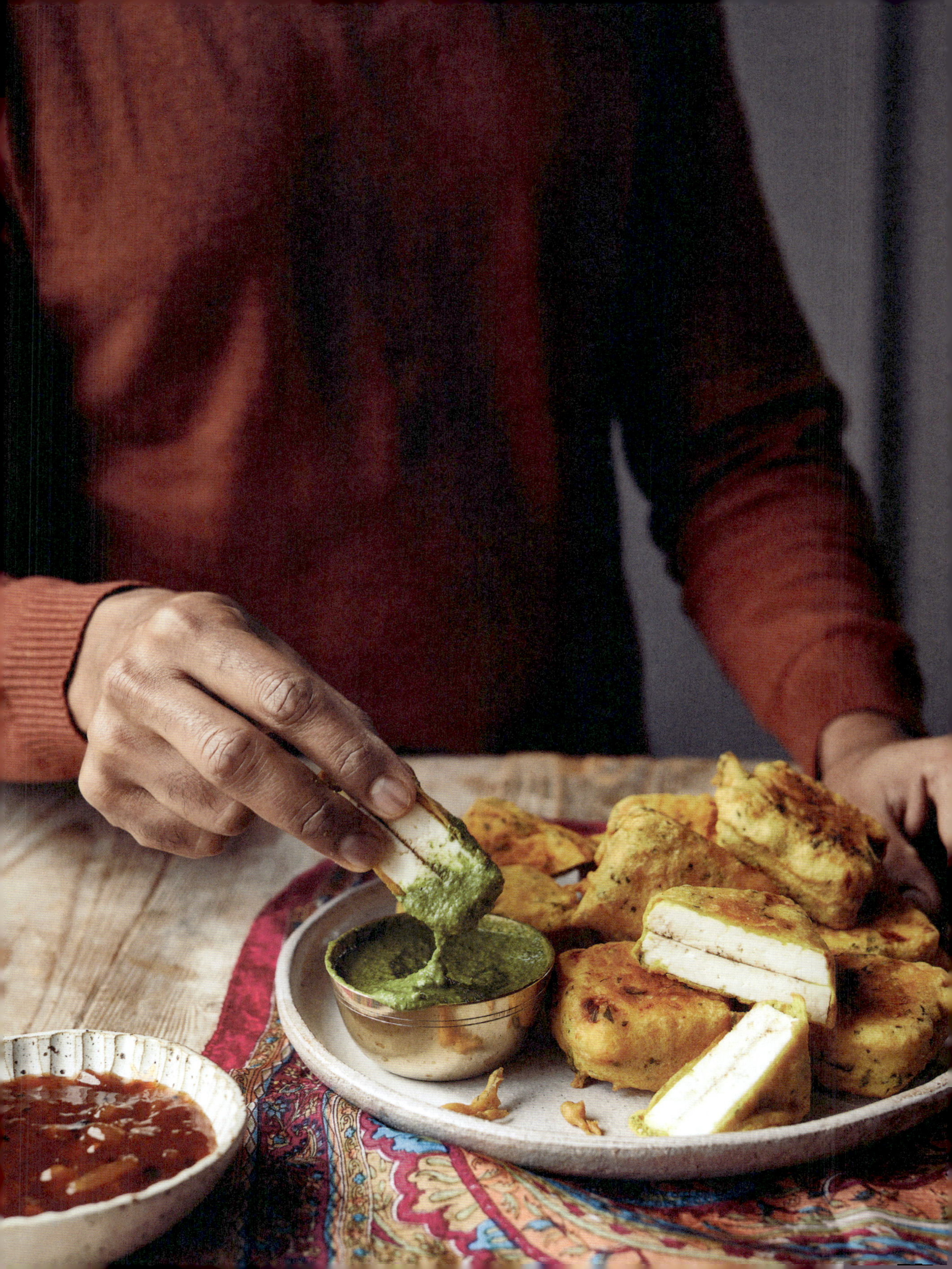

PANEER PAKORA

These paneer pakoras are as pillowy and delicious in a way you have never experienced before! Creamy, soft paneer, filled with tangy Chaat Masala, coated with golden crispy batter and dipped in mango chutney or Mint and Coriander Chutney. After reading this, you might dream of these tonight!

Makes 8–10

100g (3½oz) gram flour (besan)

50g (1¾oz) rice flour or 25g (1oz) cornflour

½ tsp salt

½ tsp ground coriander

¼ tsp ground turmeric

¼ tsp red chilli powder

4 tbsp chopped fresh coriander (cilantro)

500g (1lb 2oz) paneer

2 tsp Chaat Masala (see page 153)

Oil, for deep-frying

To serve
Mango chutney

Mint and Coriander Chutney (see page 162)

Start by making the batter. In a large bowl, combine the flours, salt and spices. Gradually add 200ml (7fl oz) of water, a little at a time, whisking until smooth, then stir in the fresh coriander. The batter should be slightly thicker than pancake batter and should be able to coat the paneer. Set aside.

Depending on the size of the paneer, cut it into 4cm (1½in) squares (about 8–10 squares in total), each 2cm (¾in thick), then slice each square in half horizontally to get 1cm (½in) thickness.

Now sprinkle a generous amount of Chaat Masala on one square of paneer and cover it with another plain square of paneer, to make a little paneer sandwich filled with Chaat Masala. Prepare the rest of the paneer squares in the same way. Set them aside for 5 minutes. The dry masala will absorb some moisture from the paneer and will work as a sticky glue for the sandwich.

Carefully dip each paneer sandwich into the batter and coat all the sides evenly. In a large pan, wok or deep-fat fryer, heat enough oil for deep-frying (remember not to fill the pan more than two-thirds full) over a medium heat to 160°C/320°F. To test if the oil is hot enough, drop a small piece of the paneer into the hot oil; it should start bubbling and float to the surface in a few seconds. Carefully slide the paneer pakoras, a few at a time, into the hot oil and deep-fry for about 3–4 minutes on each side, until they become golden and crispy.

Remove the pakoras from the hot oil using a slotted spoon and place on a plate lined with paper towels to drain off any excess oil. Repeat to cook the remaining paneer pakoras.

Serve the paneer pakoras hot and enjoy with the chutneys.

Easy swap
Use boiled potato slices in place of the paneer.

SNACKS, SOUPS & SALADS

BLACK PEPPER CRACKERS
(KALI-MIRCH MATHI)

Kali-mirch mathi are pretty much like crispy little savoury flatbreads. They can be stored in an airtight container for weeks and are wonderful snacks, especially with a cup of tea. Culturally, Indian mothers often make these and pack them up if you are going on a short trip or leaving home for university. Whenever you miss home, you can simply enjoy a couple of mathi and think of your mother. Though my mother is no longer with us in this world, with her beautiful recipes and lovely food memories, I still often feel her presence around me.

Makes 25–30

250g (9oz) plain (all-purpose) flour
½ tsp salt
½ tsp ajwain (carom seeds)
2 tbsp very coarsely crushed black pepper
60ml (2fl oz) oil, plus extra for oiling and deep-frying

To serve (optional)
Mango chutney or a dip of your choice
Indian spicy pickles

In a mixing bowl, combine all the dry ingredients, then add the oil. Rub the oil into the flour with your hands until it can hold its shape. Now gradually add 75ml (2½fl oz) of water, a little at a time, to make a dough (see page 14). Cover with a damp dish towel and leave to rest at room temperature for at least 30 minutes.

Once rested, knead the dough once again for 2 minutes, then divide it into four equal portions and roll each one into a ball.

Oil the work surface. Roll out a ball of dough to around 2–3mm (1⅛in) thick. Prick it all over with a fork. Then, using a round cutter (6cm/2.5in in diameter), cut out little circles. Don't discard the trimmings – you can knead them again with the remaining dough. Repeat with the remaining dough balls to make 25–30 little round discs in total.

In a large pan, wok or deep-fat fryer, heat enough oil for deep-frying (don't fill the pan more than two-thirds full) over a medium heat to 150°C/300°F. Test if the oil is ready (see page 113).

In batches, carefully slide a few discs of dough into the hot oil. Deep-fry them for around 6–8 minutes on each side, until the crackers are fully cooked and become golden and crispy. Using a slotted spoon, transfer the cooked crackers to some paper towels to drain off the excess oil, while you cook the rest in the same way.

Let the cooked crackers cool down completely, then enjoy them on their own, with a chutney or dip, or with Indian spicy pickles.

Tip
Use any other dried seeds and herbs, like nigella seeds or oregano.

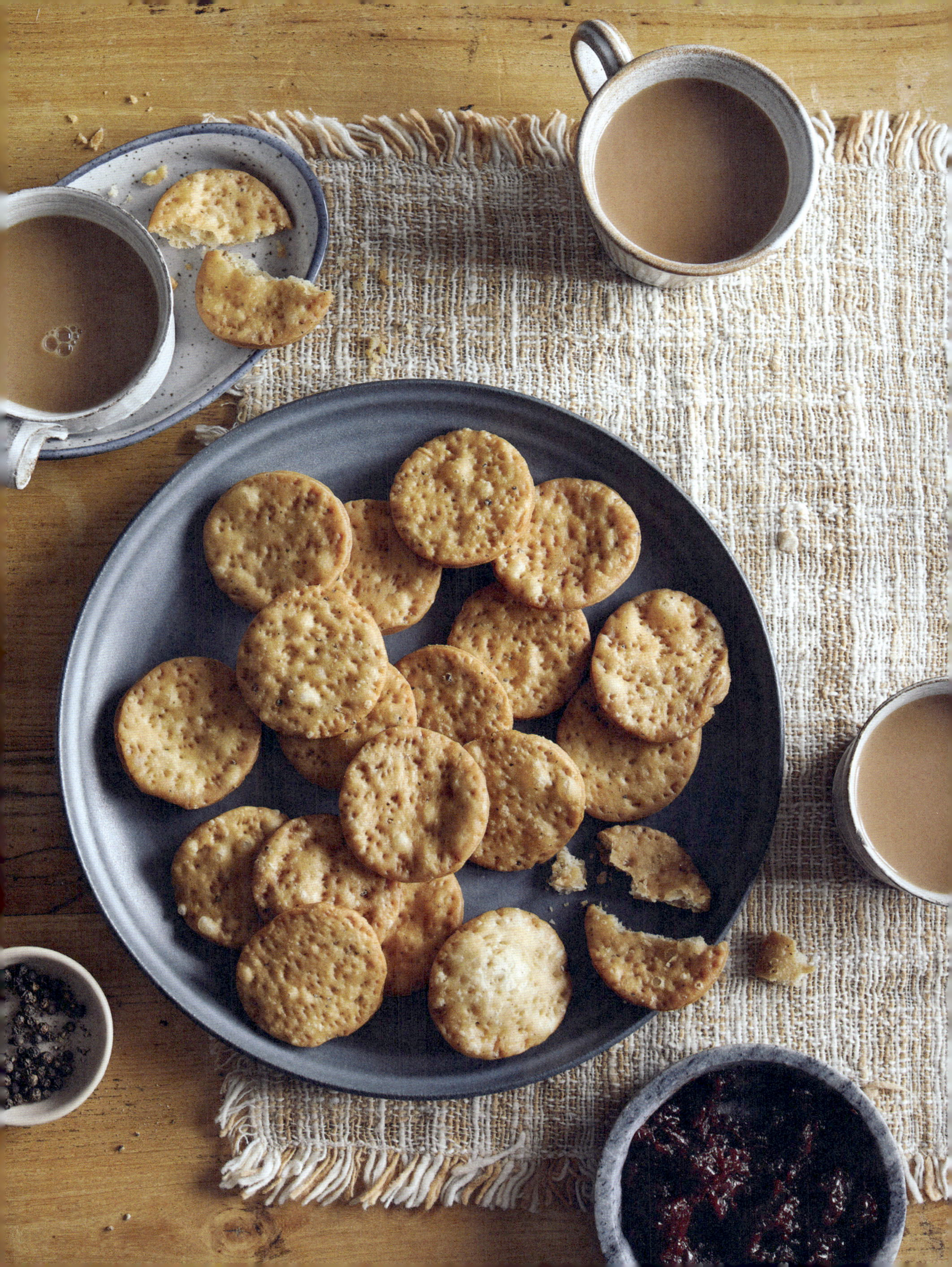

CHARRED CORN AND LETTUCE SALAD

(BHUTTA CHAAT)

This recipe is inspired by lovely memories of school summer breaks, hearing the calls from the wheel cart vendors going from one street to another, selling freshly charred corn on the cob with a sensational spice rub. My mother would cut off the kernels for me as I found it hard to eat directly from the cob. Now I do the same for my kids! The nostalgia of my childhood and those wheel cart vendors... I enjoyed writing this recipe.

The charring of the corn cobs and the spice rub using fresh lime halves are essential to this dish.

Serves 4

For the rub
1 tsp Curry Masala (see page 154)
1 tsp Chaat Masala (see page 153)
½ tsp salt

For the corn
600g (1lb 5oz) corn on the cob, husks and silks removed
2 limes
200g (7oz) iceberg lettuce, shredded
100g (3½oz) red onions, finely sliced
100g (3½oz) roasted red (bell) peppers from a jar (drained weight), sliced
2 tbsp pickled green jalapeño slices, drained
2 tbsp chopped fresh coriander (cilantro)

First, evenly char each corn on the cob over an open fire, gas stove or BBQ, turning regularly as you cook them.

Meanwhile, to make the rub, mix the Curry Masala, Chaat Masala and salt together in a bowl.

Once the corn cobs are charred all over, cut each lime in half, then dip the cut side of each lime half into the rub and rub it over the hot charred corn while gently squeezing the lime juice. This way the spice rub and lime juice will thoroughly cover the cobs and the heat will help to absorb all the flavours. Let the cobs rest for a few minutes and then apply more rub again, if required.

Now using a sharp knife, very carefully cut the kernels from the cobs – you should end up with around 300g (10½oz) of corn kernels. Keep warm.

In a large bowl, mix together the shredded lettuce, red onion, roasted red peppers, jalapeños and fresh coriander.

Just before you are ready to serve, add the warm corn kernels to the salad and gently mix to combine. The spice and warmth of the corn will taste amazing with the fresh and zingy salad.

Easy swap
Swap out the pickled jalapeños for sliced pickled baby cucumbers or gherkins.

SNACKS, SOUPS & SALADS

PUFF SAMOSA

Traditional Indian samosas are homemade deep-fried triangular pastry parcels, filled with spiced potatoes and peas. I am salivating even writing about them. But from a cooking perspective, it's tricky to get the pastry right, making sure it stays crispy and holds the filling so that during frying it doesn't burst open or absorb too much oil. My simplified recipe, which uses shop-bought puff pastry and is baked in the oven, avoids all of this – it's very hard to get wrong!

Makes 10–12

4 tbsp oil

1 tsp cumin seeds

1 tsp chopped green chilli

1 tbsp grated fresh peeled ginger

200g (7oz) white onions, finely chopped

2 tsp salt

1 tsp ground fennel

1 tsp ground turmeric

½ tsp red chilli powder

½ tsp Garam Masala (see page 155)

200g (7oz) frozen peas

500g (1lb 2oz) boiled peeled waxy potatoes, cooled and cubed

Plain (all-purpose) flour, for dusting

1 x 320g (11¼oz) ready-rolled puff pastry sheet

Milk, for brushing

To serve
Tomato ketchup
Mint and Coriander Chutney (see page 162)

Heat the oil in a pan (with a lid) over a medium heat and add the cumin seeds. Once they start popping, add the green chilli and ginger and cook for a minute. Now add the onion and sauté until translucent but without any colour. Add the salt and all the spices and cook over a high heat for 1–2 minutes. Once the spices start to stick, add the peas and a little splash of water.

Stir in the potatoes, very slightly crushing them as you go, then cover the pan and simmer for 5 minutes. The potatoes will absorb all the flavours. Remove from the heat and let it cool completely.

Preheat the oven to 180°C/160°C fan/350°F/Gas 4. Lightly dust the work surface with flour, then unroll the puff pastry sheet onto it and lightly dust the top of the sheet with flour. Roll it out evenly to increase the overall size by 10–20%. On the longer side, place the filling in the centre of the pastry so that it covers the middle third and reaches the shorter sides. Tightly fold both (uncovered) long sides of the pastry over the filling in the middle to create a log shape. Dust the log with a little more flour, if needed. Using your hands, straighten the sides, tuck in the ends and very gently roll the pastry to get an even top (without making the log bigger) to create a straight-sided square log.

Cut the rolled log across into 5–6 equal square slices, using a pizza cutter or sharp knife. Cut each square slice in half diagonally to make a nice triangular shape. Brush the samosas with a little milk and place on a lined baking sheet, leaving space between each one. Bake in the oven for 30–35 minutes (you may need to adjust this, depending on the size of your samosas), or until crisp and golden. Serve hot and enjoy with ketchup and the chutney.

Easy swap
Use paneer or cooked, shredded chicken or lamb instead of potato.

Pictured overleaf.

SNACKS, SOUPS & SALADS

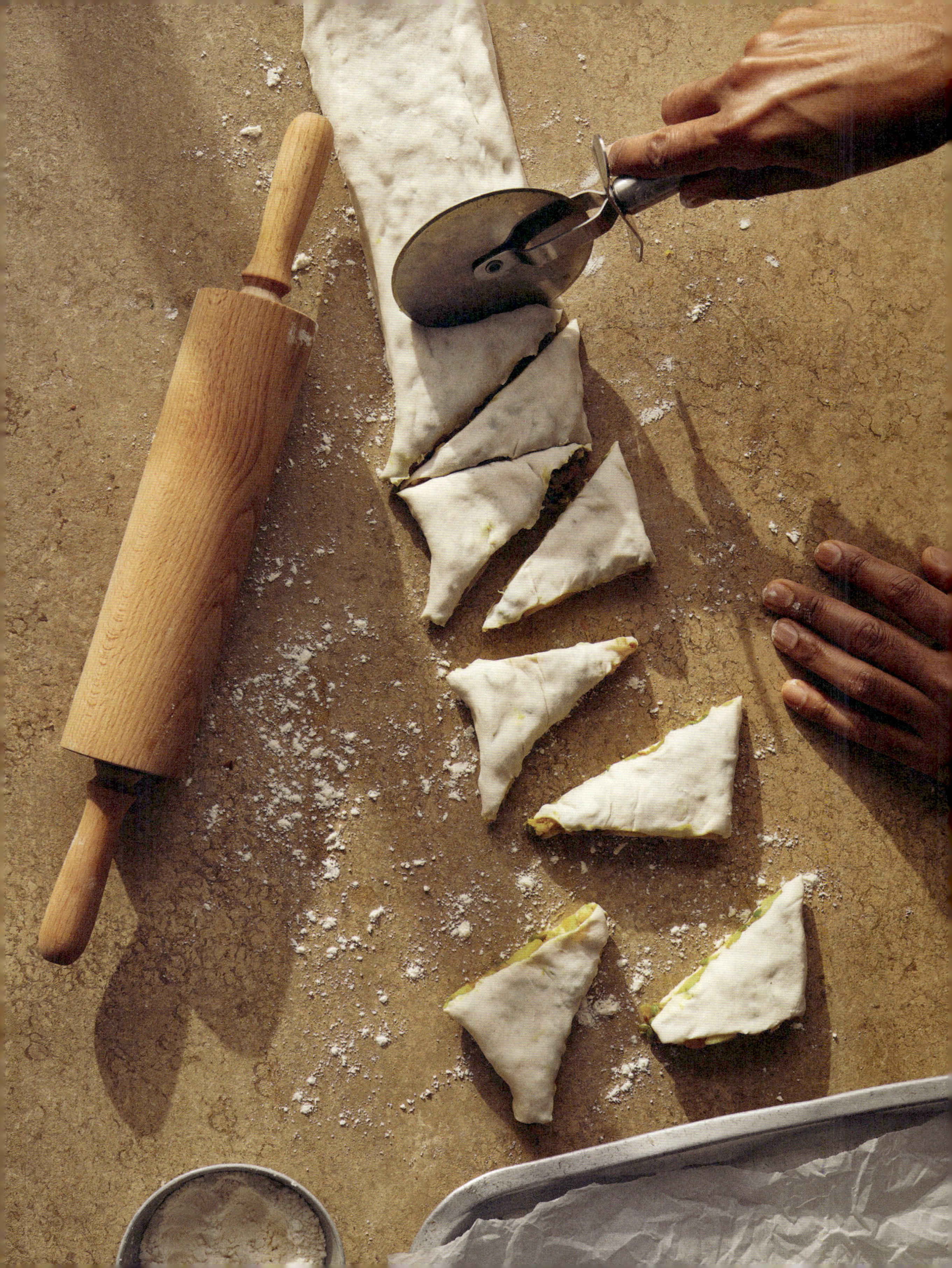

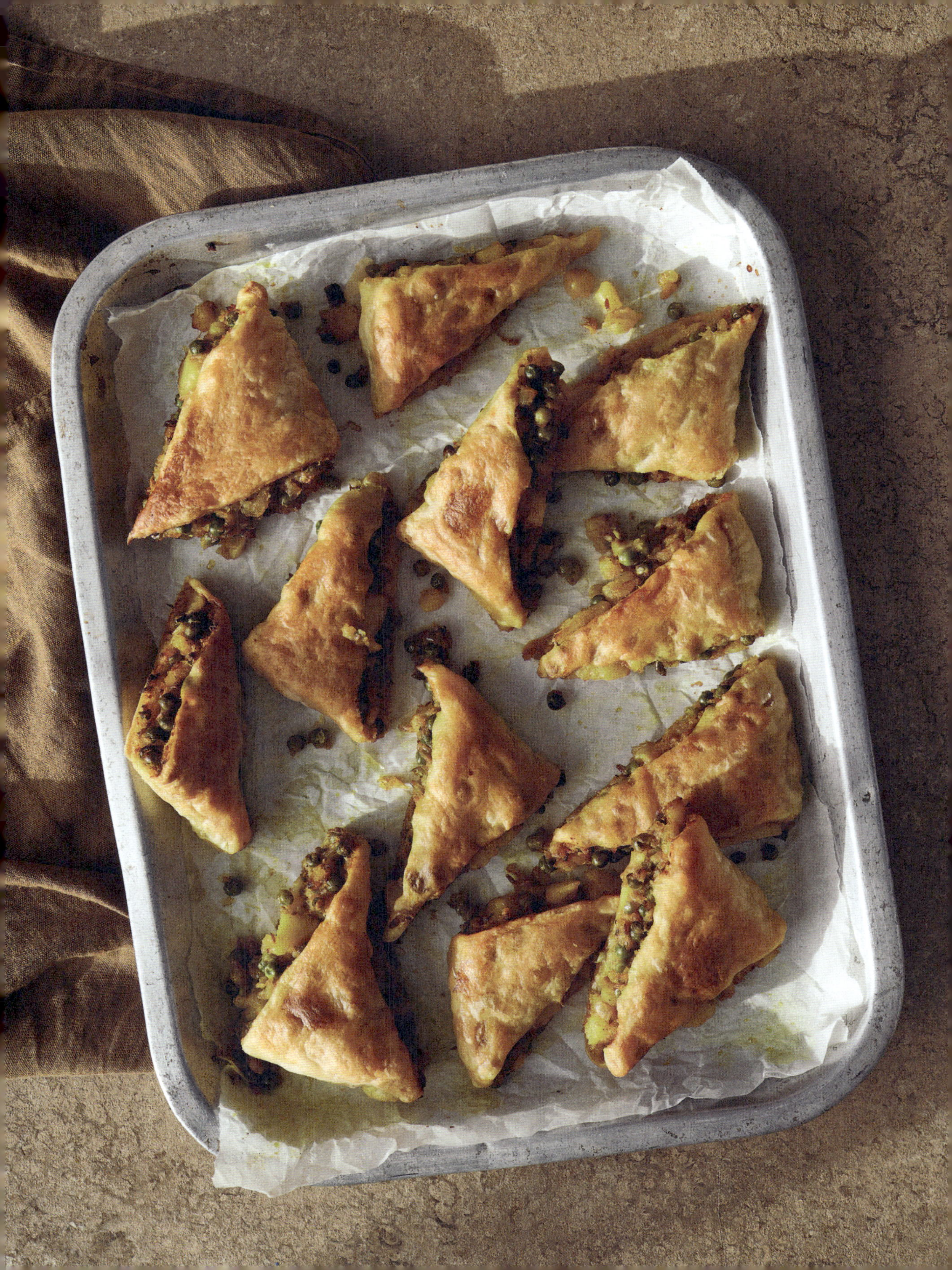

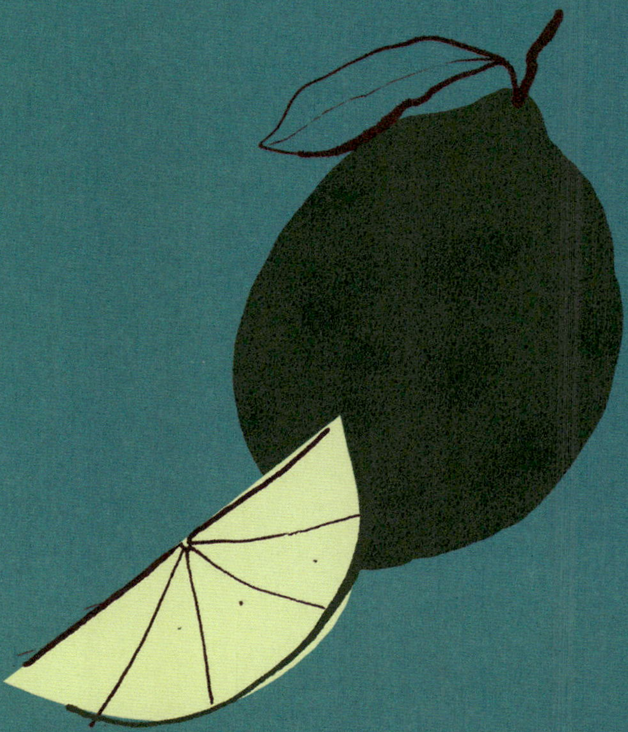

puddings
MITHA

Mitha means anything sweet in Hindi and no meal is complete without a pudding! Let me put it this way: it's not a cliché but a reality for Indians. I have a very sweet tooth, and sometimes even after breakfast I like to have a mini pudding. Continuing with the theme of Indian cuisine, most of the Indian puddings are very comforting in terms of warmth, flavours, little spice notes here and there and multiple textures.

If I must give one example of a Western pudding that can match the nostalgia of an Indian pudding, then it will be warm sticky toffee pudding with salted caramel sauce and ice cream. If you like this, then I am sure you will love the selection of recipes included in this chapter.

I look at Indian meals as an experiential journey where you enjoy the multiple flavours, textures, colours and aromas. And the destination is the pudding. So, you can imagine that it must be extra special to exceed any expectations you have already formed during the earlier courses. And it will be the perfect finale that will stay in your mind for a very long time.

There is a general perception that Indian puddings are too sweet for the Western palate. To be honest, even though I am Indian by birth, after living in the UK for such a long time, even I find them too sweet at times. Therefore, the following recipes are my take on traditional Indian puddings, making them simpler, easier and more palatable for everyone. Let's see how you feel about these delicacies, once you have had a chance to cook and taste them!

SHAHI TUKDA

'Shahi tukda' literally means 'royal piece'. As the name suggests, this is a special dessert and has earned first place in this chapter. It is also deceptively easy to make, using only a few ingredients. Imagine a crunchy sweet base with a creamy, rich topping finished with vibrant nuts. What's not to like?

Makes 8

1 tbsp ghee
200g (7oz) ricotta cheese
100g (3½oz) granulated sugar, or to taste
¼ tsp saffron threads
200ml (7fl oz) evaporated milk
½ tsp green cardamom seeds
8 medium slices of soft white bread
Oil, for frying
100ml (3½fl oz) runny honey
Milk, to loosen, if needed

To decorate
Finely chopped pistachios
Edible gold or silver leaf

In a heavy-based, non-stick pan, heat the ghee over a medium heat, then add the ricotta cheese. Using a rubber spatula, keep pressing and stirring it and very soon it will become a thick batter.

Reduce the heat to low and cook for 10–15 minutes, while stirring, until very thick, dry and grainy. Stir in the sugar, saffron threads and evaporated milk. Cook over a medium heat for another 5 minutes until you get a thick, batter-like consistency. Keep an eye on the heat – the mixture can burn very easily, which will result in a very bad taste.

Crush the cardamom using a mortar and pestle, then mix with the sweetened cheese mixture and remove from the heat.

Using a round cutter (8cm/3¼in in diameter), cut out a round from the middle of each bread slice. Heat some oil in a large frying pan (skillet) over a low–medium heat, then add the bread rounds (in batches) and fry until they are golden brown on both sides.

Remove the fried bread using tongs and transfer to some paper towels to absorb the excess oil and keep hot while you cook the rest in the same way. While the fried bread slices are still hot, carefully drizzle some honey over both sides of each slice.

Arrange the honey-soaked crunchy bread on a platter, spoon some of the sweetened cheese mixture into the centre of each slice, then spread it so that it covers most of the top of each slice. If the sweetened cheese mixture has become too thick, stir in a little regular milk to make it spreadable.

Decorate the slices with a sprinkling of vibrant green chopped pistachios and a little edible gold or silver leaf. Cool, then chill in the fridge before serving.

Easy swaps
Maple syrup will work in place of the honey.

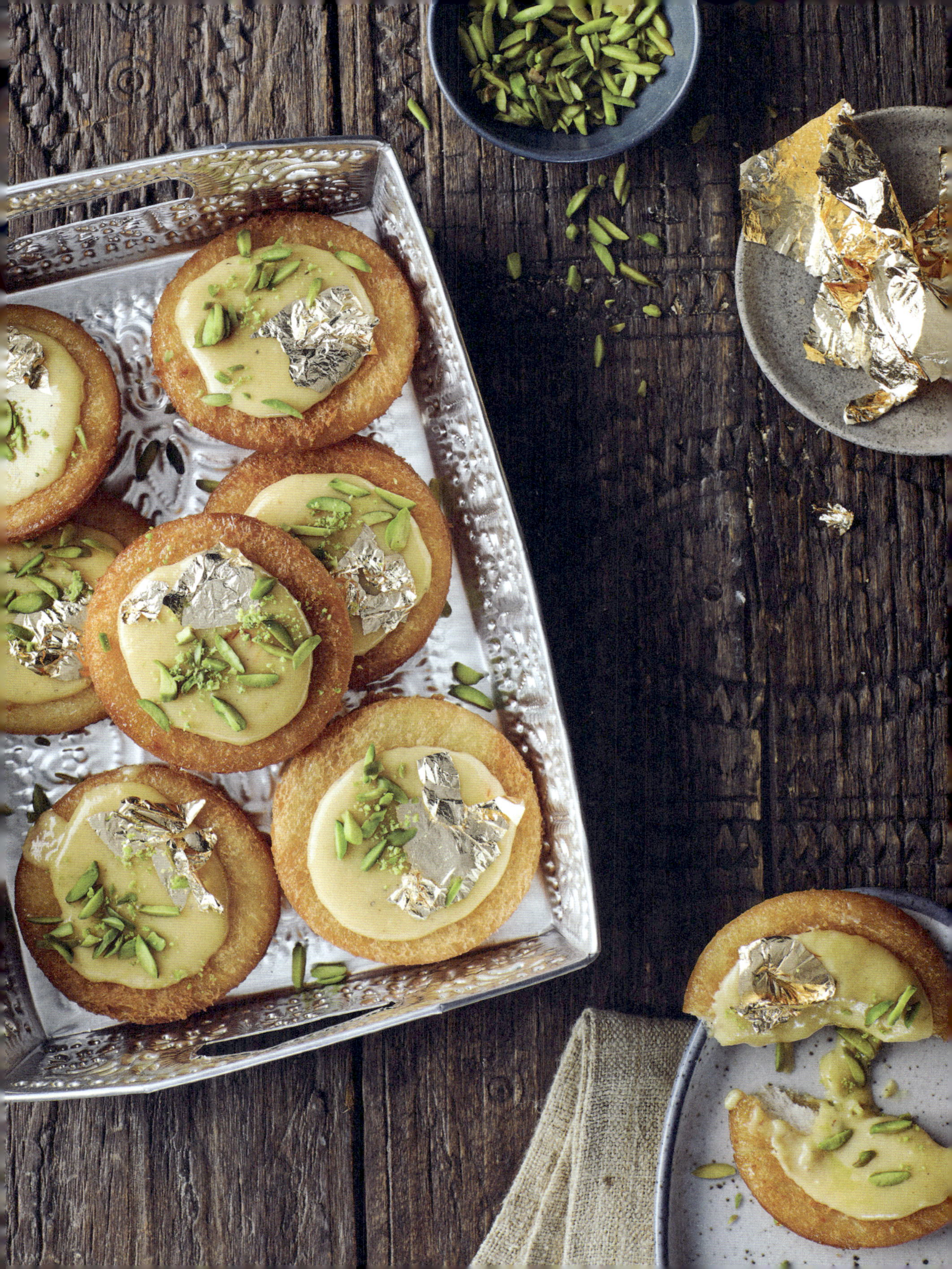

CINNAMON RICE PUDDING WITH SEASONAL BERRIES

(KHEER WITH SEASONAL BERRIES)

Kheer is one of the simplest puddings to cook as it's made in one pot and is very comforting to eat. It can be enjoyed chilled or warm, and is a wonderful base to incorporate different spices such as cinnamon, cardamom or nutmeg. Pairing it with fresh fruit adds tartness and a pop of colour. This is traditionally made as an offering during religious Indian festive celebrations, but you can indulge in it every week, if you like.

Serves 4-6

75g (2½oz) pudding rice
500ml (17fl oz) whole milk, plus up to 2 tbsp extra for loosening up
2 cinnamon sticks
2 tbsp chopped blanched almonds
75g (2½oz) granulated sugar, or to taste
2 tbsp golden sultanas
400ml (14fl oz) evaporated milk
½ tsp green cardamom seeds, crushed

To serve
100g (3½oz) fresh mixed seasonal berries, such as raspberries and blackberries
Almond slivers (with skin on)

Put the pudding rice in a bowl of cold water and leave to soak for at least 30 minutes. Drain and rinse the soaked rice.

In a heavy-based, non-stick pan, combine the whole milk, cinnamon sticks, chopped blanched almonds and soaked rice and bring to the boil over a medium heat. Reduce the heat and simmer for 15–20 minutes, until the rice is fully cooked and soft, and the milk has reduced by about a third. It should become thick, almost porridge-like in consistency. Keep an eye on the heat so the mixture doesn't burn on the bottom – this will result in a very bad taste.

Stir in the sugar, golden sultanas, evaporated milk and crushed cardamom, then cook over a medium heat for another 5–10 minutes, until thickened.

Remove from the heat. Remove the cinnamon sticks, then either serve warm or transfer the rice mixture to a heatproof bowl and let it cool completely before chilling in the fridge. After chilling, the rice pudding will thicken further: add a little extra milk to loosen it and mix it in well.

To serve, place some of the mixed berries into the bottom of 4–6 small glass bowls or martini glasses. Fill up each bowl/glass with the rice pudding, leaving a little space at the top of each one. Place some more mixed berries on top, then scatter over a few almond slivers. Congratulate yourself for giving a glamourous makeover to the humblest rice pudding with a touch of spice. Enjoy!

Easy swap
Use ground cinnamon or grated nutmeg instead of the cardamom.

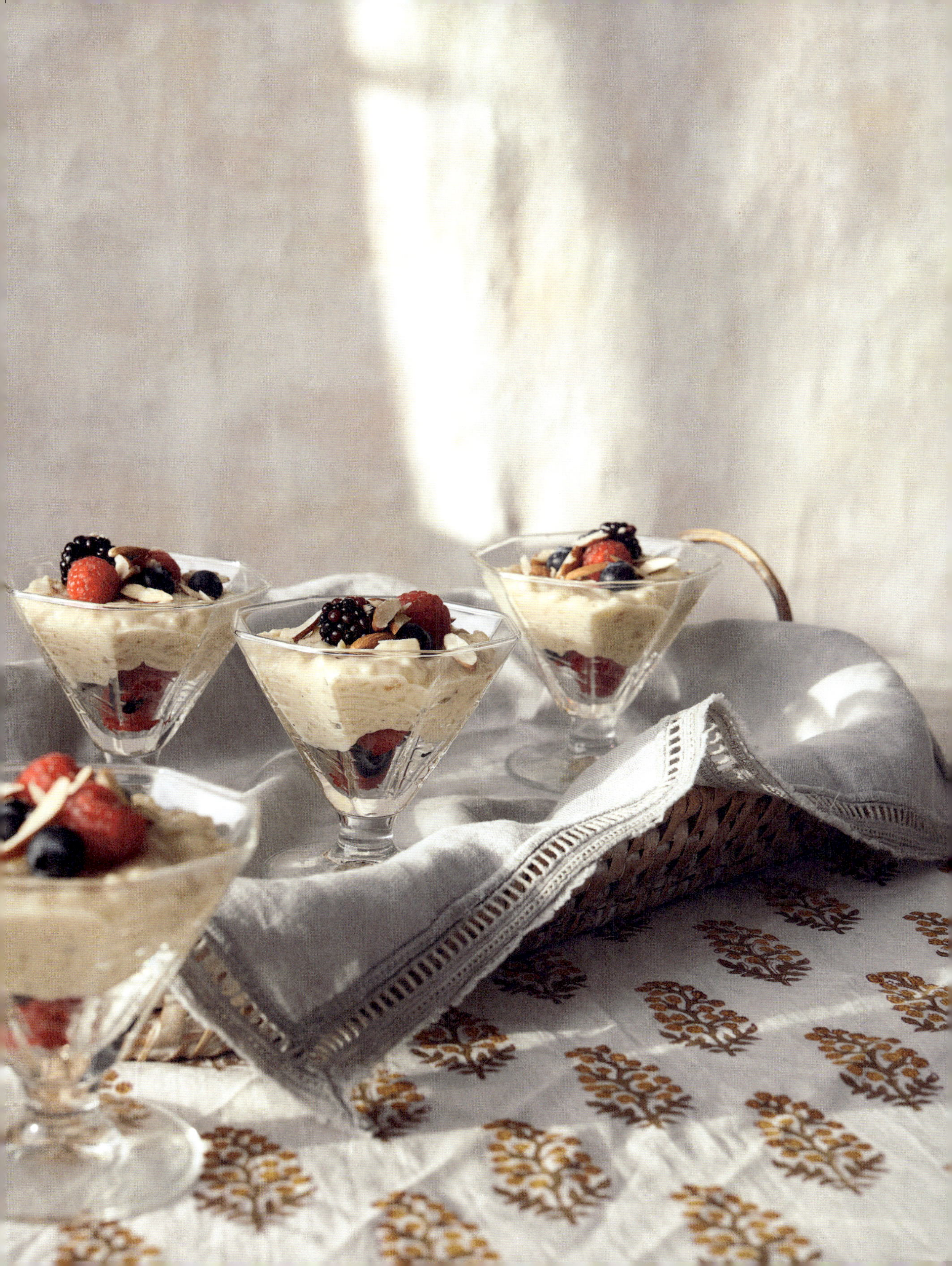

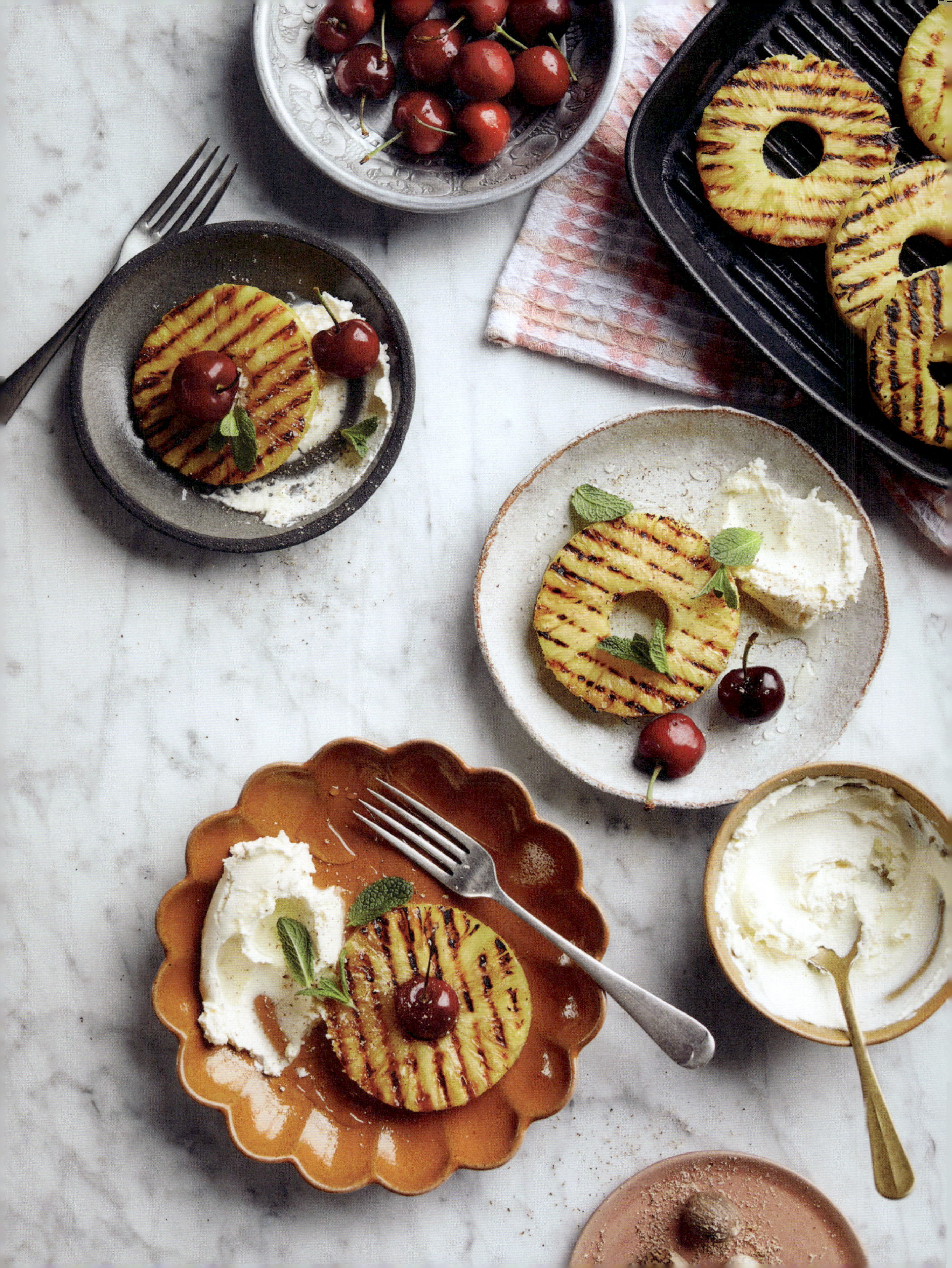

ROASTED PINEAPPLE

During the summer, when the BBQ is fired up, we like to have something simple, fresh and delicious for dessert. This quick recipe ticks all the boxes, and within a few minutes you can whip up an amazing pudding without much effort at all.

Serves 4–8

8 pineapple rings (you can use canned or fresh)

100g (3½oz) mascarpone cheese

2 tbsp stem ginger syrup (from a jar)

1 whole nutmeg

100g (3½oz) fresh cherries, with stalks

Fresh mint leaves, to decorate

Preheat the BBQ or a griddle pan until hot.

Grill the fresh pineapple rings on the BBQ or in the griddle pan over a high heat for about a minute or so on each side to get nice charred lines and caramelization. Alternatively, use a kitchen blowtorch.

To serve, place 1–2 charred pineapple rings on a small plate and scoop a dollop of mascarpone cheese on the side. Drizzle some stem ginger syrup over the top. Using a micro grater, grate over a little nutmeg to add a touch of spice. Place a fresh cherry in the centre of each pineapple ring.

Decorate with mint leaves, then serve this easy and delightful warm and cold combination to celebrate the summer!

Easy swaps
Serve with vanilla ice cream instead of the mascarpone.

Swap out the stem ginger for a mix of 1 tbsp runny honey and 1 tbsp fresh ginger juice.

ALMOND AND PISTACHIO ICE CREAM

(RABRI ICE CREAM)

Even if you are a seasoned traveller and have tried every flavour of gelato in Italy, the taste and texture of this ice cream will be a first for you. Rich, creamy and nutty, infused with fragrant cardamom and finished with pistachio 'zest', it is simply wonderful. Take a spoonful, close your eyes and let it melt in your mouth. Observe the different flavours and textures, then keep eating it very slowly. Before you know it, you might have finished two portions!

Serves 4

50g (1¾oz) blanched whole almonds

50g (1¾oz) shelled pistachios, plus 2 tbsp to decorate

200ml (7fl oz) evaporated milk

2 tbsp ghee

200g (7oz) ricotta cheese

1 tsp cornflour (cornstarch)

200ml (7fl oz) double (heavy) cream

100g (3½oz) granulated sugar, or to taste

½ tsp ground cardamom

2 tsp almond extract

Soak the blanched almonds and pistachios in the evaporated milk in a bowl in the fridge for at least an hour, or overnight. Once soaked, blitz to a smooth, fairly liquid paste using a blender.

In a heavy-based, non-stick pan, heat the ghee over a medium heat, then add the ricotta and cornflour. Stir using a rubber spatula to form a thick batter.

Lower the heat, then stir the cream, the milk and nut paste, sugar, ground cardamom and almond extract into the cheese mixture and gently heat until fully warmed through, without allowing the mixture to boil. Remove from the heat and leave to cool completely.

Transfer the mixture to an ice-cream maker, then follow the appliance instructions, churning the mixture to make a thick and creamy ice cream. Transfer the ice cream into four 6–8cm (2½–3¼in) round silicone moulds or into a shallow, freezer-proof container. Cover and freeze for about 30 minutes, or until set.

(If you don't have an ice-cream maker, transfer the cooled mixture to a shallow, freezer-proof container, cover and chill in the fridge for 1 hour. Transfer the container to the freezer and freeze the mixture, stirring it every hour or so to break down the ice crystals, until smooth and lightly set. Once ready, allow the ice cream to soften slightly before scooping.)

Unmould or scoop out the ice cream into serving dishes, then decorate each portion with some pistachio 'zest' made by finely grating the remaining 2 tablespoons of pistachios using a micro grater. Serve immediately.

SESAME AND COCONUT CHOCOLATE BALLS

(TILL LADOO)

Ladoo are dry sweet balls which can be made using so many different ingredients and flavours. These ones are very popular during Indian winters as sesame seeds provide warmth to our body. I've added chocolate to make them more fun, and to get my kids trying new flavours and textures!

Makes 16—20

125g (4½oz) sesame seeds

125g (4½oz) desiccated (dried shredded) coconut

2 tbsp ghee

200g (7oz) ricotta cheese

100g (3½oz) caster (superfine) sugar, or to taste

2 tsp ground cardamom

Oil, for greasing

300g (10½oz) dark chocolate, at least 70% cocoa solids, broken into pieces

Dry-roast the sesame seeds and desiccated coconut in a hot pan over a low–medium heat, stirring regularly, for 4–5 minutes, to get some colour. Remove from the heat and allow to cool completely. Set aside 3 tablespoons, then blitz the remaining to a very coarse powder in a small blender.

In a heavy-based, non-stick pan, heat the ghee over a medium heat, then add the ricotta. Stir using a rubber spatula to form a thick batter. Keep cooking and stirring for 10–15 minutes, until the ricotta thickens and the ghee starts to separate.

Remove the pan from the heat, then immediately add the sugar, the ground sesame seed and coconut mixture and the cardamom and mix well. The residual heat helps to melt the sugar and bring everything together to make a crumbly dough consistency.

With oiled hands, divide the mixture into 16–20 equal portions and roll them into individual balls between your palms, applying some pressure so that each ball binds perfectly. Put them on a tray and place in the freezer for 15–30 minutes to fully set.

Meanwhile, melt the chocolate in the microwave in 20-second bursts, or in a heatproof bowl set over a pan of simmering water (making sure the water doesn't touch the bottom of the bowl).

Remove the chilled ladoo from the freezer, insert a thin toothpick in each one and dip them thoroughly in the melted chocolate to coat all over. Place the dipped balls on a wire rack and sprinkle with the reserved sesame seed and coconut mix while the chocolate is still melted. Let them set at room temperature. Enjoy, and let me know if you can speak with a whole ladoo in your mouth!

Pictured overleaf.

PUDDINGS

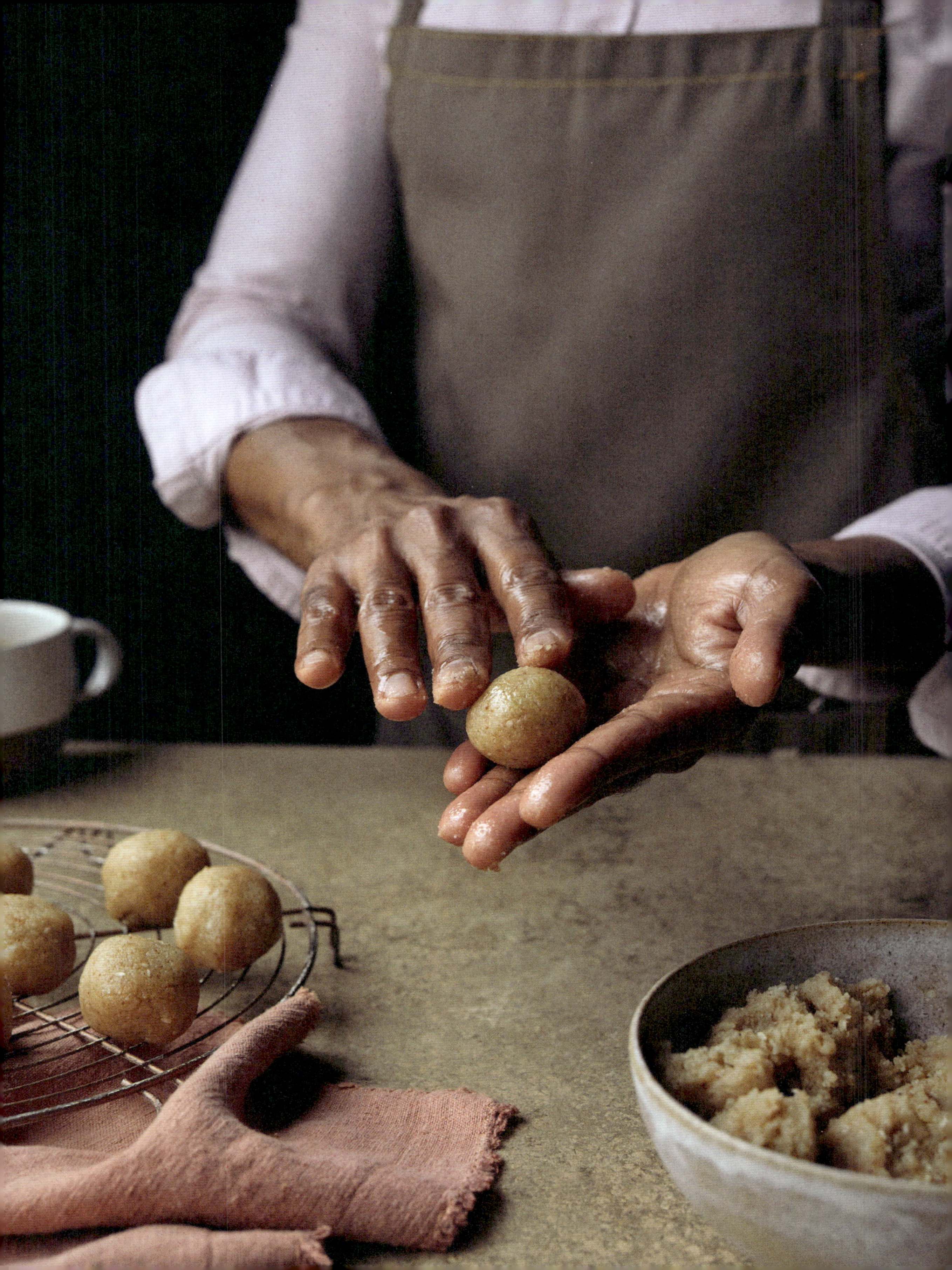

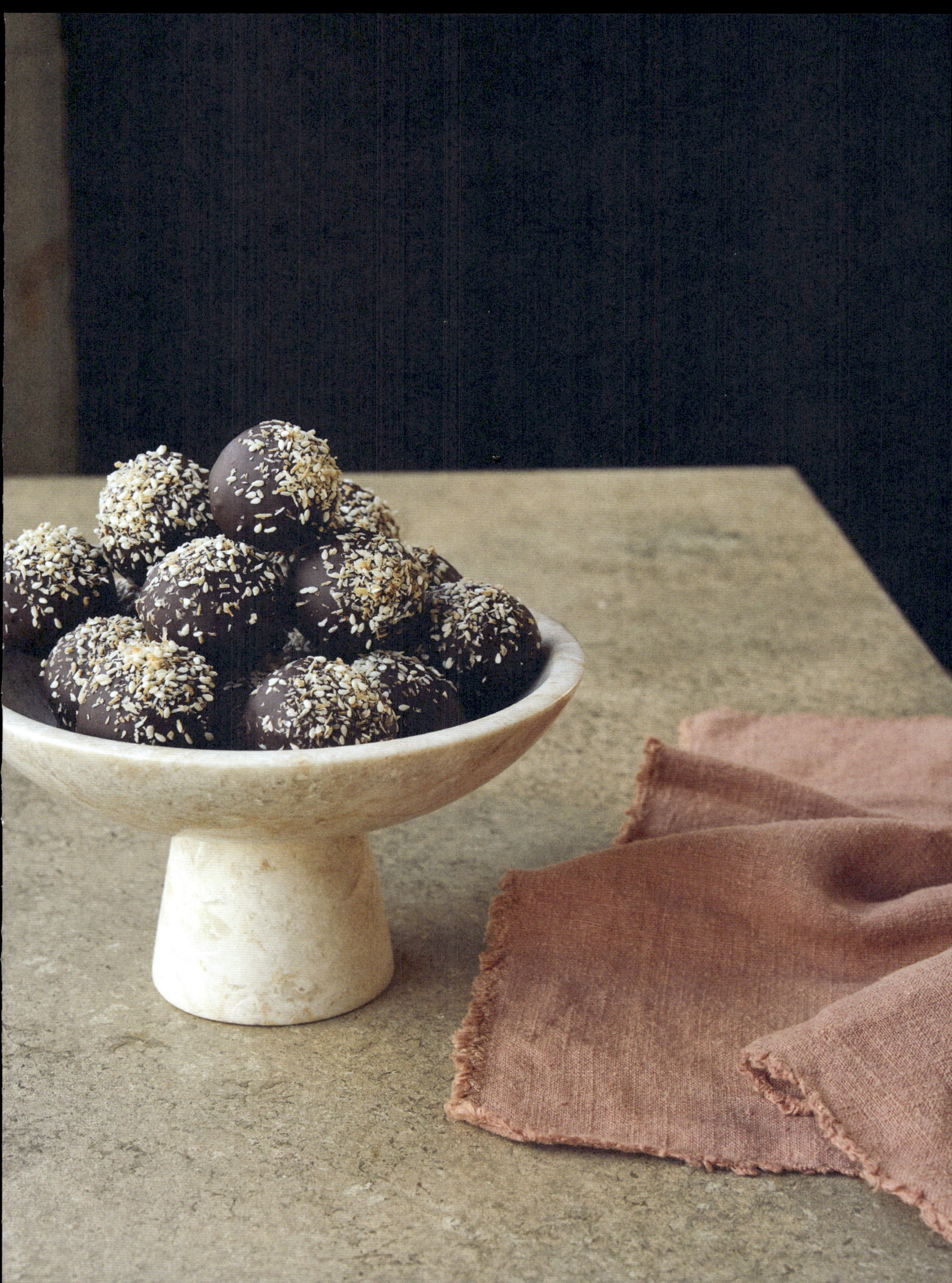

MANGO SHRIKHAND

If you close your eyes and take a spoonful of this pudding, you will be transported to a beautiful tropical island, eating something very cooling and fresh – a delicious mango and creamy yoghurt combination. I love to make this during the summer, and as well as being a pudding, I enjoy eating it as a little snack. I told you I have a sweet tooth!

Serves 6–8

1 litre (35fl oz) full-fat Greek-style yoghurt

500ml (17fl oz) fresh, unsweetened mango pulp or purée

2 tbsp runny honey

1 whole nutmeg

To decorate
Small cubes of mango flesh
Toasted dried coconut flakes

Line a large sieve (strainer) with muslin cloth (cheesecloth) and spoon the yoghurt into it. Place over a bowl, cover and leave to drain in the fridge overnight. The next morning you will be left with very thick and creamy yoghurt in the sieve. Discard the liquid in the bowl.

In a large mixing bowl, whisk the thickened yoghurt by hand for 1 minute, until smooth, then mix in 450ml (16fl oz) of the mango pulp or purée and the honey. Grate over half of the nutmeg and mix again.

Fill 6–8 ramekins each two-thirds full with the mango and yoghurt mixture. Alternatively, use small serving glasses, or just serve in one large dish.

Drizzle over the remaining mango pulp or purée, grate over a little more nutmeg and then decorate with the mango cubes and toasted coconut flakes. Serve.

This dessert can also be made in advance, covered and stored in the fridge for 2–3 days. Decorate just before serving.

Easy swap
Swap out the mango pulp and fresh mango cubes for passion fruit or strawberry pulp/purée, with extra passion fruit pulp or strawberries for decorating.

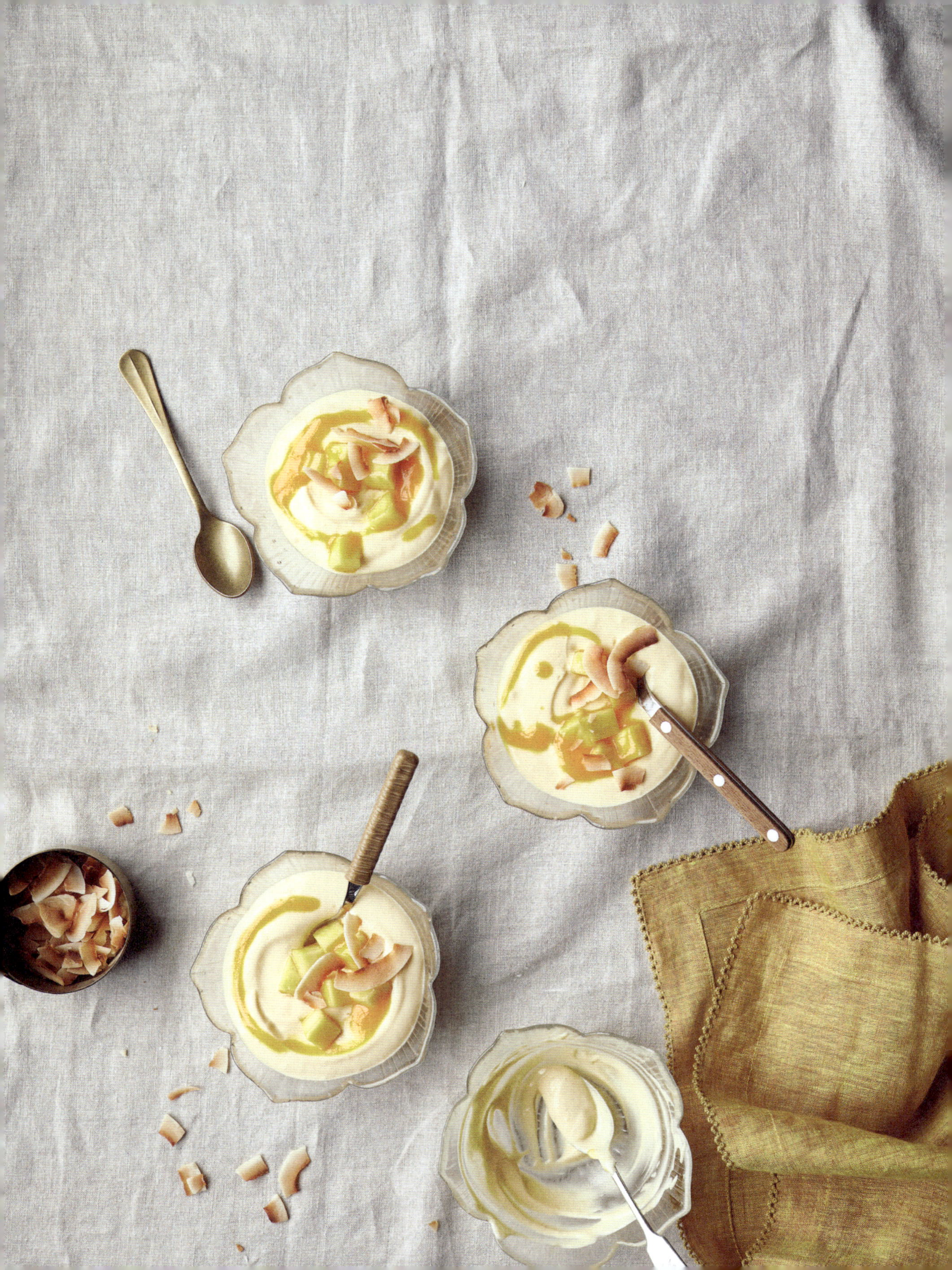

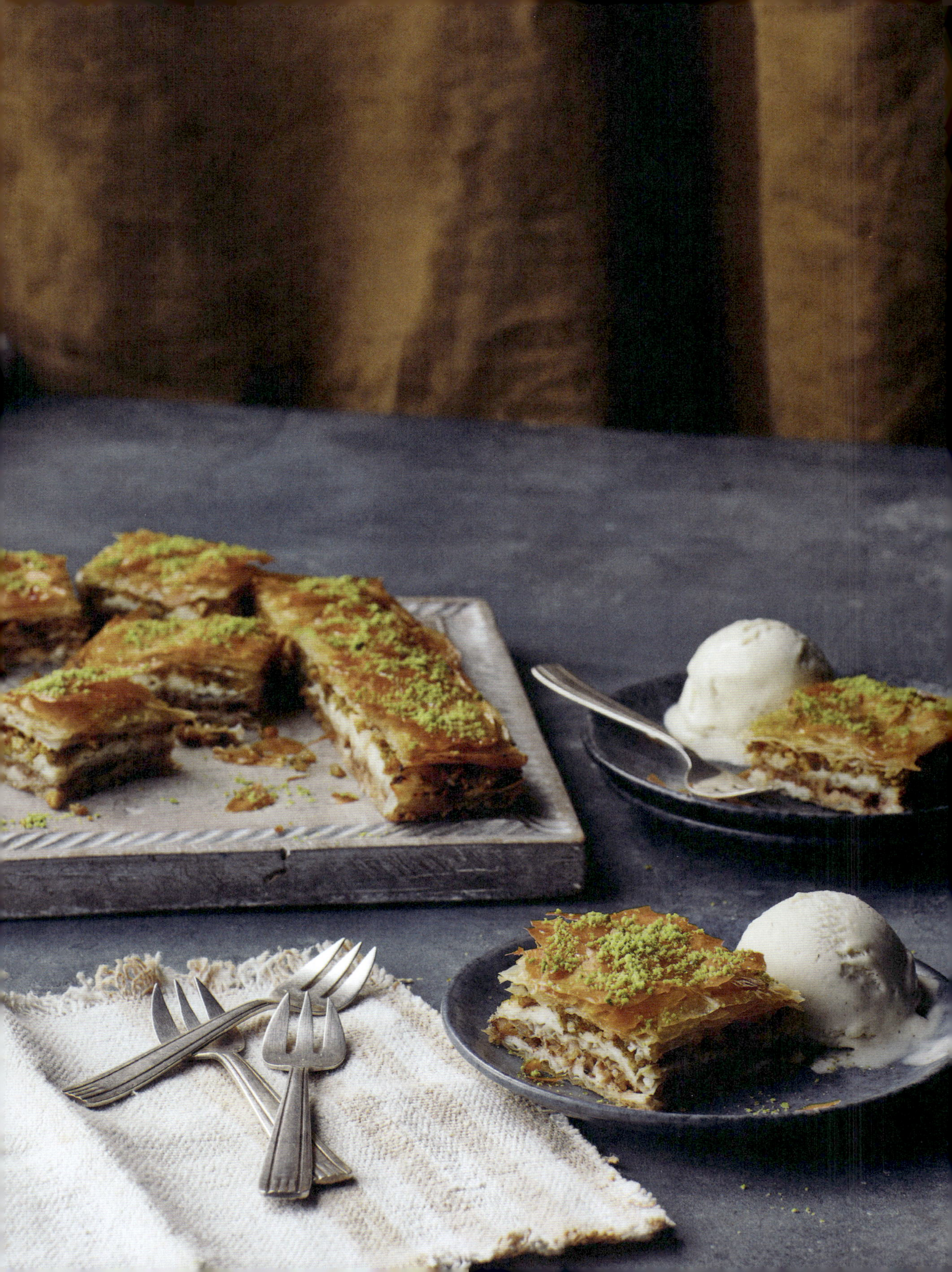

PANEER BAKLAWA

There are many similarities between Mediterranean and Indian cuisine. My travels to Greece and Turkey inspired me to come up with this perfect union of cultures and cuisines. Flaky filo pastry, oozing with butter and dressed in honey, filled with paneer and nuts with a hint of spice, then finished with a dusting of ground pistachios. This creation is a showstopper and it's perfect for entertaining a large group.

Makes 16–20

200ml (7fl oz) runny honey
½ tsp saffron threads
200g (7oz) butter, melted
12 filo pastry sheets, 20 x 30cm (8 x 12in) in size
250g (9oz) paneer, grated
100g (3½oz) walnuts, finely chopped
2 tsp ground cinnamon
100g (3½oz) shelled pistachios, finely chopped
1 tsp ground nutmeg
5 tbsp ground pistachios, to decorate
Ice cream, to serve

In a small pan, warm the honey, then remove from the heat, stir in the saffron threads and leave to infuse for at least 15 minutes.

Preheat the oven to 180°C/160°C fan/350°F/Gas 4.

Brush some melted butter over a rectangular baking dish, about 30 x 20cm (12 x 8in), then line it with 4 sheets of the filo pastry, layering them one on top of the other and brushing each one generously with melted butter as you go. Make sure you do this thoroughly or so it doesn't dry out during cooking.

Spread half of the grated paneer over the filo, followed by all the walnuts, then sprinkle over the ground cinnamon and a generous drizzle of the saffron-infused honey. Layer another 4 sheets of filo pastry on top, brushing each one generously with melted butter.

Spread over the remaining grated paneer, followed by the finely chopped pistachios, then sprinkle over the ground nutmeg and drizzle with some saffron-infused honey. Repeat the pastry layering and brushing with butter with the final 4 sheets.

Bake for 25–30 minutes, or until golden brown and crisp. Carefully take the baklawa out of the oven, then drizzle over the remaining saffron-infused honey and let it rest for 15–20 minutes.

Sprinkle over the ground pistachios to decorate. Cut the baklawa into 16–20 squares, then serve warm with any ice cream of your choice. Cinnamon ice cream complements the flavours nicely. Alternatively, keep at room temperature in an airtight container for 3–4 days. Serve chilled: simply place in the fridge for 30 minutes before serving.

Easy swaps
Use any nuts of your choice, and maple syrup in place of the honey, if you like.

PUDDINGS

CARROT FUDGE PUDDING
(GAJAR HALWA)

As a child in India, Diwali, the festival of light, which takes place in autumn, was incomplete without this amazing carrot pudding. The freshness of Indian vibrant red carrots, the creaminess of milk and the fragrance of saffron and cardamom – it's so delicious. It's very common to use humble fruit and vegetables to make something very special. This sentiment reminds me that whatever situation you are in, focus on your immediate surroundings and you can make the best out of it.

Indian carrots are very deep red in colour, so I have added beetroot purée to mimic their hue.

Serves 8–10

1kg (2lb 4oz) carrots, peeled and grated

200g (7oz) fresh beetroot (beet) purée (made by simply blitzing fresh peeled beetroot/beets)

600ml (21fl oz) evaporated milk

Pinch of saffron threads

5 tbsp ghee

250g (9oz) granulated sugar, or to taste, depending on the sweetness of your carrots

4 tbsp chopped blanched almonds

4 tbsp chopped (shelled) pistachios

4 tbsp chopped cashew nuts

4 tbsp sultanas (golden raisins)

1 tbsp ground cardamom

To decorate
Finely chopped mixed pistachios and almonds
Edible gold or silver leaf

In a large, heavy-based, non-stick pan (or karahi) with a lid, cook the grated carrots and beetroot purée over a medium heat, with the lid on, for 10–15 minutes. The carrots will release water during this time. Now cook the mixture without the lid over a high heat to evaporate the extra liquid.

Tip in the evaporated milk and saffron threads. Mix well. Keep cooking and stirring over a medium heat until you have a very loose dough. Then add the ghee and continue cooking the mixture until the ghee starts to separate. This is a long, slow process, so be patient – it may take anywhere between 15–25 minutes to reach the desired consistency.

Now add the sugar and keep stirring over a medium heat until you have a fudge-like consistency. Keep an eye on the heat, as it can burn at the bottom very easily.

Once you have a fudge-like consistency, remove from the heat. Add the chopped nuts, the sultanas and the cardamom. Mix well.

Serve warm, decorated with a sprinkling of finely chopped mixed nuts and a little edible gold or silver leaf. Leftover halwa can be stored in an airtight container in the fridge for up to 2 weeks. Simply reheat gently in a pan or microwave before serving.

Easy swap
Swap in any other nuts of your choice.

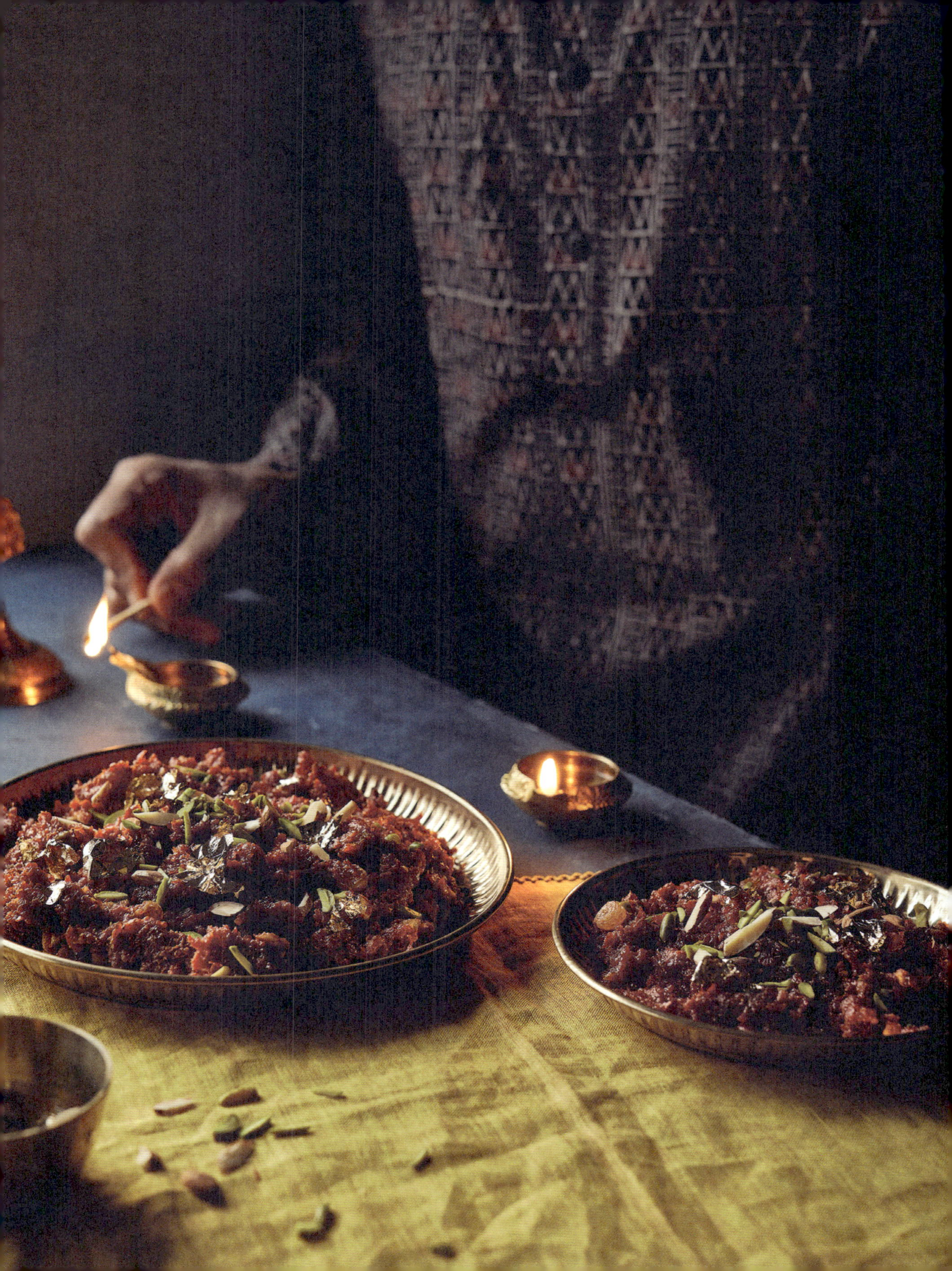

PEANUT BUTTER AND GINGER COOKIES

Crunchy peanut butter and fiery ginger go so well together. These cookies are very crispy, not doughy and soft, so they are perfect for dipping into your cup of tea. I like sweet treats with balancing flavours like the hint of spice from the ginger here.

Makes 12–16

250g (9oz) crunchy peanut butter
100g (3½oz) golden caster (superfine) sugar
1 large egg
2 tbsp grated fresh peeled ginger
Oil, for greasing
150g (5½oz) dark chocolate, at least 70% cocoa solids, broken into pieces
100g (3½oz) roasted peanuts, chopped

Preheat the oven to 150°C/130°C fan/300°F/Gas 2. Line a large baking sheet with baking paper.

In a mixing bowl, combine the peanut butter, sugar, egg and grated ginger, mixing well to make a soft, sticky dough.

Divide the dough equally into 12–16 portions. With oiled hands, roll them into balls and gently press onto the lined baking sheet.

Bake for around 25 minutes, depending on the size of your cookies, or until crispy. Remove from the oven and cool for a minute or two on the baking sheet, then transfer the cookies to a wire rack and leave them to cool completely (otherwise they will turn soggy!).

Melt the chocolate in the microwave in short 20-second bursts, or in a heatproof bowl set over a pan of simmering water (making sure the water doesn't touch the bottom of the bowl).

Dip half of each cookie in the melted chocolate and sprinkle with the chopped roasted peanuts. Return the cookies to the wire rack. Allow the chocolate to set at room temperature for 30 minutes.

Enjoy these cookies with tea or coffee. If any are left over, store them in an airtight container – they will keep for up to 5 days.

Easy swap
Try this with any nuts and nut butter of your choice.

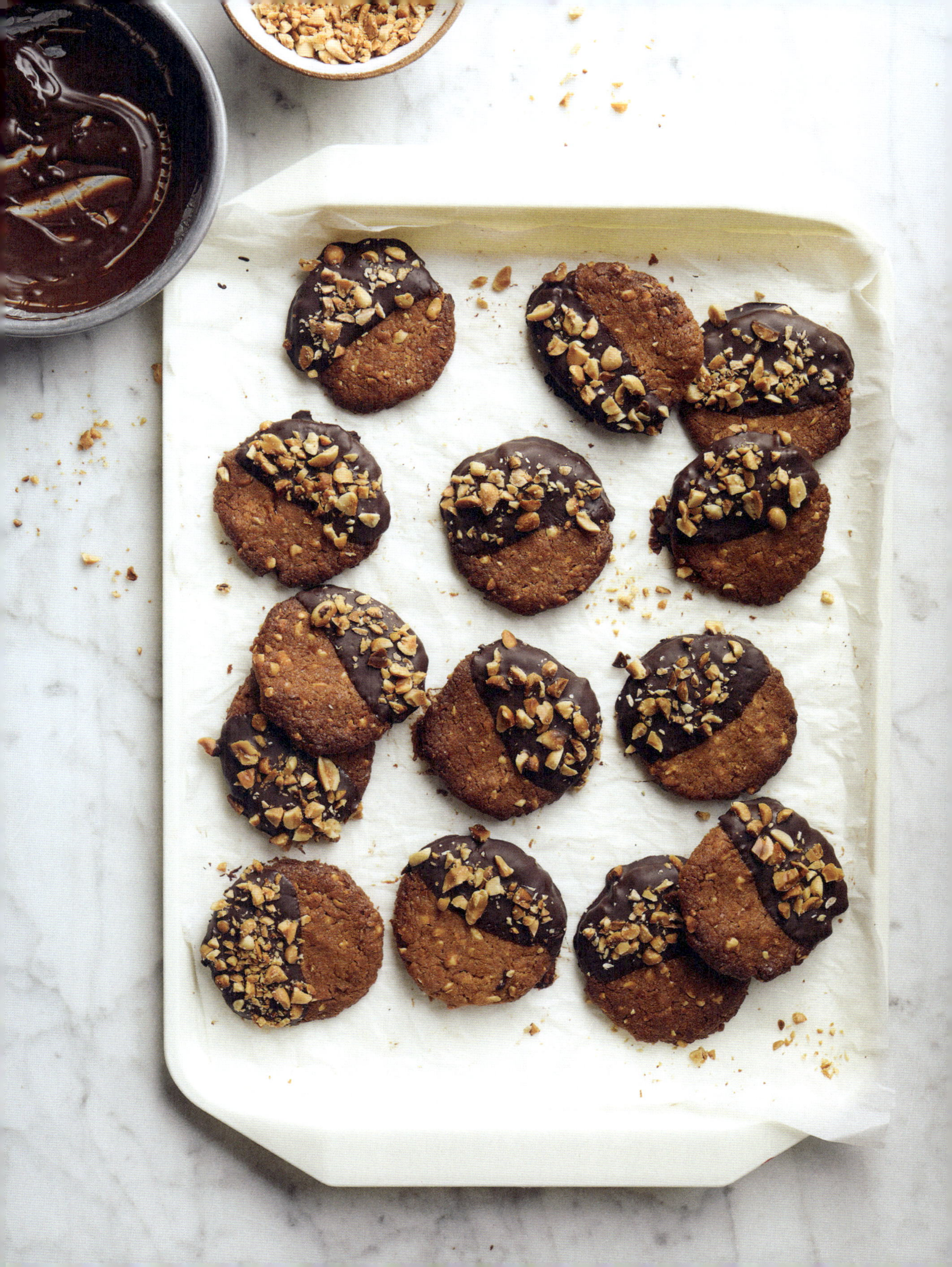

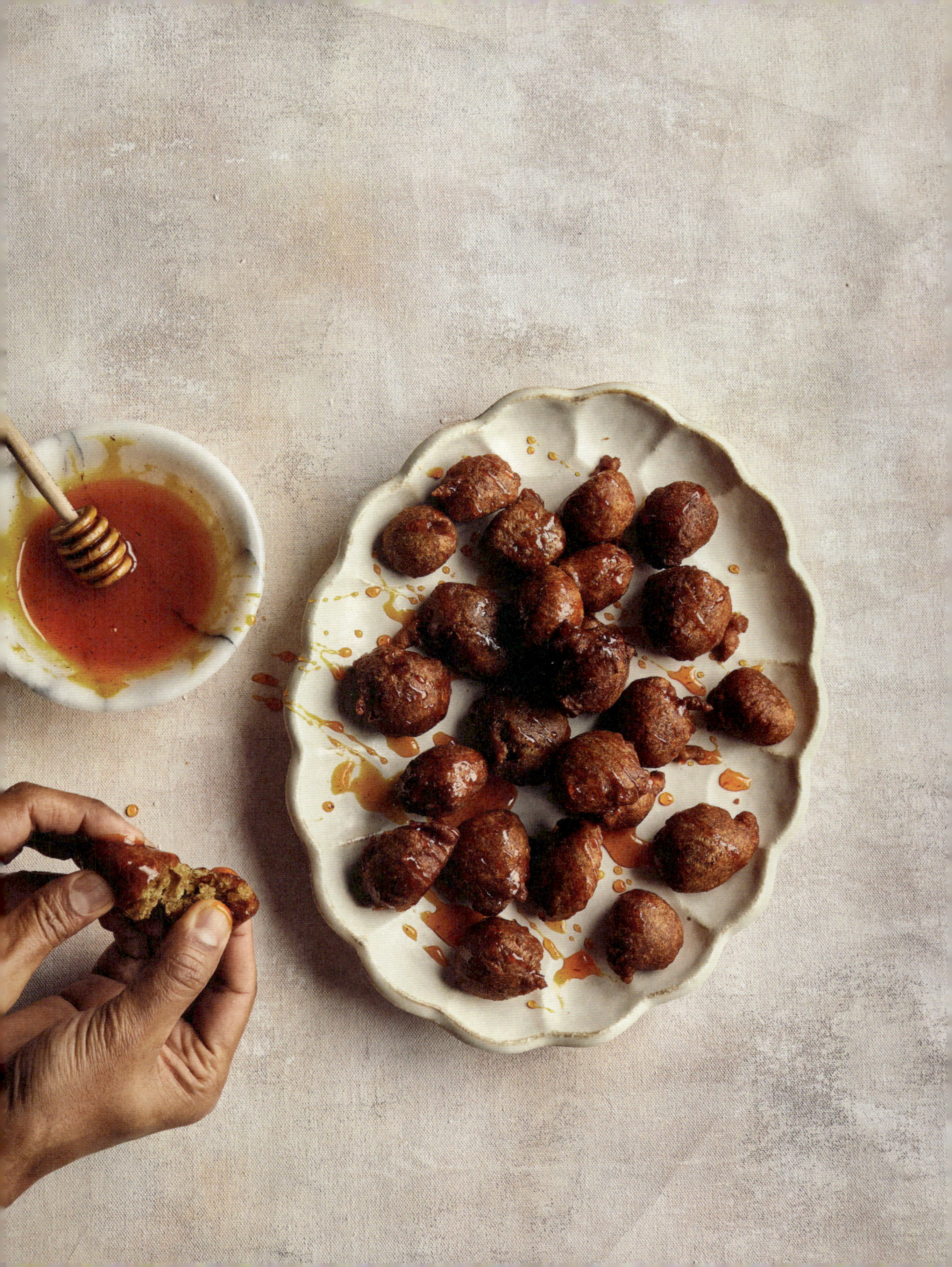

SWEET DOUGH BALLS

(GULGULLA)

Makes 20—25

100g (3½oz) jaggery

160ml (5¾fl oz) warm water

175g (6oz) atta (wheat flour)

½ tsp crushed fennel seeds

¼ tsp ground cardamom

¼ tsp bicarbonate of soda (baking soda)

Oil, for deep-frying

For the dip

½ tsp saffron threads

¼ tsp salt

100ml (3½fl oz) light-coloured runny honey

My mother used to make these specially for me so I hold this recipe very dear. Even the name itself, 'gulgulla' sounds very warm and cuddly to me. These can be compared with doughnuts, but they are a bit denser in structure and less sweet. They can be enjoyed warm or at room temperature. I must warn you that they can be very addictive – once you start eating them, it's very hard to stop!

Dissolve the jaggery in 80ml (2½fl oz) of the warm water.

In a mixing bowl, combine the atta, crushed fennel seeds, ground cardamom and bicarbonate of soda and mix well.

Now add the remaining 80ml (2½fl oz) of warm water and beat for 2 minutes to make a smooth batter. Cover and rest for 30 minutes and then beat again for a minute to get an airy texture. The consistency is important here: it should be thick enough to hold its shape, not runny at all, so add more flour if needed.

In a large pan, wok or deep-fat fryer, heat enough oil for deep-frying (don't fill the pan more than two-thirds full) over a medium heat to 160°C/320°F. Test if the oil is hot enough (see page 113).

In batches, either with wet hands or a spoon, carefully scoop small dollops of the batter, a few at a time, into the hot oil. Do not stir – they will float to the surface in a minute. Stir and gently flip them over. Keep frying them for 2–3 minutes or so, until golden brown.

Use a slotted spoon to carefully remove the dough balls from the oil. Drain on paper towels. Keep them warm while you deep-fry the rest.

Meanwhile, to make the dip, using a mortar and pestle, crush the saffron threads with the salt until it turns into a powder. Gently heat the honey in a small pan, then remove from the heat, stir in the saffron/salt powder and allow to rest for 10 minutes.

Serve the gulgulla warm, drizzled with the honey and saffron dip.

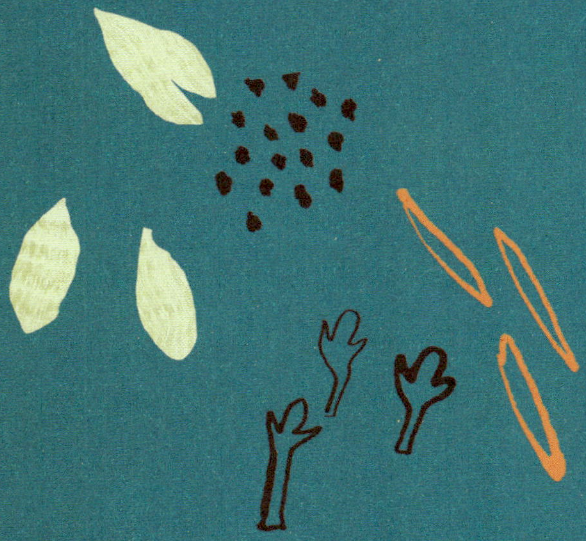

spice blends, sauces & ACCOMPANIMENTS

If I must give you an analogy to explain this section, then I will say that spice blends and sauces are the DNA of Indian cuisine. Just as DNA is unique for every individual, these blends are unique for families. They are also well guarded secrets. You know how much I love you all, therefore I wanted to share a sneak peak of this treasure from my home.

There is no set recipe for these: once you start understanding the flavour profile of different blends, then you can always adjust the recipe as per your personal preferences. And you will end-up creating your own personal well-guarded secret!

These are delicious and stay good for long time. I think in the old times, they were very much like frozen food – you can eat them whenever you don't want to cook.

ROASTED GROUND CUMIN

(BHUNA JEERA)

Makes about 100g (3½oz)

100g (3½oz) whole cumin seeds

It's amazing how the flavour and properties of a spice can change based on the form we use it in for our cooking. For example, dry roasted cumin seeds taste so different from regular ground cumin. This works brilliantly as a sprinkle on yoghurt-based street food and even on salads.

In a heavy-based frying pan (skillet), dry-roast the whole cumin seeds over a low-medium heat. Keep stirring occasionally to make sure the seeds at the bottom don't get burnt. It should take 3–5 minutes to get a nice dark brown colour and smoky aroma.

Remove from the heat and transfer the hot roasted seeds to a plate, then let them cool down completely.

Using a spice grinder or a small powerful blender like a bullet blender, blitz the seeds just slightly to get a very coarse powder.

Store the ground cumin in an airtight container and use within 6 months for the best flavour.

SPICE BLENDS, SAUCES & ACCOMPANIMENTS

CHAAT MASALA

Makes about 200g (7oz)

30g (1oz) dried pomegranate seeds (anardana)

10g (¼oz) fennel seeds

10g (¼oz) ajwain (carom seeds)

10g (¼oz) black peppercorns

40g (1½oz) Roasted Ground Cumin (see opposite)

50g (1¾oz) amchoor (dried mango powder)

30g (1oz) black salt, or to taste

10g (¼oz) red chilli powder, or to taste

10g (¼oz) Garam Masala (see page 155)

Chaat refers to the Indian street food dishes and it literally means 'to lick'. The idea is that the street food is so out of this world that you end up licking the plate itself, so that not even a little drop is wasted. This masala is the heart of all the chaat recipes and is a blend of different Indian spices. It tastes very sharp, salty, tangy, earthy and fragrant with a gentle kick of heat, but not too much. You can easily buy this blend in Indian stores or online. Even some of the big supermarkets sell it as well.

Make sure all the whole seeds/spices (pomegranate seeds, fennel seeds, ajwain and peppercorns) are perfectly dry. If not, spread them out on a baking sheet and place in a preheated oven at 100°C/80°C fan/212°F/Gas ¼ for 5 minutes, then leave them to cool completely.

Add all the ingredients to a spice grinder or a small powerful blender like a bullet blender and blitz to a fine powder.

Store the chaat masala in an airtight container and use within 6 months for the best flavour.

This recipe can easily be doubled/halved to make a larger/smaller quantity of this spice mix.

SPICE BLENDS, SAUCES & ACCOMPANIMENTS

CURRY MASALA

Makes about 250g (9oz)

10g (¼oz) green cardamom pods
10g (¼oz) cloves
60g (2¼oz) ground cumin
60g (2¼oz) ground coriander
30g (1oz) ground turmeric
20g (¾oz) red chilli powder
20g (¾oz) freshly ground black pepper
20g (¾oz) ground ginger
20g (¾oz) ground cinnamon

Curry masala is a blend of different whole and ground spices that works as the base flavouring for most Indian curries. Using it in varying proportions with other whole spices for a particular dish can produce distinct flavour profiles. It is always used at the start of the cooking process and is very different to Garam Masala (see opposite).

Using a spice grinder or a small powerful blender like a bullet blender, grind the cardamom pods and cloves together.

Add all the remaining ground spices and blitz to a fine powder.

Store the curry masala in an airtight container and use within 6 months for the best flavour.

This recipe can easily be doubled/halved to make a larger/smaller quantity of this spice mix.

GARAM MASALA

Makes about 250g (9oz)

50g (1¾oz) coriander seeds
50g (1¾oz) cumin seeds
40g (1½oz) black peppercorns
4 dried red chillies
6 star anise
7.5cm (3in) piece cinnamon stick
3 blades of mace (javitri)
6 black cardamom pods
30g (1oz) green cardamom pods
2 whole nutmegs
30g (1oz) cloves
8 dried bay leaves
20g (¾oz) ground ginger

Garam masala must be one of the most famous spice blends in Indian cuisine and it's used for its highly aromatic composition. There will be countless recipes for this and everyone will prefer their own blend. If you buy it from a shop, you will notice that it varies from one brand to another. This is my own blend based on the recipe I have inherited from my family, with a few changes for my own preference. In comparison to the Curry Masala (see opposite), garam masala is usually added towards the end of cooking to add maximum aroma to the dish.

Place all the ingredients, except the ground ginger, in a heavy-based frying pan (skillet) over a very low heat and dry-roast for 5 minutes. Alternatively, spread the spices out over a baking sheet and roast in a preheated oven at 160°C/140°C fan/320°F/Gas 3 for 4 minutes.

Let the spices cool down completely, then, using a spice grinder or a small powerful blender like a bullet blender, blitz them into a coarse powder. Add the ground ginger and blitz briefly to mix.

Store the garam masala in an airtight container and use within 6 months for the best flavour.

This recipe can easily be doubled/halved to make a larger/smaller quantity of this spice mix.

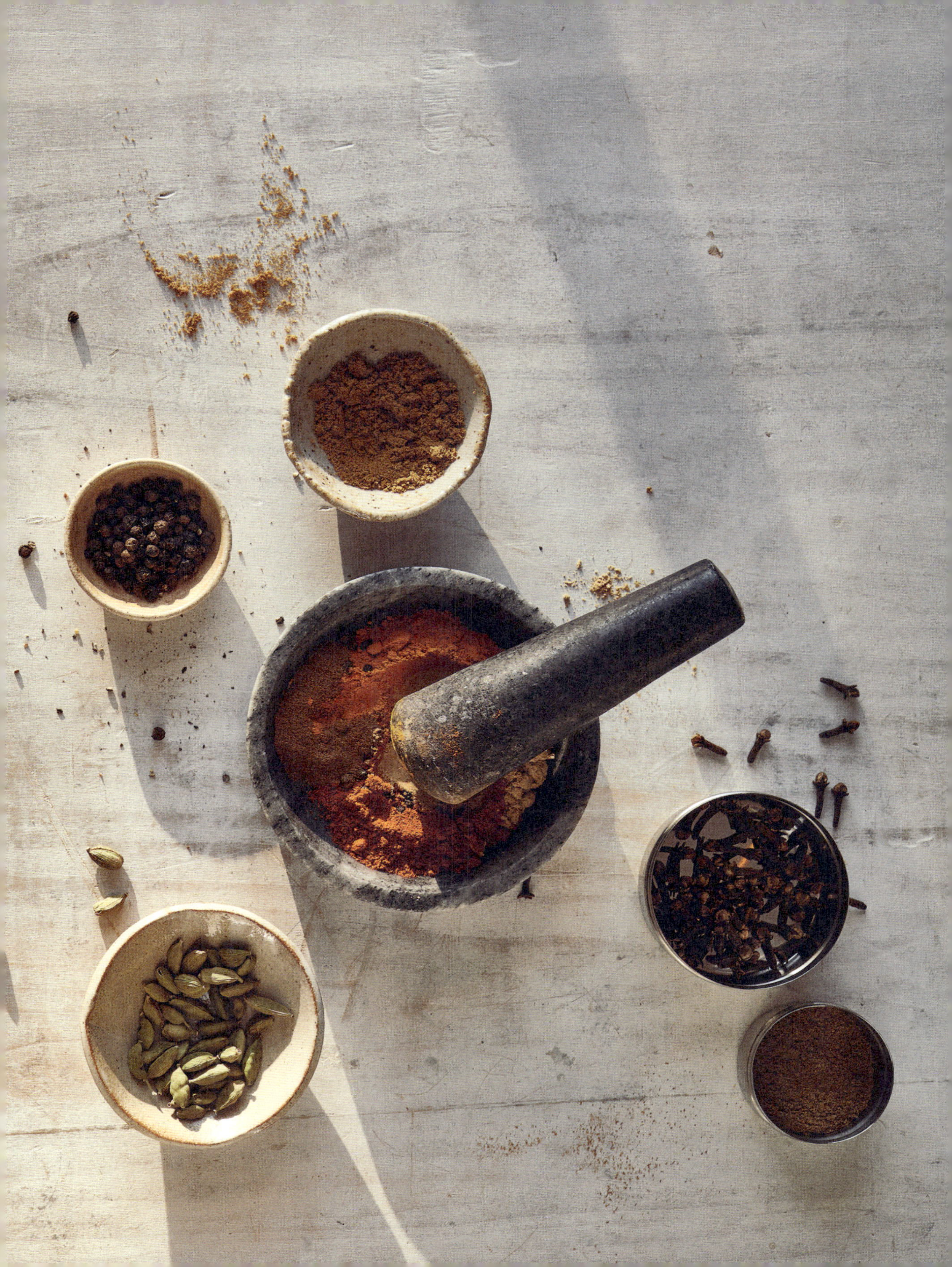

BASE SAUCE FOR CURRIES

Most Indian curries use a base sauce made up of onions, tomatoes, ginger, garlic and different spices. Here, I am suggesting this very generic recipe that you can make in bulk and refrigerate or freeze for later use, allowing for some customization for the dish you are cooking.

Makes about 600g (1lb 5oz)

100ml (3½fl oz) oil

500g (1lb 2oz) onions, finely chopped

100g (3½oz) Ginger Garlic Paste (see opposite)

2 tbsp ground coriander

1 tbsp ground cumin

1 tbsp ground turmeric

1 tsp red chilli powder

200g (7oz) tomato purée (paste)

In a heavy-based pan, heat the oil over a medium heat, then add the onions and sauté until they start getting some colour, about 5 minutes.

Add the Ginger Garlic Paste and cook for another 2 minutes, then add all the spices. Keep cooking until the spices start to stick at the bottom of the pan.

Stir in the tomato purée (paste) and add a splash of water, if needed. After a few minutes of cooking over a medium heat, the oil will start separating.

Remove from the heat and let it cool down completely.

Store in an airtight container in the fridge for up to 5 days, or freeze and use within 3–4 weeks for the best flavour. You can freeze it into an ice cube tray to make this really easy to use.

Depending on the curry or dish you plan to make, use this sauce as a base and add other spices and salt. Just add veg, meat or lentils and some water, cook through and you'll have your fresh Indian curry ready before you know it.

GINGER GARLIC PASTE

This is another staple in Indian curries and other dishes. You can also buy it from Indian stores, supermarkets or online, but I feel that this homemade version is more flavourful and fresh, plus it's much cheaper.

Makes about 250ml (9fl oz)

150g (5½oz) fresh peeled ginger
100g (3½oz) peeled garlic cloves
20ml (½fl oz) white wine vinegar

Roughly chop the ginger and add it to a small powerful blender like a bullet blender. Add the garlic cloves and vinegar and blitz to a smooth paste. Add a splash of water, if needed.

Store in an airtight container in the fridge for up to 5 days.

SPICED OIL

(TADKA)

Tadka is tempered oil or ghee, with different combinations of whole and dry spices. Generally, in Indian cuisine, we use it to enhance flavour and add another visually vibrant layer on top of lentil and other sauce-based dishes. It's hard to come up with a universal tadka, but the following can very much go with many dishes, or you can mix and match what you want to add to it, based on the basic recipe below

Makes about 200ml (7fl oz)

200ml (7fl oz) oil or ghee
2 tbsp cumin seeds
¼ tsp asafoetida (hing)
2 red chillies, chopped
2 green chillies, chopped
4 tbsp curry leaves, chopped
2 tbsp grated fresh peeled ginger
2 tbsp finely chopped garlic
1 tbsp ground turmeric
1 tsp salt

In a small pan, heat the oil or ghee over a medium heat, then add the cumin seeds and asafoetida. Once they start sputtering, add the red and green chillies and the curry leaves and cook for 1 minute.

Add the ginger and garlic and keep cooking for about 2 minutes, or until everything gets some colour, being careful not to let the mixture burn.

Remove from the heat, add the turmeric and salt and mix well. Leave to cool completely.

Store in an airtight container in the fridge for up to 5 days.

Depending on the flavours and quantity of the curry or dish you have made, add 1 or 2 tablespoons of this tadka (the oil with the bits in) on top of the dish when serving. Make sure you gently warm the tadka before use, or make it fresh.

TAMARIND PASTE

Tamarind paste is a must for street food and can be used as a dipping sauce as well. I personally prefer this to tomato ketchup with snacks or fried foods. It's very tangy, sweet and earthy and has a fresh feel to it. Consider the light and heavy aspects of different dishes – see page 175!

Makes about 300ml (10½fl oz)

100g (3½oz) jaggery or soft dark brown sugar

250ml (9fl oz) tamarind pulp

1 tbsp salt

1 tbsp Roasted Ground Cumin (see page 152)

1 tsp freshly ground black pepper

1 tsp ground cardamom

In a small pan, dissolve the jaggery or brown sugar in the tamarind pulp over a medium heat.

Stir in the salt, Roasted Ground Cumin and ground black pepper and cook for 10 minutes, or until it reaches a ketchup consistency – when you touch it, it should feel a bit sticky.

Mix in the ground cardamom, then remove from the heat. Leave to cool completely.

Store in an airtight container in the fridge for up to 5 days.

SPICE BLENDS, SAUCES & ACCOMPANIMENTS

MINT AND CORIANDER CHUTNEY

(HARI CHATNI)

This is a must-have in my home, and with a beautiful herb patch in my garden, I am never short of fresh mint and coriander. Being Indian, my palate craves spices and freshness in whatever I eat. I find that mint and coriander chutney does that job perfectly. When serving it with any snacks, meals or street food, this chutney holds a special place for me. This recipe is a simplified version of one I used to make many years ago, which contained between 15–20 ingredients. I am sure that once you make this, you will never buy a jar of mint chutney again!

Makes about 250g (9oz)

- 100g (3½oz) fresh mint
- 50g (1¾oz) fresh coriander (cilantro)
- 4 garlic cloves, peeled
- 2.5cm (1in) piece of fresh ginger, peeled
- 4–6 hot green chillies, or to taste
- 1 tsp salt, or to taste
- ½ tsp granulated sugar
- 3 tbsp lemon juice, or to taste
- 2 tbsp extra virgin olive oil

Take the fresh mint, separate the leaves from the stalks and wash thoroughly. Discard the stalks. The coriander (cilantro) can be used with the stalks.

Add all the ingredients to a small powerful blender like a bullet blender, then blitz at a high speed, adding some ice-cold water every now and then to stop the mixture from getting warm next to the motor and losing its vibrant colour.

Taste for salt and lemon and adjust accordingly.

Store in an airtight, sterilized jar in the fridge for 1–2 weeks.

Enjoy this chutney with almost anything. I love eating it with most things, especially pakoras!

Tip
Add ice-cold water while blitzing and do not blend it for a long time, otherwise, due to the heat, you won't get the vibrant green colour.

Pictured overleaf.

ONION TOMATO CHUTNEY

(TAMATAR PYAZ CHATNI)

This chutney is simple yet delicious. It goes so well as a dip with snacks or with stuffed parathas.

Makes about 250g (9oz)

4 tbsp oil

2 dried red chillies, broken into pieces

1 tbsp chopped garlic

200g (7oz) red onions, finely chopped

200g (7oz) tomatoes, chopped

3 tbsp tamarind pulp, or to taste

2 tbsp jaggery or soft dark brown sugar

1 tsp salt, or to taste

½ tsp red chilli powder

½ tsp ground turmeric

In a pan, heat the oil over a medium heat, then fry the broken red chillies and garlic until the garlic takes on some colour, about 2 minutes.

Add the red onion and cook until translucent, then increase the heat to medium high and stir in the tomatoes. Keep cooking for another 3–5 minutes, until the tomatoes start to dry.

Stir in the tamarind pulp, jaggery or brown sugar, salt, red chilli powder and turmeric. Reduce the heat and simmer for 5 minutes, until you end up with a loose paste. Taste and adjust for salt and tamarind.

Remove from the heat and leave to cool completely.

You can use this chutney in this rustic form, or if you like it smooth, blend it with a little water (while still hot) using a stick blender to make a fine paste.

Store in an airtight, sterilized jar in the fridge and use within 1–2 weeks for the best flavour.

Pictured overleaf.

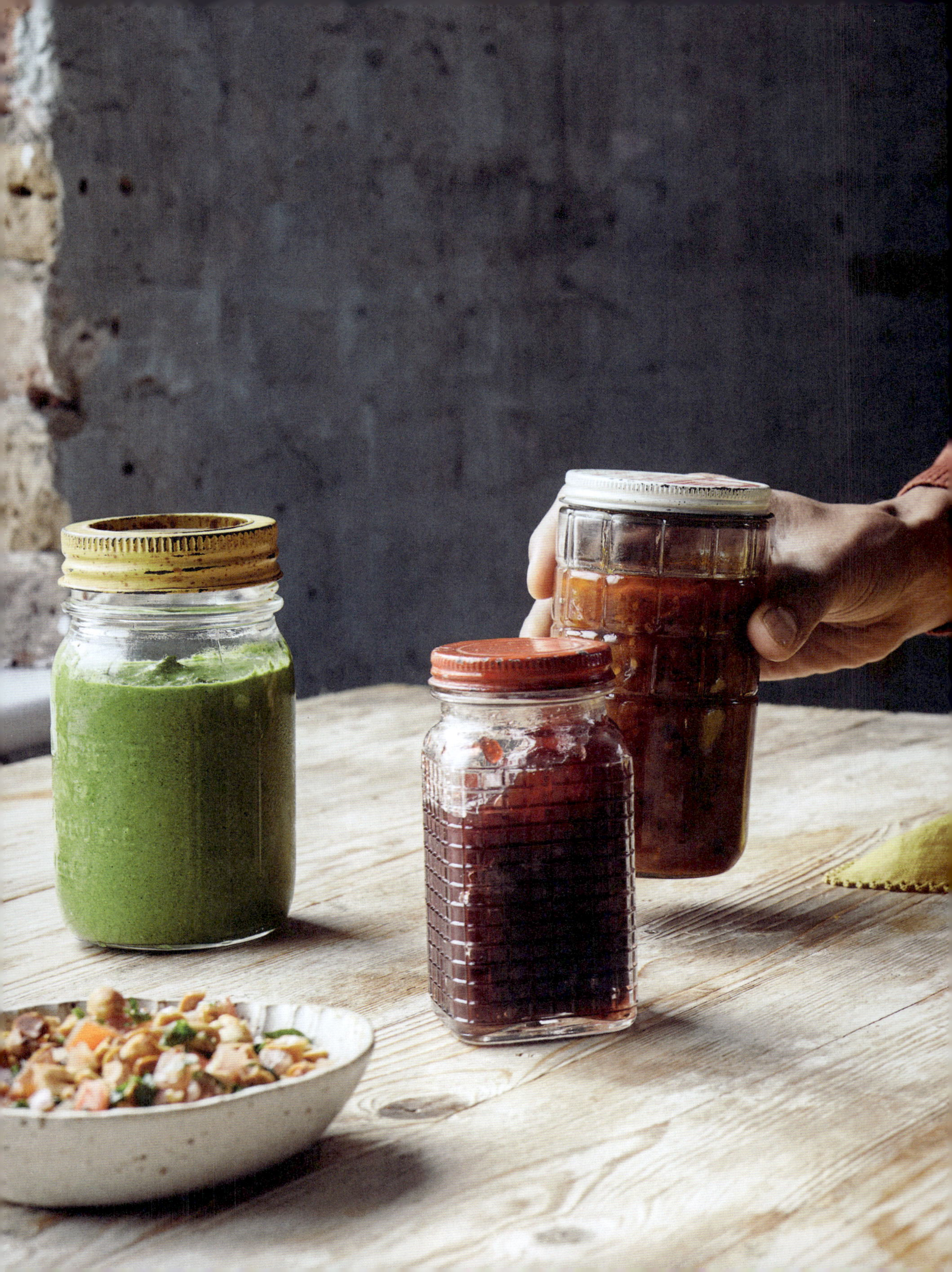

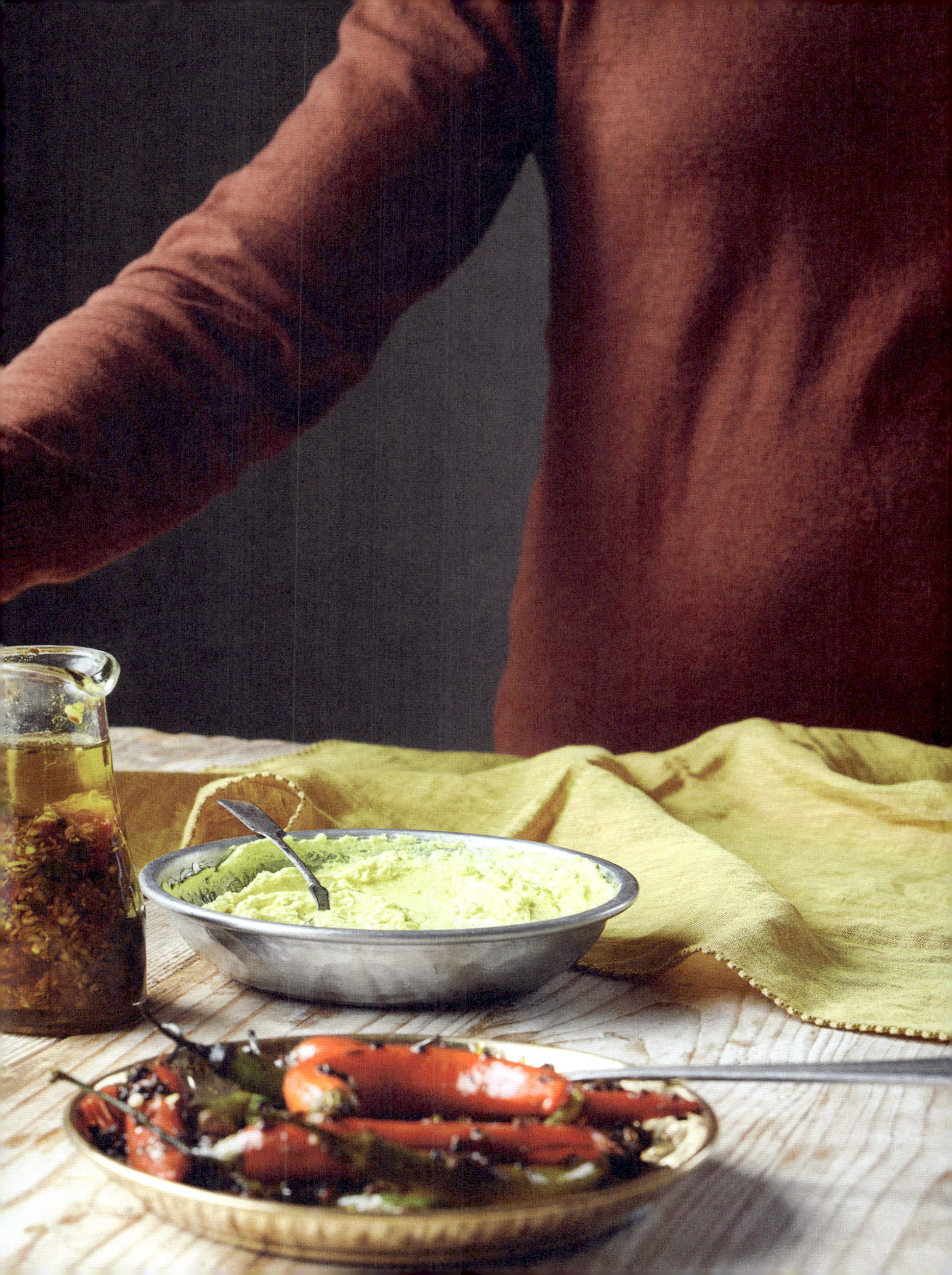

CHILLI PICKLE
(TAJA MIRCH KA ACHAR)

Serves 8–10

8–10 large mixed chillies
5 tbsp oil
1 tsp small mustard seeds (rai)
1 tsp cumin seeds
1 tsp nigella seeds (kalongi)
1 tsp salt
½ tsp red chilli powder
½ tsp ground turmeric
4 tbsp lemon juice

I love eating homemade Indian pickles as I can make them to my preference without them being overpowered with lots of spices and preservatives. This is yet another very simple recipe and you can also use it for pickling other veg, like carrots, radishes and turnips, too.

Make a cut along one side of each chilli and set aside.

In a small pan (with a lid), heat the oil over a medium heat and add the mustard, cumin and nigella seeds. Once the seeds start to pop, add the chillies and toss them in the hot seed mix. Stir in the salt and ground spices and mix well, then cover and simmer for 5 minutes.

Now drizzle in the lemon juice and cook, uncovered, for another 3–5 minutes, until all the spices and seeds are absorbed by the chillies with the help of the lemon juice.

Remove from the heat and leave to cool completely.

Store in an airtight, sterilized jar in the fridge and use within 2–3 weeks for the best flavour.

Pictured on page 177.

CRANBERRY RELISH

Makes about 200ml (7fl oz)

250g (9oz) fresh cranberries

2 tbsp oil

100g (3½oz) soft dark brown sugar

1 tsp salt

1 tsp ground ginger

1 tsp ground cinnamon

½ tsp Garam Masala (see page 155)

½ tsp ground nutmeg

½ tsp smoked paprika

I love Christmas time when you get many unique seasonal ingredients like beautiful fresh cranberries. They are such a delicious berry with contrasting sour and sweet notes. That's what inspired me to come up with this recipe for a relish with a hint of warming spices. This goes so well with crackers, roasts or even as a side with regular Indian dinners.

Add the cranberries to a pan (with a lid) with the oil and toss together over a medium heat for 2 minutes, or until thick and jammy.

Now tip in the sugar, salt and all the spices and mix well. Keep cooking over a medium heat for 3–5 minutes, then once the sugar begins dissolving and the mixture starts bubbling, cover the pan and simmer for 3–5 minutes. Check the consistency; it should be like a runny jam.

Eat the cranberry relish warm, or cool it down completely and store in an airtight, sterilized jar in the fridge for up to 2 weeks.

Pictured on pages 164–165.

MUSTARD GARLIC YOGHURT

Creamy, tangy and fresh, that's how I like to describe this. It couldn't be simpler, and this yoghurt can happily replace any mayo or cheese dip in your cupboard or fridge!

Makes about 250ml (9fl oz)

500ml (17fl oz) full-fat Greek-style yoghurt

2 tbsp neutral oil

1 tbsp finely chopped garlic

1 tbsp mustard powder

½ tsp ground turmeric

½ tsp salt

A little extra virgin olive oil (optional)

Line a large sieve (strainer) with muslin cloth (cheesecloth) and spoon the yoghurt into it. Place over a bowl, cover and leave to drain in the fridge overnight. The next morning you will be left with a very thick, creamy yoghurt in the sieve. Discard the liquid in the bowl. Transfer the yoghurt to a mixing bowl and set aside.

In a small pan, heat the oil over a medium heat and once it starts smoking, add the garlic, then remove the pan from the heat. Now add the mustard powder and turmeric, mix carefully as they will start bubbling in the hot oil. Immediately add this to the yoghurt in the bowl.

Add the salt and mix well using a whisk. If it is too thick, add a little extra virgin olive oil or a splash of water.

Store in an airtight container in the fridge and use within 4–6 days.

Pictured on pages 164–165.

PEANUT AND CHILLI SALSA

Roasted peanuts are a great source of protein and they have a very nutty flavour. That's why I have made this rustic salsa using peanuts, onions, tomatoes, chillies and lots of fresh coriander (cilantro). You can use it on top of roasted meats, serve it as a side dish or use it to make an Indian-style bruschetta! It is best served freshly made.

Serves 4–6

4 tbsp neutral oil

200g (7oz) raw, skinned peanuts

100g (3½oz) red onions, finely chopped

200g (7oz) deseeded tomatoes, finely chopped

50g (1¾oz) chopped fresh coriander (cilantro)

1 tsp chopped green chilli

1 tsp Chaat Masala (see page 153)

½ tsp salt

1 tbsp extra virgin olive oil

1 tbsp lime juice

In a small pan, heat the oil over a low-medium heat, add the peanuts and fry until they become golden brown, about 3–5 minutes. Remove from the heat and transfer the peanuts to paper towels, then let them cool down completely.

Roughly chop the cooled peanuts or slightly crush them using a mortar and pestle.

In a mixing bowl, combine the red onion, tomatoes, coriander (cilantro), green chilli, Chaat Masala and salt, mixing well.

Add two-thirds of the peanuts, the extra virgin olive oil and lime juice and mix well.

Sprinkle the rest of the peanuts on the top and serve immediately, before the peanuts become soggy!

Pictured on pages 164–165.

SPICE BLENDS, SAUCES & ACCOMPANIMENTS

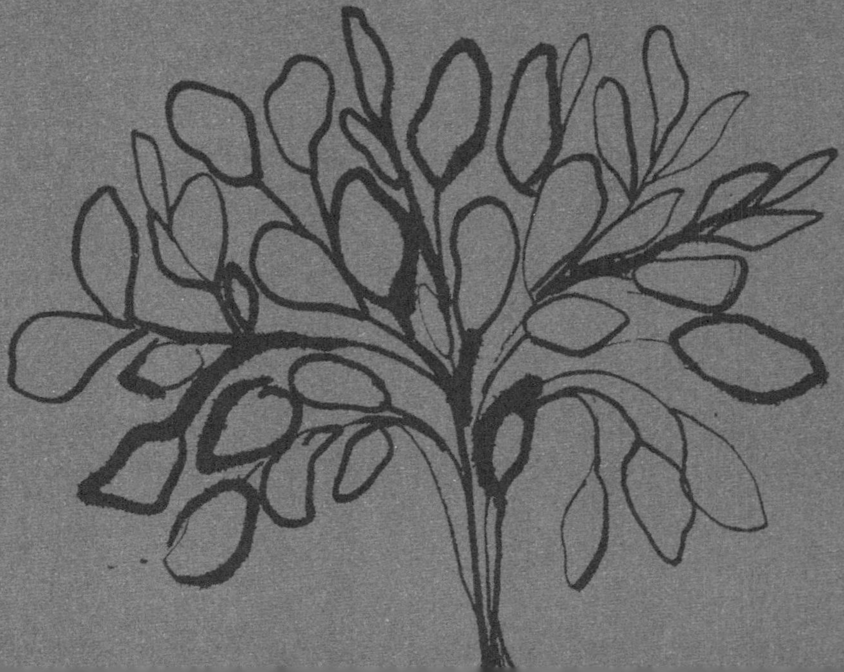

meal COMBINATIONS

Indian cuisine is all about sharing and this is very much evident in the way each dish is presented and served. Pairing different dishes together can make a wonderful and homely meal. This way of eating promotes a balanced diet, as the proportion of carbs, protein and fats is always considered. It is also very exciting due to the variety of foods you can introduce into your meals by mixing and matching dishes.

In this section, I will explain the key fundamentals of food pairing from an Indian cuisine perspective and propose meal combinations using some of the individual dishes covered in earlier chapters.

FUNDAMENTALS OF FOOD PAIRING IN INDIAN CUISINE

NUTRIENTS

While individual requirements differ significantly from person to person, broadly speaking, a balanced diet contains carbs (including complex carbohydrates like vegetables, fruits, whole grains and legumes/pulses, as well as refined grains like rice, breads and desserts), fats (from meat and dairy, such as ghee, as well as vegetable and coconut oils) and protein (Indian cuisine makes use of a wide range of animal and plant proteins, including meat, fish, lentils, soya and dairy like paneer), and a whole range of colours and textures. Also, a meal will be most enjoyable when it contains variety, so use this information to help you decide which components to combine for a filling, balanced meal.

COLOURS

Nature gives us many clues about how and what we should eat. Look for the beautiful colours of different ingredients and make a meal which is colourful. Without even realizing, you will end up enjoying a variety of nutrients, including vitamins and minerals.

Indian cuisine offers such a wide variety of colours in terms of multiple spices, the use of so many fresh vegetables and an emphasis on regional and seasonal produce. All these components add to the overall taste of the dish. I believe that one should aim to have at least three colours in every meal. We eat with our eyes as well as our mouths, after all!

MEAL COMBINATIONS

TEXTURES

The next aspect is the texture of different elements within a dish or meal. No one likes to eat gloopy baby food, except babies (although we can't say that for sure, as babies can't speak!). Experiencing food is about how our different perceptions react. The perception of touch is crucial, after the colour. As soon as we touch any food with our fingers or mouth, our mind starts to get ready to process and digest that food in the most optimal way to get the best out of it.

In Indian cuisine, we sometimes have a tendency to overcook things like vegetables. This compromises the texture, but most importantly, we may also lose many good nutrients if our food is overcooked. Therefore, when making dishes, always pay some attention and respect to the different ingredients you are using.

Personally, when I create a dish, I always make sure that it has at least three of the following textures: crisp (toasted or fried), soft (roti, rice), fresh (raw veg, salad, herbs), dry (seasonings, nuts), sticky (sauces), oily (oils/fat), liquid (dressing) and hot/cold.

MEAT AND VEGETABLES

Eating meat and veg can be influenced by your lifestyle, health, culture or even geography (I talk more about this on page 63). Therefore, there is no right or wrong. Always remember, when we talk about food, no one size fits all.

It doesn't need to be complicated! Meat is full of protein and is therefore filling, but this book is full of naturally vegetarian meals that are just as satiating. You can always choose from lentils and other legumes/pulses, dairy products, etc, rather than eating fish, poultry or red meat.

BALANCE OF FLAVOURS

I talked about the role of our sense of perception when it comes to food. The taste of the food does take the top spot in the process of deciding what to eat. We can forget the name, look or the texture of a dish, but will remember the flavours for a long time. Sweet, salty, sour, bitter and umami are the five taste elements that build our overall perception of flavour.

To make a good dish, ensure there is a balance of different flavour elements. Depending on the dish, a few elements can dominate, but there should be some balance coming from others. For example, an Indian curry might be dominated by the chilli flavour, but to enjoy the dish it must be balanced with something sour/sweet/salty. Otherwise, your mouth will be on fire and you won't enjoy the meal at all.

This aspect is applicable to individual dishes as well as to the whole meal. That's why most of the curries are paired with plain rice, salads and/or yoghurt, to incorporate different flavours into the whole meal.

HEAVY AND LIGHT

This aspect is very intangible and is a mix of the five earlier aspects I have covered in this chapter so far. Very often we say that today I would like to eat something light. We're not usually referring to the actual weight of the food item, rather we're referring to the feel of what we experience after eating something. For example, if we eat molten chocolate/lava cake, we will probably feel heavy afterwards, in contrast to how we feel after eating an apple.

For any dish, and especially for a meal, the balance between heavy- and light-feeling elements is crucial to ensure an enjoyable experience.

Indian curries are typically very rich and heavy, so always pair them with balancing elements like plain rice rather than biryani, fresh salads, cooling yoghurt, and so on.

SUGGESTED MEAL COMBINATIONS

On the previous pages, I have focused on six aspects of meal combinations that are easy to understand and implement in day-to-day planning, cooking and eating.

Overleaf, you will find examples of meal combinations with a variety of colours, flavours, textures and nutrients, for truly enjoyable and satisfying meals. These all contain complementary dishes suitable for different meals and occasions, and you will find photographs of these meal combinations throughout the chapters in this book.

I would like to emphasize that meal planning is not rocket science! If you overthink it, then not only does it kill the whole fun of cooking and eating, it is also not sustainable in the long run. Therefore, find what works for you.

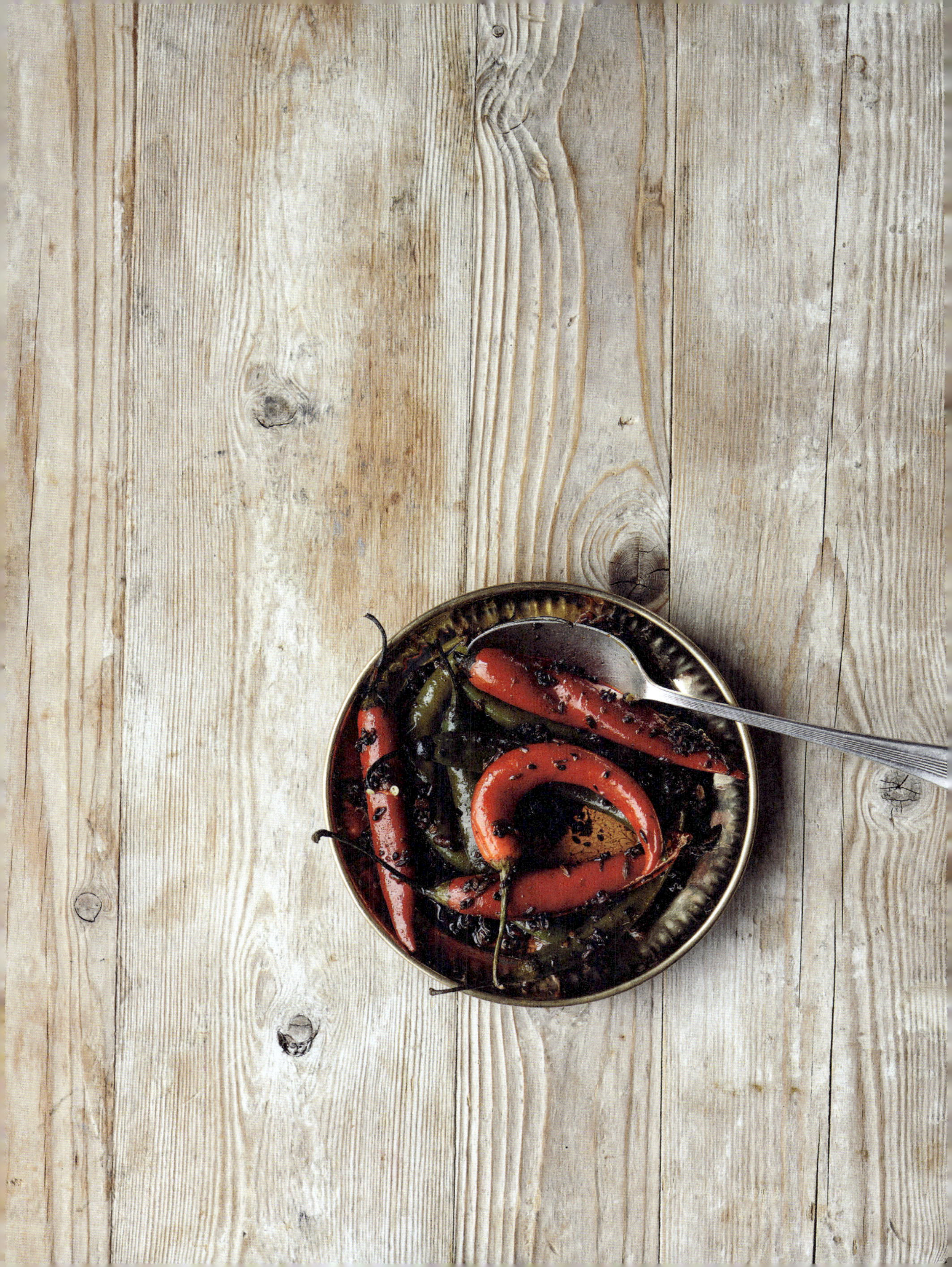

Breakfast of champions

Masala Chai (see page 34)

Savoury Vegetable Flattened Rice with Peanuts (Poha) (see page 29)

Spiced Egg Rolls (Egg Bhurji Pav) (see page 33)

Black Chickpea and Spinach Salad (Palak Chana Chaat) (see page 110)

Mint and Coriander Chutney (see page 162)

Pictured on pages 30–31.

Light lunch

Coconut Trout Curry (see page 72)

Steamed Semolina Cake (Idlis) (see page 22)

Mixed Salad (see page 59)

Peanut and Chilli Salsa (see page 169)

Picnic

Tomato Soup (see page 116)

Chicken Rolls (see page 117)

Charred Corn and Lettuce Salad (Bhutta Chaat) (see page 124)

Mustard Garlic Yoghurt (see page 168)

Peanut Butter and Ginger Cookies (see page 146)

Pictured overleaf.

Friday night curry

Home-style Chicken Curry (see page 64)

Naan Bread (see page 98)

Roasted Cauliflower (Tandoori Gobhi) (see page 42)

Cucumber Raita (see page 59)

Mixed Salad (see page 59)

Cinnamon Rice Pudding (Kheer) (see page 132)

Vegetarian dinner

Potato and Pea Curry (Aloo Matar) (see page 40)

Paneer Tikka (see page 52)

Roti (see page 88)

Cucumber Raita (see page 59)

Mixed Salad (see page 59)

Comfort food

Lentil Flatbread (Daal Paratha) (see page 93)

Courgette Curry (Turiya) (see page 58)

White Butter (Makkhan) (see page 36)

Black Chickpea and Spinach Salad (Palak Chana Chaat) (see page 110)

Cranberry Relish (see page 167)

Pictured on pages 60–61.

MEAL COMBINATIONS

Nostalgic dinner

Kidney Bean Curry (Rajma) (see page 46)

Cumin (Jeera) Rice (see page 105)

Carrots and Beans (Gajar Fali) (see page 48)

Cucumber Raita (see page 59)

Mixed Salad (see page 59)

Sweet Dough Balls (Gulgulla) (see page 149)

Anytime meal

Masala Lamb Chops with Mustard Potatoes (see page 68)

Cucumber Raita (see page 59)

Mixed Salad (see page 59)

Pictured on page 69.

Summer BBQ

Paneer Tikka (see page 52)

Charred Corn and Lettuce Salad (Bhutta Chaat) (see page 124)

Pan-fried Flatbread (Plain Paratha) (see page 90)

Cucumber Raita (see page 59)

Mint and Coriander Chutney (see page 162)

Roasted Pineapple (see page 135)

Street food vibes

Chicken Keema with Peas (Murg Matar Keema) (see page 79)

Pan-fried Plain Paratha (Sada Paratha) (see page 90)

Roasted Potato Chaat (Aloo Chaat) (see page 118)

Mixed Salad (see page 59)

Almond and Pistachio Ice Cream (Rabri Ice Cream) (see page 136)

Pictured on pages 80–81.

Traditional celebration meal (like for Diwali)

Spinach and Indian Cottage Cheese Curry (Palak Paneer) (see page 45)

Roasted Cauliflower (Tandoori Gobhi) (see page 42)

Chickpea Curry (Chole) (see page 56)

Veg Rice (Mix Veg and Paneer Pulav) (see page 100)

Puffed Fried Bread (Poori) (see page 94)

Roasted Potato Chaat (Aloo Chaat) (see page 118)

Cucumber Raita (see page 59)

Mixed Salad (see page 59)

Shahi Tukda (see page 130)

MEAL COMBINATIONS

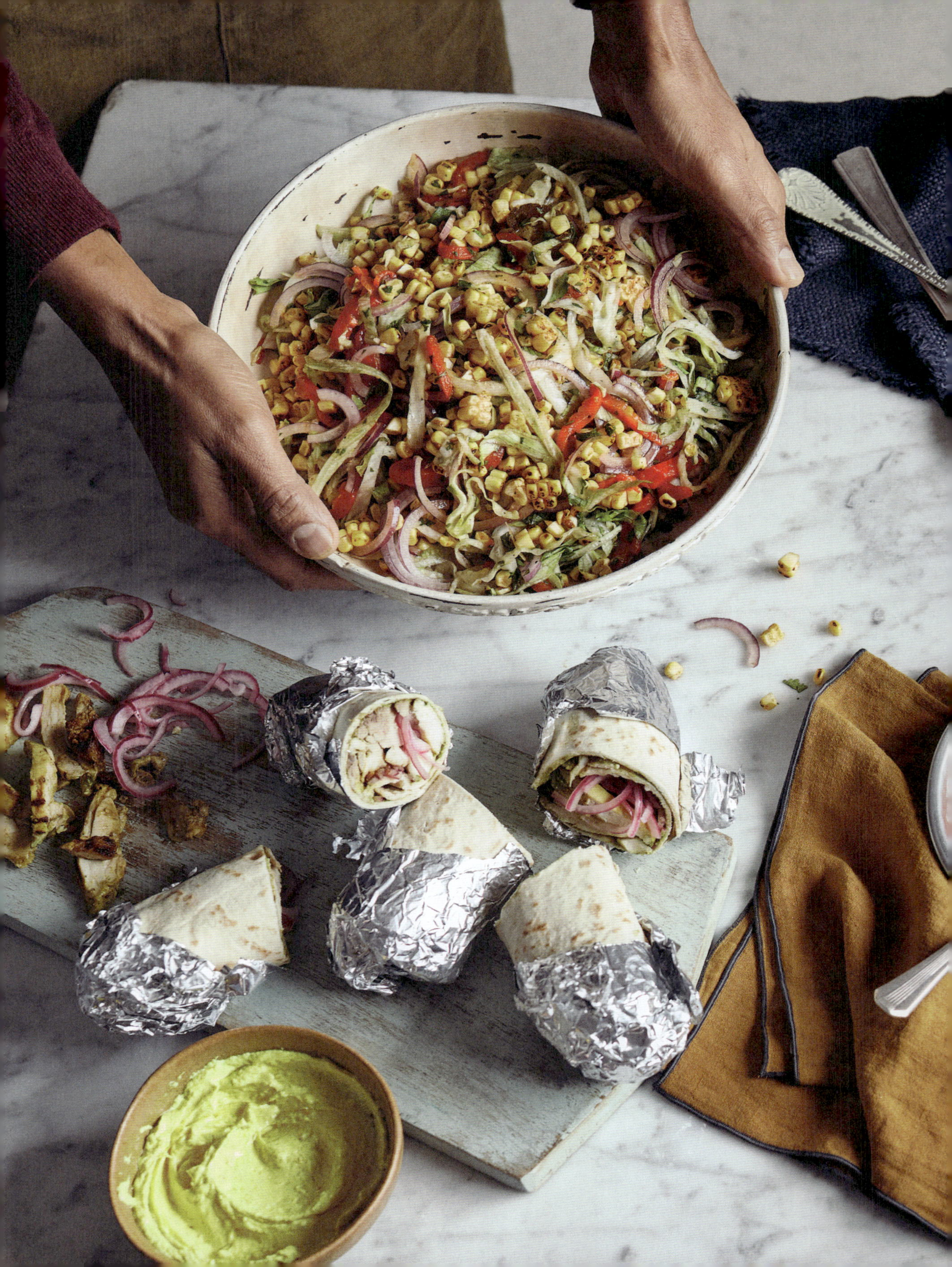

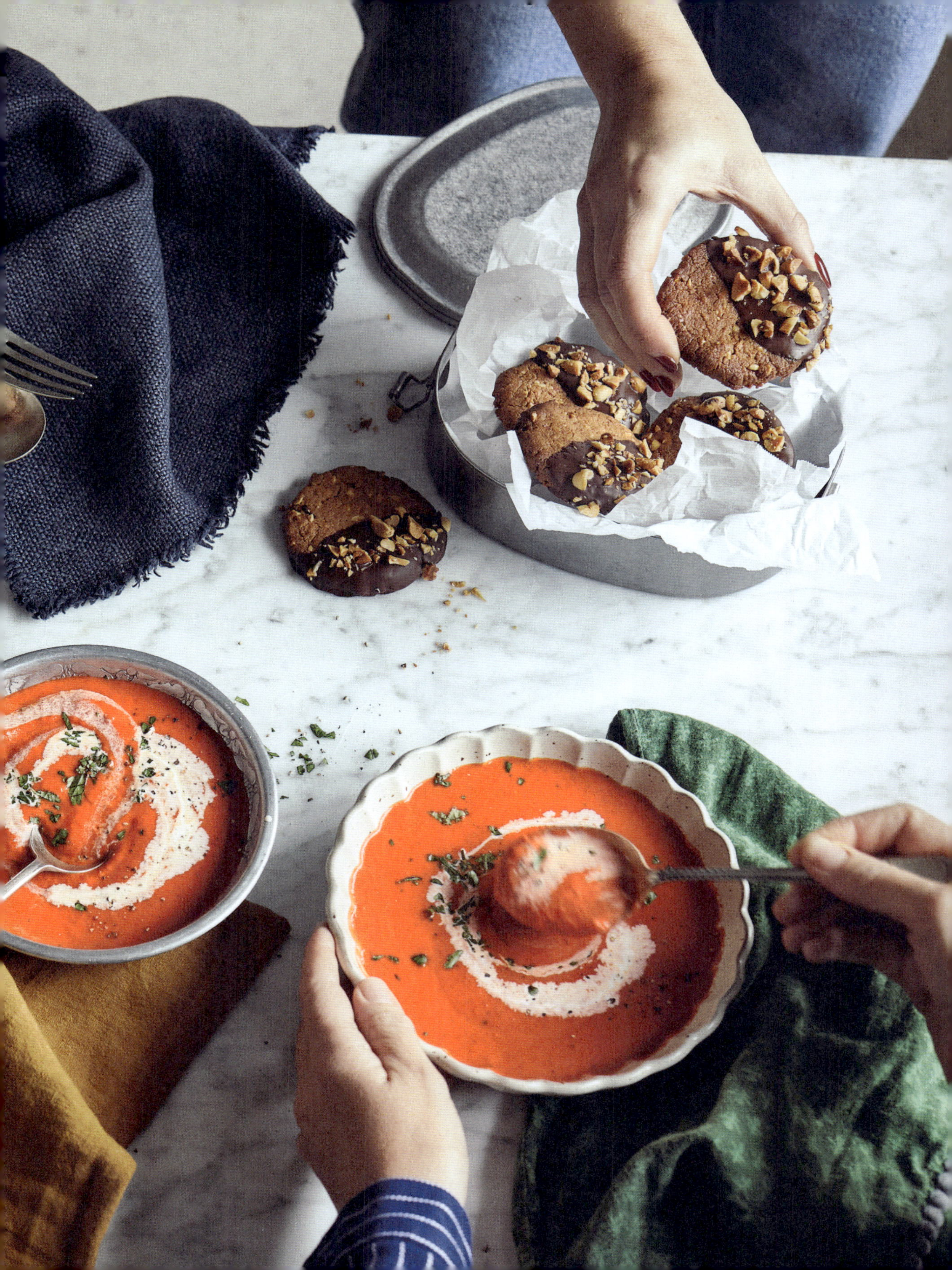

INDEX

A

ajwain seeds (carom seeds) 10
   chaat masala 153
almonds
   almond and pistachio ice cream 136
   carrot fudge pudding 144
   cinnamon rice pudding with seasonal berries 132
aloo chaat 118
aloo matar 40
aloo sandwich 20
amchoor (dried mango powder) 11
   chaat masala 153
anardana (dry pomegranate seed powder) 11
anda curry 71
asafoetida (hing) 11
atta (wheat flour): sweet dough balls 149
aubergines (eggplants): bashed aubergine 49

B

baingan bharta 49
baklawa, paneer 143
base sauce for curries 158
bashed aubergine 49
bay leaves: garam masala 155
beans, carrots and 48
beetroot (beet)
   carrot fudge pudding 144
   tomato soup 116
beetroot (beet) juice: slow-cooked lamb shoulder in rogan josh sauce 74–6
belan (rolling pin) 17
berries, cinnamon rice pudding with seasonal 132
besan (gram or chickpea flour) 10
   besan chilla 26
   gram flour pancakes 26
   mixed veg pakora 113
   paneer pakora 121
bhuna jeera 152
bhutta chaat 124
biryani, simple chicken 102
black chickpea and spinach salad 110
black lentils, chicken thighs with vegetables and 83
black pepper
   black pepper crackers 122
   chaat masala 153
   curry masala 154
   garam masala 155
black salt 11
   chaat masala 153
blackberries: cinnamon rice pudding with seasonal berries 132
bread
   chicken keema with peas 79
   lentil flat bread 93
   naan bread 98
   pan-fried bread 36
   pan-fried plain paratha 90
   pea-stuffed flat bread 25
   potato toasties 20
   puffed fried bread 94
   shahi tukda 130
   spiced egg rolls 33
   thin flat breads 88
breakfast 18–37
butter
   clarified butter 8
   paneer baklawa 143
   white butter 36

C

cardamom
   carrot fudge pudding 144
   curry masala 154
   garam masala 155
   home-style chicken curry 64
   Indian aromatic tea 34
   lamb and potato curry 77–8
   simple chicken biryani 102
carom seeds *see* ajwain seeds
carrots
   carrot fudge pudding 144
   carrots and beans 48
   chicken thighs with vegetables and black lentils 83
   mixed veg pakora 113
   red lentil soup 114
   tomato soup 116
   veg rice 100
cashew nuts
   carrot fudge pudding 144
   simple chicken biryani 102
cauliflower, roasted 42
celery: tomato soup 116
chaat masala 153
   black chickpea and spinach salad 110
   charred corn and lettuce salad 124
   paneer pakora 121
   paneer tikka 52
   peanut and chilli salsa 169
   roasted potato chaat 118
   veg rice 100
chapati flour 8
   lentil flat bread 93
   pan-fried plain paratha 90
   puffed fried bread 94
   thin flat breads 88
charred corn and lettuce salad 124
cheese 8
   chicken thighs with vegetables and black lentils 83
   paneer baklawa 143
   paneer pakora 121
   paneer tikka 52
   spinach and Indian cottage cheese curry 45
   veg rice 100
cherries: roasted pineapple 135
chicken
   chicken keema with peas 79

chicken rolls 117
chicken thighs with vegetables and black lentils 83
home-style chicken curry 64
simple chicken biryani 102
chickpea flour (besan) 10
  besan chilla 26
  gram flour pancakes 26
  mixed veg pakora 113
  paneer pakora 121
chickpeas (garbanzo beans)
  black chickpea and spinach salad 110
  chickpea curry 56
  spiced crust sea bass with chickpea salad 84
chillies 11
  chilli pickle 166
  coconut trout curry 72
  curry masala 154
  garam masala 155
  lemon rice 105
  mint and coriander chutney 162
  mixed salad 59
  onion tomato chutney 163
  peanut and chilli salsa 169
  smoked paprika tiger prawns with red and green peppers 67
  spiced oil 160
chocolate
  peanut butter and ginger cookies 146
  sesame and coconut chocolate balls 137
chole 56
chutney
  mint and coriander chutney 162
  onion tomato chutney 163
cilantro *see* coriander
cinnamon
  cinnamon rice pudding with seasonal berries 132
  curry masala 154
  garam masala 155
clarified butter 8
cloves
  curry masala 154

garam masala 155
Indian aromatic tea 34
coconut: sesame and coconut chocolate balls 137
coconut milk: coconut trout curry 72
colours 172
cookies, peanut butter and ginger 146
coriander (cilantro) 10
  base sauce for curries 158
  black chickpea and spinach salad 110
  curry masala 154
  garam masala 155
  masala omelette 28
  mint and coriander chutney 162
  mixed salad 59
  naan bread 98
  paneer pakora 121
  peanut and chilli salsa 169
  savoury vegetable flattened rice with peanuts 29
corn on the cobs: charred corn and lettuce salad 124
courgette (zucchini) curry 58
crackers, black pepper 122
cranberry relish 167
cream
  almond and pistachio ice cream 136
  home-style chicken curry 64
  tomato soup 116
  white butter 36
cream of wheat *see* semolina
cucumber
  cucumber raita 59
  mixed salad 59
cumin
  base sauce for curries 158
  chaat masala 153
  cumin rice 105
  curry masala 154
  garam masala 155
  roasted ground cumin 152
  spiced oil 160
  tamarind paste 161
curry
  base sauce for curries 158
  chickpea curry 56

coconut trout curry 72
courgette curry 58
curry masala 154
egg curry 71
home-style chicken curry 64
kidney bean curry 46
lamb and potato curry 77–8
potato and pea curry 40
spinach and Indian cottage cheese curry 45
curry leaves 10
  coconut trout curry 72
  lemon rice 105
  smoked paprika tiger prawns with red and green peppers 67
  spiced oil 160
  tadka daal 55
curry masala
  home-style chicken curry 64
  lamb and potato curry 77–8
  potato and pea curry 40
  spinach and Indian cottage cheese curry 45

D
daal paratha 93
daal shorba 114
desi chicken 64
dhaniya 10
dough
  making a dough 14
  sweet dough balls 149
dried split red lentils: red lentil soup 114
drinks: Indian aromatic tea 34

E
eggplants *see* aubergines
eggs
  egg bhurji pav 33
  egg curry 71
  egg rice 99
  masala omelette 28
  spiced egg rolls 33
eno 11
evaporated milk

INDEX

almond and pistachio ice cream 136
carrot fudge pudding 144
cinnamon rice pudding with seasonal berries 132
shahi tukda 130

F
fennel seeds: chaat masala 153
fenugreek leaves (kasoori methi) 11
   roasted cauliflower 42
feta cheese: chicken thighs with vegetables and black lentils 83
filo pastry: paneer baklawa 143
fish
   coconut trout curry 72
   spiced crust sea bass with chickpea salad 84
flat breads
   lentil flat bread 93
   naan bread 98
   pan-fried plain paratha 90
   pea-stuffed flat bread 25
   thin flat breads 88
flavours, balance of 174–5
flour, roti/chapati 8
food pairing 172–5
French (green) beans: carrots and beans 48
fudge: carrot fudge pudding 144

G
gajar fali 48
gajar halwa 144
garam masala 155
   chaat masala 153
   chickpea curry 56
   lamb and potato curry 77
   simple chicken biryani 102
garbanzo beans *see* chickpeas
garlic
   ginger garlic paste 159
   mustard garlic yoghurt 168
   onion tomato chutney 163
   spiced oil 160
ghee 8
   pan-fried bread 36

spiced oil 160
ginger
   chickpea curry 56
   curry masala 154
   garam masala 155
   ginger garlic paste 159
   Indian aromatic tea 34
   kidney bean curry 46
   mint and coriander chutney 162
   peanut butter and ginger cookies 146
   roasted pineapple 135
   spiced oil 160
   tadka daal 55
ginger garlic paste 159
   base sauce for curries 158
   chicken rolls 117
   egg curry 71
   home-style chicken curry 64
   masala lamb chops with mustard potatoes 68
   paneer tikka 52
   roasted cauliflower 42
   slow-cooked lamb shoulder in rogan josh sauce 74
golden sultanas
   carrot fudge pudding 144
   cinnamon rice pudding with seasonal berries 132
   simple chicken biryani 102
gram flour (besan) 10
   besan chilla 26
   gram flour pancakes 26
   mixed veg pakora 113
   paneer pakora 121
gud (jaggery) 10
   onion tomato chutney 163
   sweet dough balls 149
   tamarind paste 161
gulgulla 149

H
hari chatni 162
hing (asafoetida) 11
home-style chicken curry 64
honey

mango shrikhand 140
paneer baklawa 143
shahi tukda 130
sweet dough balls 149

I
ice cream, almond and pistachio 136
idli 22
idli mould 17
imli (tamarind) 10
   onion tomato chutney 163
   tamarind paste 161
Indian aromatic tea 34
ingredients 8–13

J
jaggery (gud) 10
   onion tomato chutney 163
   sweet dough balls 149
   tamarind paste 161
jalapeños: mixed salad 59
javitri (mace): garam masala 155
jeera rice 105

K
kali-mirch mathi 122
kalongi (nigella seeds): naan bread 98
kasoori methi (dried fenugreek leaves) 11
   roasted cauliflower 42
keema: chicken keema with peas 79
kheer with seasonal berries 132
kidney bean curry 46

L
laal maas 74–6
lal jheenga 67
lamb
   lamb and potato curry 77–8
   lamb masala 68
   masala lamb chops with mustard potatoes 68
   slow-cooked lamb shoulder in rogan josh sauce 74–6
lemon rice 105
lentils

INDEX

chicken thighs with vegetables and black lentils 83
lentil flat bread 93
red lentil soup 114
lettuce: charred corn and lettuce salad 124
lime juice: home-style chicken curry 64

M
mace (javitri): garam masala 155
makkhan 36
mango powder, dried (amchoor) 11
  chaat masala 153
mango shrikhand 140
masala
  chaat masala 153
  curry masala 154
  masala chai 34
  masala fish fry 84
  masala lamb chops with mustard potatoes 68
  masala omelette 28
mascarpone cheese: roasted pineapple 135
matar paratha 25
meal combinations 176–9
measuring tools 15
meat 173–4
  meat-based dishes 62–85
  see also chicken; lamb, etc
milk: cinnamon rice pudding with seasonal berries 132
mint
  cucumber raita 59
  mint and coriander chutney 162
  mixed salad 59
  mixed veg pakora 113
mint and coriander chutney 162
  chicken rolls 117
  roasted potato chaat 118
mixed salad 59
mixed veg and paneer pulav 100
mixed veg pakora 113
moong (yellow lentils)
  lemon rice 105

lentil flat bread 93
  tadka daal 55
murg daal 83
murg matar keema 79
mustard: mustard garlic yoghurt 168
mustard seeds: mustard potatoes 68
mutton aloo 77–8

N
naan bread 98
nariyal machhi jhol 72
nashta 18–37
nigella seeds (kalongi): naan bread 98
non-stick pans 15
nutmeg: garam masala 155
nutrients 172

O
oils 8
  spiced oil 160
omelette, masala 28
onions
  base sauce for curries 158
  bashed aubergine 49
  black chickpea and spinach salad 110
  charred corn and lettuce salad 124
  chicken keema with peas 79
  chicken rolls 117
  chicken thighs with vegetables and black lentils 83
  coconut trout curry 72
  egg curry 71
  egg rice 99
  gram flour pancakes 26
  home-style chicken curry 64
  kidney bean curry 46
  lamb and potato curry 77–8
  lentil flat bread 93
  masala omelette 28
  mixed salad 59
  mixed veg pakora 113
  onion tomato chutney 163
  peanut and chilli salsa 169
  potato and pea curry 40
  potato toasties 20
  puff samosa 125

red lentil soup 114
savoury vegetable flattened rice with peanuts 29
simple chicken biryani 102
slow-cooked lamb shoulder in rogan josh sauce 74–6
spiced crust sea bass with chickpea salad 84
spiced egg rolls 33
spinach and Indian cottage cheese curry 45
tomato soup 116
veg rice 100

P
pakoras
  mixed veg pakora 113
  paneer pakora 121
palak chana chaat 110
palak paneer 45
pancakes, gram flour 26
paneer 8
  paneer baklawa 143
  paneer pakora 121
  paneer tikka 52
  spinach and Indian cottage cheese curry 45
  veg rice 100
pans 15
paprika
  slow-cooked lamb shoulder in rogan josh sauce 74–6
  smoked paprika tiger prawns with red and green peppers 67
parathas
  chicken rolls 117
  lentil flat bread 93
  pan-fried plain paratha 90
  pea-stuffed flat bread 25
pav: spiced egg rolls 33
peanut butter and ginger cookies 146
peanuts
  lemon rice 105
  peanut and chilli salsa 169
  peanut butter and ginger cookies 146

savoury vegetable flattened rice with peanuts 29
peas
  chicken keema with peas 79
  egg rice 99
  pea-stuffed flat bread 25
  potato and pea curry 40
  puff samosa 125
  savoury vegetable flattened rice with peanuts 29
  veg rice 100
peppercorns: black pepper crackers 122
peppers
  charred corn and lettuce salad 124
  egg rice 99
  paneer tikka 52
  potato toasties 20
  smoked paprika tiger prawns with red and green peppers 67
  veg rice 100
peri-peri marinade: simple chicken biryani 102
pickle, chilli 156
pineapple, roasted 135
pistachios
  almond and pistachio ice cream 136
  carrot fudge pudding 144
  paneer baklava 143
poha 10
  savoury vegetable flattened rice with peanuts 29
pomegranate seed powder (anardana) 11
pomegranate seeds
  chaat masala 153
  mixed salad 59
poori 94
potatoes
  black chickpea and spinach salad 110
  chicken thighs with vegetables and black lentils 83
  lamb and potato curry 77–8
  masala lamb chops with mustard potatoes 68
  potato and pea curry 40

potato toasties 20
puff samosa 125
roasted potato chaat 118
savoury vegetable flattened rice with peanuts 29
spiced crust sea bass with chickpea salad 84
veg rice 100
prawns (shrimp): smoked paprika tiger prawns with red and green peppers 67
pressure cookers 15–17
puddings 128–49
puff pastry: puff samosa 125
puffed fried bread 94
pulav, veg rice 100

R

rabri ice cream 136
radishes: mixed salad 59
raita, cucumber 59
rajma 46
raspberries: cinnamon rice pudding with seasonal berries 132
red lentil soup 114
relish, cranberry 167
rice
  cinnamon rice pudding with seasonal berries 132
  cumin rice 105
  egg rice 99
  lemon rice 105
  savoury vegetable flattened rice with peanuts 29
  simple chicken biryani 102
  veg rice 100
ricotta cheese
  almond and pistachio ice cream 136
  sesame and coconut chocolate balls 137
  shahi tukda 130
rogan josh sauce, slow-cooked lamb shoulder in 74–6
rolling pin 17
roti flour 8
  lentil flat bread 93

pan-fried plain paratha 90
pea-stuffed flat bread 25
roti 88
thin flat breads 88
runner (string) beans: chicken thighs with vegetables and black lentils 83

S

sada paratha 90
salads
  black chickpea and spinach salad 110
  charred corn and lettuce salad 124
  mixed salad 59
  spiced crust sea bass with chickpea salad 84
salsa, peanut and chilli 169
salt, black 11
  chaat masala 153
samosa, puff 125
sandwiches, aloo 20
sauce: base sauce for curries 158
savoury vegetable flattened rice with peanuts 29
sea bass: spiced crust sea bass with chickpea salad 84
semolina (cream of wheat) 10
  puffed fried bread 94
  steamed semolina cakes 22
sesame and coconut chocolate balls 137
shahi tukda 130
shrikhand, mango 140
shrimp see prawns
simple chicken biryani 102
slow-cooked lamb shoulder in rogan josh sauce 74–6
smoked paprika
  slow-cooked lamb shoulder in rogan josh sauce 74–6
  smoked paprika tiger prawns with red and green peppers 67
sooji 10
soups
  red lentil soup 114
  tomato soup 116

INDEX

spice grinder and blenders 17
spiced crust sea bass with chickpea salad 84
spiced egg rolls 33
spiced oil 160
spices and spice blends
   chaat masala 153
   curry masala 154
   garam masala 155
   roasted ground cumin 152
spinach
   black chickpea and spinach salad 110
   gram flour pancakes 26
   lentil flat bread 93
   mixed veg pakora 113
   spinach and Indian cottage cheese curry 45
star anise: garam masala 155
steamed semolina cakes 22
steamers 17
sultanas (golden raisins)
   carrot fudge pudding 144
   cinnamon rice pudding with seasonal berries 132
   simple chicken biryani 102
sweet dough balls 149
sweetcorn: charred corn and lettuce salad 124

T
tadka 160
   tadka daal 55
taja mirch ka achar 166
tamarind (imli) 10
   onion tomato chutney 163
   tamarind paste 161
tamatar payag chatni 163
tandoori gobhi 42
tava (non-stick pan) 15
tea
   chickpea curry 56
   Indian aromatic tea 34
techniques 14
textures 173
tikka, paneer 52
till ladoo 137

toasties, potato 20
tomatoes
   base sauce for curries 158
   bashed aubergine 49
   black chickpea and spinach salad 110
   chicken thighs with vegetables and black lentils 83
   coconut trout curry 72
   courgette curry 58
   egg curry 71
   home-style chicken curry 64
   kidney bean curry 46
   lamb and potato curry 77–8
   masala omelette 28
   mixed salad 59
   mustard potatoes 68
   onion tomato chutney 163
   peanut and chilli salsa 169
   potato and pea curry 40
   red lentil soup 114
   roasted cauliflower 42
   savoury vegetable flattened rice with peanuts 29
   simple chicken biryani 102
   smoked paprika tiger prawns with red and green peppers 67
   spiced crust sea bass with chickpea salad 84
   spiced egg rolls 33
   spinach and Indian cottage cheese curry 45
   tomato soup 116
tools 15
tortillas: chicken rolls 117
trout: coconut trout curry 72
turiya 58
turmeric
   base sauce for curries 158
   curry masala 154
   smoked paprika tiger prawns with red and green peppers 67
   spiced oil 160

V
vegetables 173–4
   chicken thighs with vegetables and black lentils 83
   mixed veg pakora 113
   savoury vegetable flattened rice with peanuts 29
   veg rice 100
   see also individual types of vegetable

W
walnuts: paneer baklawa 143
white butter 36

Y
yellow lentils (moong)
   lemon rice 105
   lentil flat bread 93
   tadka daal 55
yoghurt
   cucumber raita 59
   gram flour pancakes 26
   home-style chicken curry 64
   lamb and potato curry 77–8
   mango shrikhand 140
   mustard garlic yoghurt 168
   naan bread 98
   slow-cooked lamb shoulder in rogan josh sauce 74–6
   steamed semolina cakes 22

Z
zucchini see courgettes

ACKNOWLEDGEMENTS

Life is a whole series of experiences, where the expression of oneself with others makes up a significant part. For me, food is a medium to express my being, my love for art and culture and to share the nostalgia that I have experienced throughout my life.

I would like to dedicate this book to my dear late mother, Sushila Aggarwal, who is the only reason that I exist in the first place and she is the greatest source of nurturing my passion for food from the very early days of my childhood. She never taught me cooking in a systematic way, but actions do speak louder than words. Growing up in a loving family and seeing her taking care of us in every aspect of life, including what we ate, says a lot about her unconditional love and her fondness for cooking. I can still remember the taste of all the dishes she used to make in my head. And it's impossible to make them again, even if I follow the exact same recipes. It was her simplicity and honest heart that used to work as the magic ingredients in whatever she used to cook.

A few years ago, I couldn't have imagined that I would be pursuing my passion for food as a full-time professional and would even write a cookbook one day. The seed of this passion was sown in my heart and nurtured by my mother — she has given me the clarity to see things in real terms and to have the courage to own my dreams. For this support and unconditional love, I sincerely thank her from the bottom of my heart. Though she is physically not with us, I can still feel her presence around and I am sure she has a beautiful smile on her face, seeing me drafting these acknowledgments. I will always love you, mummy!

This is my first cookbook, and it means a lot to me. It enables me to express my story, passion and art with so many of you, whom I have never met, but who share some kind of connection via our love for food. Being able to truly express myself is priceless and gives me a sense of liberation. I often say that food and stories are interlinked. As a human civilization, we have evolved over billions of years. Food plays a major role in that evolution, as it is used to transfer the knowledge from one era to the next from all aspects, including culture, technology, science, lifestyle and human values. Without stories, food is meaningless, and without food, stories will be lost.

In the beautiful journey of life, we all follow multiple paths, meet many individuals and encounter diverse situations. Whatever happens in life is neither good or bad, it's right for you and it's meant to be like that. Meeting Pooja, my wife, through a traditional Indian arranged marriage route was not a coincidence. From day one, we clicked on so many levels, and one of them was food. She is my support system and pillar of strength for enabling me to take this pivotal decision mid-life to switch from the corporate to the culinary world. I couldn't have done it without her support and I am greatly thankful for her trust in my dreams. Children have no filters, and at times that could become a bit tricky, but in my case for my two boys, their daddy is the world's best chef! It's not about what they say related to my food, it's about them looking up to me regarding any aspect of everyday life that is the greatest reward for me as a parent. They do inject a lot of energy and motivation into my personality, too. Thank you to my lovely boys for being my cheerleaders!

When we go to a large party, if there is no music playing in the background, it feels very empty. Some music in the background plays an important role as 'white noise' to liven up the party. In a similar fashion, the 'white noise' in my life is made up of the feedback about my love for food, the little compliments here and there, and the constructive comments and excitement that I have received from my extended family, friends and work colleagues. This gives me fulfilment about my passion and plays an important part in my own journey. Therefore, I would like to extend sincere thanks to each one of you who has contributed to this 'white noise' in my life, either in a negative or a positive way. Without it, my life would be like a party without the music!

Next, I would like to thank MasterChef UK for giving me an opportunity to express my passion for cooking on such a grand platform. This final push gave me immense inner acknowledgment. With the valuable exposure and experience, I now feel fearless to be my true self. From the judges to the casting team, production, directors and each member of the crew, they all played an important role, allowing me to recognize the theme of my remaining life journey, which is food and cooking.

Like the saying goes, it takes an army to build a village. My dream of writing this cookbook has involved the whole publishing house. My sincere thanks to the Quadrille team at Penguin Random House for believing in my vision for this book, to Sofie Shearman for guiding me every step of the way, to Alicia House for such a warm and impactful design, Rita Platts for capturing my thoughts via beautiful shots and almost seeing through my eyes for every dish, Libby Silbermann for creating magic in the kitchen through your styling, Rebecca Newport for all the beautiful props and backdrops, and to many more who worked very hard behind the scenes to manifest my love for food into the beautiful book you are holding right now.

My last thank you is the most special one, because without this my expressions become meaningless. I would like to thank all the lovely audiences who have supported me throughout my recent culinary journey via TV, social media, supper clubs, corporate client events and print media readers. Even if I have never met them and have shared messages/comments with very few, their good wishes, vibes and support mean a lot to me.

Thank you. I feel very blessed to be able to follow my passions!

ACKNOWLEDGEMENTS

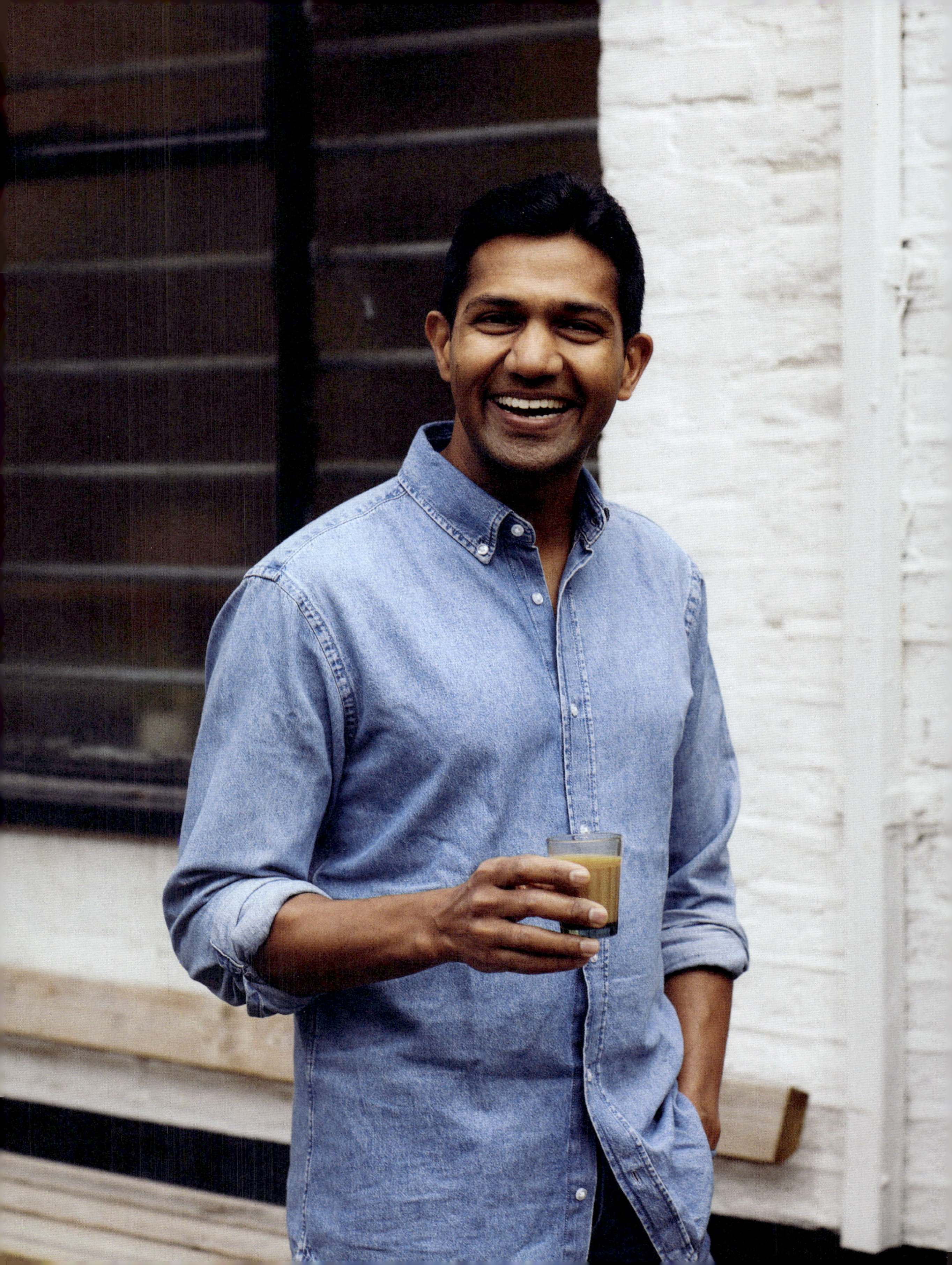

ABOUT THE AUTHOR

Anurag Aggarwal was born and raised in Gurgaon, north India, where food was synonymous with family. He moved to the UK in 2010, and despite enjoying a successful career in finance, he longed for the nostalgic flavours of home.

In 2023, he made it to the final of MasterChef UK, and he now runs a successful food business POD and gives motivational talks about turning your passion into a profession. Success to him is beyond titles, industry, or the bottom line. It's all about being genuinely happy and feeling confident that you have given your best in a particular situation, whether personal or professional."

Follow his journey @anuragfoodstory

Quadrille, Penguin Random House UK, One Embassy Gardens, 8 Viaduct Gardens, London SW11 7BW

Quadrille Publishing Limited is part of the Penguin Random House group of companies whose addresses can be found at global.penguinrandomhouse.com

Penguin Random House UK

Text © Anurag Aggarwal 2025
Illustrations © Jordan Amy Lee 2025
Photography © Rita Platts 2025
Design and layout © Quadrille 2025

Anurag Aggarwal has asserted his right to be identified as the author(s) of this Work in accordance with the Copyright, Designs and Patents Act 1988

Penguin Random House values and supports copyright. Copyright fuels creativity, encourages diverse voices, promotes freedom of expression and supports a vibrant culture. Thank you for purchasing an authorized edition of this book and for respecting intellectual property laws by not reproducing, scanning or distributing any part of it by any means without permission. You are supporting authors and enabling Penguin Random House to continue to publish books for everyone. No part of this book may be used or reproduced in any manner for the purpose of training artificial intelligence technologies or systems. In accordance with Article 4(3) of the DSM Directive 2019/790, Penguin Random House expressly reserves this work from the text and data mining exception.

Published by Quadrille in 2025

www.penguin.co.uk

A CIP catalogue record for this book is available from the British Library

ISBN 978 1 83783 3016

10 9 8 7 6 5 4 3 2 1

Managing Director Sarah Lavelle
Editor Sofie Shearman
Designer Alicia House
Cover Illustration Jordan Amy Lee
Photographer Rita Platts
Food Stylist Libby Silbermann
Prop Stylist Rebecca Newport
Head of Production Stephen Lang
Production Manager Sabeena Atchia

Colour reproduction by F1

Printed in China by C&C Offset Printing Co., Ltd.

The authorised representative in the EEA is Penguin Random House Ireland, Morrison Chambers, 32 Nassau Street, Dublin D02 YH68.

Penguin Random House is committed to a sustainable future for our business, our readers and our planet. This book is made from Forest Stewardship Council® certified paper.

MIX
Paper | Supporting responsible forestry
FSC® C018179